Making Your Point

A Practical Guide to Persuasive Legal Writing

◆ ◆ ◆

Kenneth F. Oettle

Member of New Jersey and California Bars

www.lawcatalog.com

Cover Design: *Ehren Seeland*

Interior Page Design: *Paige Hinkle*

Library of Congress Cataloging-in-Publication Data

Oettle, Kenneth F.
Making your point : a practical guide to persuasive legal writing / Kenneth F. Oettle.
p. cm.

ISBN 978-1-58852-135-4 (pbk.)

1. Legal composition. 2. Law—United States—Language. 3. Law—United States—Methodology. I. Title.

KF250.O384 2007
808'.06634—dc22

2007001197

Dedication

To my Wife, Robin,
and my Son, Colin

Acknowledgements

Books don't get written without support. I am most grateful to Rob Steinbaum, the Publisher of the New Jersey Law Journal, and Ron Fleury, the Editor-in-Chief, for authorizing the "Making Your Point" columns and for continual encouragement; to my Editors at the Law Journal, Lou Tafuri and Bridget Bosworth, who taught me things I didn't know I didn't know; to my editor at American Lawyer Media, Ellen Greenblatt, for helping shape this book and keep it on message; to my secretary, Sherry Lord, for dutifully processing my seemingly interminable edits and for letting me know, without hesitation, when something didn't ring true; to the members of my informal polling group for their insights and opinions; and last, but not least, to everyone who gave me permission, always graciously, to use their work as examples.

Contents

Introduction

Only for the blessed few is persuasive legal writing easy. Initial drafts take a serious act of will, and editing can be a grind. That's one reason I write the New Jersey Law Journal's Making Your Point columns—to analyze a challenging discipline. I also write the columns to vent frustration with lawyers on my side who weaken our case with unfinished thinking and unclear prose and lawyers on the other side who make blatantly bogus arguments. Both try my patience. Finally, I write the columns to spread the gospel—the belief that persuasive legal writing requires a compelling theme, impeccable logic, clarity, and candor with the court and with oneself.

Because brief writing is so important in litigation and, for some lawyers, so essential to their status within the firm, I long wondered if I could find the "secret" to persuasive legal writing—some element of the product or the process whose mastery would enable any lawyer to write persuasively. I sought a unifying truth for persuasive legal writing—the rhetorical counterpart, as it were, to "string theory" for subatomic particles.

Initially, I thought the secret might lie in one of the qualities of a good brief, such as a strong theme, logic, clarity or even brevity. After due consideration, I eliminated brevity, notwithstanding judges' universal complaint that briefs are too long, because brevity didn't seem dominant. Though it helps the writer deliver the message, it isn't the message, and it doesn't ensure victory.

Theme, as experienced lawyers know, is crucial. Arguments are built around theme. In fact, if you were to contend that the secret of persuasive legal writing is a strong theme, I would not argue with you. It's close enough. The theme orders the facts. Typically, courts don't look to the law to determine how an issue should be resolved; they look to the facts. When the law permits, as it usually does, courts rule against litigants who deserve to lose and in favor of litigants who deserve to win. They work "backwards" from the facts to the law because the facts show the court what is fair, and judges, being human, want to do what is fair. They want to do the right thing. In most cases, the law just serves as a hook for the court to hang its hat on once it determines the right result. Precedent gives the court comfort that it is making the right decision and that it won't be reversed.

The term "theme" as I use it means the amalgam of moral principle and operative fact that establishes why your client deserves to win and why the adversary's client deserves to lose. Ideally, a theme persuades merely in the articulation, without need of elaboration, as in the following argument by a construction company seeking summary judgment against an injured trespasser: "An inebriated daredevil who sneaks into a construction site after dark despite an eight-foot-high chain-link fence and well-illuminated warning signs can't blame the construction company when he topples off a bulldozer and breaks his leg."

Themes that have worked for me include: "Plaintiff's claim to priority for sewage treatment capacity under a ten-year old agreement with the Municipal

Utilities Authority can't have ripened if plaintiff isn't ready to use the capacity"; "A missing line item worth two percent of the bid isn't *de minimis* in a bid contest decided by less than one percent of the bid"; and, "It can't be 'forum shopping' to sue a defendant in the state where it is headquartered."

Behind each theme is a moral principle, usually reflected in a moral failing such as "thou shalt not deceive" (defendant deserves to lose because he lied); "people should be careful" (plaintiff deserves to lose because her sloppiness caused the problem); or "sloth is sinful" (plaintiff deserves to lose because he dropped the ball). Experienced writers build fact scenarios around moral principles to trigger judges' moral attitudes.

In some cases—actually most—advocates fault each other to the same end (*e.g.*, "He failed to turn over an e-mail"; "Her interrogatory answers were evasive."). Litigators know that in a close case, a judge may rule for the party whose counsel appears to have been more diligent and forthcoming. Diligence shows respect for the court, and candor begets trust. Justice is blind not only in the sense that the court is supposed to be neutral but also in the sense that the court can't see what the litigants won't show it. Whether consciously or unconsciously, courts tend to punish litigants who appear to be trying to keep the adversary, and thus the court, in the dark.

Logic and Clarity

If a strong theme isn't the secret of persuasive legal writing—I'm not saying it's not—what other qualities of a good brief might be the secret?

Logic is obviously important. It draws the reader inexorably from your premise to your conclusion. But that's no secret. No one doubts that logic is essential to a good brief. The same is true for clarity, which depends on logic, precision and brevity, among other things. A reader can't be persuaded by what the reader can't understand. Logic and clarity are *sine qua non's* of persuasive legal writing, and everyone knows it. When litigators are illogical and unclear, the reason is often that they are trying to make a point that is weak or downright unmakeable.

The Principal Tasks of the Writing Process

Besides the traditional qualities of good persuasive writing (*e.g.*, theme, logic, clarity), viable candidates for the secret of persuasive legal writing include the principal tasks of the writing process: finding the facts; researching the law; outlining your arguments; thinking hard—really hard—before you write; beginning powerfully; laying out the facts in a manner that makes the court want to rule for you; showing how your case fits within the fabric of precedent or how the other side's case doesn't (also called "applying the law to the facts"); relentlessly polishing your work; and seeking feedback at all stages, from the beginning of the writing process to the end.

Like the qualities of good persuasive writing, these tasks are candidates for the secret of persuasive legal writing more because they are important to the process than because writers are unaware of them. Lawyers know, for example, that they have to develop the facts and research the law. They learn that in law school. They also know they should think very hard before they write and should at least roughly outline their ideas, though they don't always do either. In fact, in one Making Your Point column, I referred to such pre-writing tasks as the "secret" of persuasive legal writing, largely because the tasks are important but partly because, paradoxically, they aren't the actual writing. Upon reconsidering the meaning of "secret" (something more undisclosed than paradoxical), I no longer view the pre-writing stage of the writing process as a secret, at least not "the" secret. Writers know that the more facts and law they gather before they write, the more options they have in shaping their argument. And they know that the more they plan, the more powerful they can make their prose.

The Statement of Facts

Writing a Statement of Facts that makes the court want to rule for you comes very, very close to the secret of persuasive legal writing. The Statement of Facts is an extrapolation of your theme, which, as I said, is so close to the secret of persuasive legal writing that I wouldn't argue the point. Many lawyers believe the Statement of Facts is the most important section of a brief because it tells the court how your client's ox was gored. It wins the court's sympathy. Some say that if you haven't persuaded the court by the end of the Statement of Facts, then you are in trouble.

Because a good Statement of Facts creates the impression that your side deserves to win and that the other side deserves to lose, experienced litigators view the Statement of Facts as more important than the Argument, where the law is applied to the facts. This hierarchy is evidenced in part by the typical allocation of brief-writing tasks: The Argument tends to be assigned to a lower or mid-level associate, whereas the Statement of Facts is written by a partner or senior associate. (The relative difficulty of these brief-writing jobs may also have something to do with the division of labor. Writing a forceful, coherent Argument can be tedious. The writer must diligently analyze the case law, make sure all facts are accounted for, and test every link in the logical chain. In contrast, writing a Statement of Facts is, if not a pleasure, at least relatively painless for an experienced attorney having record references conveniently at hand.)

The Preliminary Statement

Important as the Statement of Facts may be—and all agree it is crucial—I know several lawyers who think the Preliminary Statement is even more important. This is where you present your theme. If the theme is strong, you can win right there. Readers want to be persuaded, and the sooner the better. Once they are persuaded, they view everything through a filter favorable to you. That is, they look to reinforce their first impression. In contrast, if your theme is weak, you will underwhelm the reader, lose the reader's attention, and probably lose the case. One way to discover if your theme is weak is to try to write a Preliminary Statement.

The importance of the Preliminary Statement and Statement of Facts is well accepted by lawyers at all levels above novice. Each of these sections of the brief is attended by significant lore, and each has many proponents. Writing them, on the other hand, requires skills that for most lawyers develop slowly. The secret of persuasive legal writing, as we shall see, may provide some guidance.

But let's finish surveying the candidates.

Improving the Draft

Many writers don't realize how much they can improve their work by editing. Others do little editing because they have little time, or the client won't pay for the work. Similarly, many writers don't realize how valuable feedback can be, whereas others suppress the realization. They don't want to experience the pain of criticism, and they don't want to create the impression that they need help. Consequently, many writers rationalize that they don't have time to seek feedback or respond to it.

So much avoidance is associated with editing and feedback that either process could be a reasonable candidate for the secret of persuasive legal writing by reason of the self-deception (keeping a secret from oneself). Still, nobody says "Ah hah! I never thought of that!" when I expound the virtues of editing and feedback. They know, at least theoretically, that the processes are useful, and they acknowledge, if pressed, that they should give them more attention. Editing and feedback are no secret.

Getting Outside Oneself

One final candidate for the secret of persuasive legal writing is neither an element of the product nor a stage in the process. It's a mindset—the willingness and capacity to shift perspective and "get outside oneself" in two ways: to identify with the reader and see the reader from the inside out, and to monitor one's own agenda and see oneself from the outside in.

A writer has to see through the reader's eyes to understand the reader's preconceptions and concerns and to bridge the gap between the reader's limited knowledge of the case and the writer's intimate familiarity with it. The writer must continually ask what the reader needs to know, wants to know and is willing to know. Being able to identify with the reader is a critical skill. Even so, being able to identify with the reader doesn't ensure victory. One still has to have a point.

One also has to know oneself to guard against the siren songs of assumption and wishful thinking. Because the writer wants so badly to win and to please clients, superiors, and peers, the temptation to self-deceive is almost overwhelming. A writer can easily slip into thinking that an opponent's position is as weak as the client and the senior partner say it is, or into pretending that a sweet-sounding dictum will carry the day even though the facts on which the putative precedent is based diverge from the facts of the writer's case.

Self-deception is so prevalent in the adversarial context and so insidious that one could reasonably call the need to be wary of it a secret. By definition, the writer who is self-deceiving is unaware of the danger, which makes it, in a sense, a secret. But overcoming self-deception doesn't ensure victory. To the contrary, the scrupulously self-honest are sometimes scrupulously concessionary. Candid to a fault, they become "devil's advocates" and can't persuade.

The Secret of Persuasive Legal Writing

Without intending to diminish any of the important elements discussed above, I have settled on an aspect of persuasive legal writing that absorbs and transcends these elements and fits my criteria for a secret, that is, a dominant technique not widely understood and, for the most part, not consciously applied. The secret of persuasive legal writing is that the writer must tell the reader a story.

It's the same advice given to trial lawyers—tell the jury a story.

A story centers around theme, but it's more than theme. Just as a bomb needs a rocket, a theme needs a story—a way to deliver the theme and embed it. The story engages the reader as a movie engages a viewer. It captures and holds the reader's attention so the theme can do its work. The Preliminary Statement previews the story, and the Statement of Facts presents it. The Statement of Facts is not a chronology but a tale. The resourceful writer presents a complete, consistent and credible narrative to draw the reader in, crafting trim, rhythmic sentences to maintain the pace. The writer spins a yarn, guiding the reader to see the facts the writer's way.

The importance of telling a story is a secret because many writers have no idea that this is the best way to present their case. The advice seems to conflict with the easy fall-back of a chronology in the Statement of Facts and the traditional task of articulating a legal test and showing how the facts satisfy it in the Argument. Yet story-telling infuses good persuasive legal writing. As a story has a moral, a brief has a theme. The theme articulates why the other side deserves to lose and why your side deserves to win.

One of the great virtues of the story is that it encourages readers to draw their own conclusions about how the issues should be resolved. In the Statement of Facts, you don't say, "We should win because . . . ." You just tell the story. If the story is compelling, the reader will reach the conclusion you advance and will "own" it for having arrived at it independently. A well-known axiom of persuasion is that an audience is persuaded best if it reaches the desired conclusion on its own.

Like juries, readers draw moral conclusions about human interaction. They identify with the parties and imagine being the victim of the wrongdoer's behavior. From that perspective, they see behavior as good or bad, moral or immoral. This is why the writer shapes a story to show who deserves to win and who deserves to lose—to tap into the reader's tendency, if not compulsion, to approve or disapprove of behavior that could, if aimed in the reader's direction, cause harm.

In short, the secret of persuasive legal writing is to tell a story that shows who deserves to win and who deserves to lose. Once you have absorbed that truth, you will be writing on another level.

Ken Oettle
January 2007

1

Composition

Understanding the Writing Process

Composition

Understanding the Writing Process

Persuasive legal writing emerges from a methodical process, not unlike the Scientific Method, of formulating a thesis, gathering and analyzing data, confirming or revising the thesis, gathering more data, and so forth through successive cycles. Because the process involves much more than writing, legal writers have to be much more than wordsmiths. Among other things, they have to be good listeners, questioners, researchers, note-takers, issue spotters, hypothesizers, distillers, compilers, organizers, tacticians, networkers and politicians.

They have to be honest with themselves and admit when they don't have the answer and haven't made a point, and they have to fight a constant back-channel war with their greatest enemy—wishful thinking—which tempts them with flawed arguments, causes them to misread cases, loads their briefs with vigorous but conclusory statements, and terminates the writing process before they have made a point. They need to suppress their own viewpoints to fathom the reader's confusions and concerns, and they need to be confident enough to seek and accept help.

The writing process is multi-faceted, and writing is not easy. Nevertheless, anyone who graduated law school and passed the Bar can become a better writer. Their motivation, of course, is their own concern.

The Writing Process Begins with Getting the Assignment Straight

Smart writers stop and ask for directions

> Two roads diverged in a wood, and I—
> I took the one less traveled by,
> And that has made all the difference.
> —Robert Frost, from *The Road Not Taken*

The road less traveled may have been good to Robert Frost, but it may not be good to you if your assignment was to explore the beaten path. A written product serves little purpose if it is off point. To begin on point, you must get the assignment straight.

Here are some hints to help you accomplish that.

- Bring pen and paper to the meeting where you receive the assignment. This seems obvious, but people forget. If the assigning attorney grabs you in the hall, borrow materials.
- As you receive the assignment, restate the facts as you understand them. The assigning attorney may think you are slow on the uptake, but the importance of getting the facts overrides appearances. If you are unfamiliar with the area, such as securities regulation, franchise agreements or environmental enforcement, acknowledge this and request a replay of any portions of the story you missed.

  You are understandably reluctant to appear naive, and you are afraid, not without reason, that the attorney assumes you came fully programmed with the appropriate database. But candor will protect you. By being honest and assertive, you can recover as many points as you lose for being unfamiliar with the subject matter.
- Before you leave the initial meeting, ask permission to restate the issues as you understand them. Few assigning attorneys are in such a hurry as to deny you this.
- Also before you leave the initial meeting, make sure you know how the assigning attorney wants the research presented—photocopies of cases, oral report, memo, brief, or combinations thereof. If the attorney hasn't decided, your question will help him or her focus.
- Immediately after the meeting, write a memo or an e-mail confirming the assignment. If your firm doesn't require assignment-confirming memos, ask if the attorney would mind your writing one.

Possible Roadblocks

After beginning the assignment, you may find things aren't going smoothly. Typical problems and possible solutions are as follows:

- The assigning attorney said your issue is "legal only" and gave you only skeletal facts. An issue may be legal only (e.g., "What does the statute say?"), but more often it is factual even though the assigning attorney says it is not. You may not understand this until you begin the research and realize you cannot determine if the cases are relevant without knowing more facts.

  Suggested Solution: Ask for the kind of facts you think you are missing. This is easier said than done, of course. The assigning attorney is busy and doesn't want to be disturbed. But do it anyway. The price of admission is your being able to summarize—orally or in writing—at least one case that led you to ask for more facts. It shows you are diligent, assertive and sincere.

- The assigning attorney says you will find law favorable to your client, but the law appears unfavorable. You don't know what to do. You are afraid the assigning attorney will kill the messenger.

  Suggested Solution: The assigning attorney will not kill the messenger just because you find bad law, though the attorney will suspect, at least briefly, that you are a double agent. After all, you are suggesting their instinct was wrong. Assigning attorneys don't like to be wrong, and they think, sometimes correctly, that they know more than you.

  If you believe a case hurts your position, re-read it to confirm your belief and then report that you have found harmful precedent that does not seem distinguishable. Be prepared, as many are not, to summarize the case and explain your concern.

  Ask the assigning attorney if additional facts can be brought to bear that might enable you to distinguish the case. Generally, if you find harmful law, you should forewarn the assigning attorney so your memo or draft brief does not become a bombshell.

- The assigning attorney may have mischaracterized the issues. Formulating issues takes time, and attorneys often give assignments off the cuff.

  Suggested Solution: The first checkpoint is the assignment-confirming memo, which gives the assigning attorney an opportunity to change course. If you feel an issue has been improperly drawn, propose a reformulation and be prepared to defend your proposal. Again, preparation is the price of admission. Preparation is so impressive to assigning attorneys that it may even get you a lunch.

- Notwithstanding all your efforts, the assignment remains unclear. In your considered judgment, if you go back to the assigning attorney, you will look stupid.

Suggested Solution: Get smart on the subject by reading a treatise or a law review article or by consulting another attorney who is working on the same case and is familiar with the facts and the law. You may wish to look for a "translator," a person who regularly works with the assigning attorney and understands the attorney's methods.

As a last resort, consult any attorney with whom you are comfortable who may know something about the area. Don't proceed alone, and don't proceed with uncertainty. Roads diverge, and the longer you stay on the wrong one, the farther you drift from the correct path.

In sum, stay in touch with the assigning attorney or, in an emergency, with someone else. Begin with the assignment-confirming memo and continue with periodic reports on your progress. Even a busy attorney will make course corrections if you provide new information, a new perspective and an incentive to adjust.

Puzzler

How would you tighten and sharpen the following sentence?

Anyone that has looked at or traveled on this site would tell you that for the past 85 years it is part and parcel of the barrier island of Brigantine.

Say "anyone who" rather than "anyone that" because you are speaking of people. Place the traveling concept first and the viewing concept second, using "even" to emphasize how little it takes to come to this conclusion (*i.e.,* just looking). Drop the "on" after "traveled" because it is implicit. Change "for" to "in" (few have viewed the site for 85 years) and move "in the past 85 years" ahead of "would tell you" because nobody can tell from one look what the site's status has been for the past 85 years. "Parcel" is unnecessary, as is the second "that."

The revised version:

Anyone who has traveled this site or even viewed it in the past 85 years would tell you it is part of the barrier island of Brigantine.

Your Writing Is a Barometer of Your Thinking

Drafts reveal when you haven't grappled with or mastered an issue

Just as industry uses gauges to determine whether things are hot or cold, full or empty, brief writers can use gauges to determine if their thinking is accurate and complete. A writer's gauges are, ironically, the obfuscations and evasions he or she uses to hide, or hide from, tough issues. The following gauges are gathered as a checklist.

1. Watch for emphatics that declare the unassailability of your position, such as "clearly," "obviously" or "simply." Odds are that you are using emphatics because you haven't made your point clear, obvious or simple.

2. If you begin a sentence with "It is important to note" or "Significantly," you may not understand how the idea you are about to note relates to the one before it. You deem the idea important, but you don't know why. If you knew why, you would not resort to "important" or "significant," which do little more than ask the reader to pay attention to what you are about to say.

3. If you cannot create a transition between paragraphs, you may not know how the ideas in the paragraphs relate. If you don't know, the reader won't know, either.

4. If your draft seems disorganized, you may have written in haste before reasoning the problem through, fearing that you might have nothing in hand when the deadline arrives.

5. If you default to "In *Smith v. Jones*" to begin a paragraph, your failure to create a topic sentence may signal that you don't know what your point is.

6. If you connect independent clauses with "and," consider whether you aren't just tacking loosely related thoughts together, possibly to create the appearance of a causative relationship. Consider subordinating one thought to the other. If you can't, then maybe they don't belong in the same sentence.

7. If you have a desire to drop a footnote, you may be avoiding an issue—trying to bury it, as it were, at the bottom of the page.

8. If you are using underlining in the text of your brief (as opposed to using it to highlight words in a quotation), ask yourself whether the underlining isn't an attempt to cure a lack of clarity or emphasis.

9. If you have several arguments to support your position and merely list them ("This is the correct result for five reasons"), you may not know what your strongest argument is, and you may be diluting it by giving subordinate points equal time.
10. If you begin a brief noncommittally with, "This is a brief in opposition to defendant's motion for summary judgment," you may be avoiding the challenge of determining your best fact and building a theme around it. At the very least, you are forfeiting the opportunity to use the premier sentence in your brief—the opening sentence—for persuasive purposes.
11. If your prose seems wordy, quantity may be masking lack of quality. Writing instructors say that pruning should be the last step in the writing process short of proofing. This is generally good advice, but you may wish to trim your prose along the way because verbosity can conceal (from you, not from the reader) the absence of a decent argument.
12. If you quote from a judicial opinion without characterizing the content (*e.g.,* instead of introducing the quotation with, "The trial court relied heavily on the disparity in bargaining power," you merely say, "As the court said"), then you may not have read the passage carefully, and it may be off point. At the very least, you are failing to extract full value from the quotation, forfeiting the opportunity to put your own spin on it, to gain credibility by characterizing it fairly, and to achieve emphasis through repetition.
13. If you are making an argument that seems weak, ask yourself whether you have maximized your strong arguments. If you had, you might not be grasping at straws. Perhaps you need to improve your theme or bring more facts and law to bear. Maybe (and now I speak the unspeakable) you should even concede a point.
14. If you find yourself restating your conclusion several times in the same paragraph, you may have no support for it, or if you have support, you may not have figured out what it is.
15. If you think that the other side's position is unreasonable and that yours is a matter of "common sense," ask yourself why. The debate is never concluded with the labeling or, if you are angry, with the name-calling. Your job may require you to identify with your client and feel indignant on their behalf (a paradox of our adversary system is that opposing lawyers can feel indignant for different sides on the same facts), but the indignation you feel does not confirm the validity of your argument.
16. Generic intensifiers such as "whatsoever," "in any way," "utterly," "completely" and "never" don't persuade. They merely give voice to your indignation. If you find yourself using these words, ask whether your facts can persuade without the purported boost.

17. If you can't answer the question, "What is my point?" then you may not have one.

Puzzler

How would you tighten and sharpen the following sentence?

In its opinion, the Appellate Division disagreed with the trial court and reversed the decision below.

Where would the Appellate Division express itself other than in its opinion? Drop "In its opinion" because it is implicit, just as you would drop "In his brief" if you were referring to the opposing party's argument. If the Appellate Division reversed a decision, then necessarily (a) the court disagreed with the trial court, and (b) the reversed decision was "below." You can drop "the trial court" and "the decision below" because both are implicit.

The revised version:

The Appellate Division reversed.

Thorough Editing Proceeds in Stages

Your initial changes may reveal more opportunities for improvement

The editing process should consist of more than one read-through of what you dictate or type. Sometimes you have to make one change before you see the possibility of another.

Consider the following sentence from a brief in which counsel contended that a partnership never arose between Jones and Smith:

A partnership between Jones and Smith was never thought of and never came into existence.

What problems do you notice with this sentence?

Did you notice that the phrase "was never thought of and never came into existence" is wordy? That the verbs are passive, not active? Or did you notice that the phrases "never thought of" and "never came into existence" are connected merely by "and," neither phrase being featured over, or subordinated to, the other.

You could emphasize the absence of a partnership by saying that not only didn't the partnership exist, but Jones and Smith never even thought of creating one. If the parties never thought about creating a partnership, they could hardly have entered into one.

Initially, you might not spot this possibility in a wordy sentence where the verbs are passive. Your first reaction may be to trim the sentence or to see if you can make the verbs active rather than passive.

For discussion purposes, let's trim the sentence, recognizing that if we looked initially to change the verbs from passive to active, the progression would be different:

A partnership between Jones and Smith was neither contemplated [instead of "never thought of"] nor created [instead of "never came into existence"].

"Contemplated" and "created" are more compact than what they replace, and they form a nice alliterative combination. I prefer "created" to "commenced," which would be too formal. "Neither . . . nor" improves on the two "nevers," at least in this version.

Shortening the sentence helps us see that one thought can be subordinated to the other:

A partnership between Jones and Smith was never even contemplated, let alone created.

"Never even" and "let alone" accomplish the subordination, and "neither . . . nor" falls away in deference to the stronger relationship.

Having produced subordination for emphasis, you would now ask whether the verbs can be made active (e.g., "created") rather than passive ("was . . . created"). If the verbs stay in the same order, the active voice may not be a good option:

Jones and Smith never even contemplated a partnership, let alone created one.

"Let alone created one" is awkward. Perhaps we can improve the sentence by moving "partnership" to the end:

Jones and Smith never even contemplated, let alone created, a partnership.

This seems like too much action ("never even contemplated, let alone created") before the reader finds out what is being acted upon (the partnership). Also, the phrase "let alone created" is still awkward.

Suppose we reverse the order of the verbs:

Not only did Jones and Smith never create a partnership, but they never even contemplated one.

This formulation is not bad, but it is long. Let's delete "not only . . . but they" and drop one of the "nevers":

Jones and Smith never created a partnership or even contemplated one.

That is the shortest of the active versions, but I prefer the passive construction because it allows me to highlight the phrase "was never even contemplated," which sets forth my most emphatic fact. After running all the possibilities, I choose the passive voice:

A partnership between Jones and Smith was never even contemplated, let alone created.

As editing processes go, this one was relatively brief. First, the prose was streamlined. Then one part of the sentence was subordinated to another for emphasis. Finally, we considered converting the verbs from passive to active but didn't.

As in most editing opportunities, even individual word choice was at issue. Contemplated and created were chosen for brevity and alliteration. Each reduced a phrase to one word.

Every sentence in a brief should go through this process, even language that you lift from judicial opinions but don't quote. The longer the sentence, the greater the number of variables and the more combinations you have to consider.

It's no wonder that a lawyer reviewing someone else's work product can almost always improve it. Legal issues generate sentences and paragraphs with so many combinations that one mind can rarely master them.

The active/passive issue is to some degree a matter of taste (with a strong bias toward the active), but subordination is a different story. When you find yourself connecting two thoughts with "and," look for subordination opportunities.

Often you will merely be tacking one idea to another where you could create a tighter relationship between them. The stronger the relationships you create among thoughts, the easier you make the reader's task and the more successful you will be in directing the reader to the conclusion you seek.

Puzzler

How would you tighten and sharpen the following sentence?

Plaintiff seeks to recover damages on his own behalf without alleging any specific harm that he purportedly suffered that is distinct from that allegedly suffered by ABC Corp.'s other shareholders.

This sentence appeared in the argument section of a brief in support of a motion to dismiss an individual action that should have been brought as a derivative action, in other words, as an action by one shareholder for the benefit of all. The opening clause ("Plaintiff seeks to recover damages on his own behalf") is unnecessary because plaintiff's having brought suit as an individual has undoubtedly been mentioned earlier. Here, it is used merely as a warm-up.

"That he purportedly suffered" is implicit, as is "specific." "That is" is unnecessary in front of "distinct." "Alleges no" is stronger than "without alleging."

The revised version:

Plaintiff alleges no harm distinct from that allegedly suffered by ABC Corp.'s other shareholders.

Writing Is a Self-Analytical Process

Quiz yourself relentlessly and without mercy as you compose

The quality of your brief is a function of the questions you ask yourself during the writing process. If you respond honestly and assiduously to the following questions, you will markedly increase your chances of writing something good.

- What is my point?
  No question could be more important. Everything flows from it. Your point isn't, for example, that the other side "fails to state a claim" or "fails to prove that any material facts are contested." Your point is that the low bidder's proposal was defective because it omitted a $70,000 line item or that an employee was fired because his incompetence ruined seven batches of product, not because he turned in somebody for stealing scraps. Your point must be premised in fact.
- Is my point credible?
  The answer is usually yes. Most points are credible. The problem is that the other side's point may be more credible.
- What will the other side argue?
  Put yourself in the other side's position. What would you argue? Whatever it is, confront it. Don't hide with the ostriches—*i.e.,* put your head in the sand. (I know they don't really put their heads in the sand.) The other side is competent, and they want to win, too.
- What have I done to win the reader over as soon as possible? Is my opening persuasive? If not, is it at least interesting? Does it build toward something persuasive?
  This is crucial. Readers are busier and more impatient than ever. They want to be persuaded, but they don't want to wait for the warmth of your argument to spread slowly through them. They want action. If you give them action, you may get them on your side early. Once converted, they will be more indulgent of what follows because readers, like jurors, interpret new evidence to support their working hypotheses.
- Have I been careful not to assume that the reader knows everything I know about the subject? Do I need to educate the reader?
- Is the reader likely to have preconceptions I need to dispel? If so, how do I handle them?
- If I were the reader, what would be going through my mind right now?
  Ask yourself this question frequently. Continually put yourself in the place of the reader.

- Have I given the reader reason to distrust me? That is, have I exaggerated? Ignored bad facts? Mischaracterized my adversary's arguments? Drawn unsupported conclusions? Restated my conclusions instead of presenting fact or argument to support them? Used intensifiers like "clearly" and "obviously" instead of presenting fact or argument? Made weak arguments?
- Have I made the most of my case law? Even if the facts of a case with good dicta are largely different from the facts of my case, can I find meaningful similarity?
- How about cases cited by my adversary? Am I truly distinguishing them or just pointing out immaterial differences?
- Does a common thread run through my cases? Through my adversary's?
- Have I mastered my facts? That is, have I reviewed all the documents and affidavits and read all the transcripts? Have I asked myself if each fact is good or bad for my case?
- Am I missing any facts that I could fill in by means of another affidavit?
- Have I used all my good facts to support my argument?
  You may wish to create working lists of good and bad facts to assist in determining how to feature or neutralize each of them.
- Am I merely reciting dicta, or am I tying the facts of my case to the facts of the cases I cite?
- Am I being clear? Can I make the reader's job easier?
- Do the sentences flow smoothly, or are they disjointed?
- Does each paragraph flow into the next?
- Am I repeating myself not for emphasis but as a substitute for factual support and analysis?
- Can I eliminate words without losing substance? (You can. Do it.)
- Can I be more precise? (You probably can. Give it some thought.)
- Can I find stronger words (*e.g.,* defendant "committed" rather than "agreed" to do something). Do any of my words carry connotations that hurt my argument?
- Have I checked my punctuation? If I don't understand punctuation, have I asked someone knowledgeable to check it for me?
- Have I tested every passive construction ("a meeting was held") to see if it works better in active form ("the parties met")?

- Is my tone appropriate? Am I being sarcastic? Strident? Cute? Whiney?
- Have I shown why the other side deserves to lose?
  This is a watershed question. Even if the court decides the case on a technical point, it needs the comfort of believing it is doing the right thing. If the other side deserves to lose, then the court is only rendering a judgment that is, in effect, pre-ordained, which means the court does not have to feel responsible for the litigant losing.
- Have I persuaded the court by the end of my preliminary statement? (If not, that's one strike against you.)
- Am I merely reiterating my equities without accounting for my adversary's? (If so, that's two strikes against you.)
- Have I made the result I advocate look fair? (If not, then it's strike three. You will almost certainly lose.)
- Finally, have I failed to think anything through?
  You usually know the answer to this question, but you may not be willing to face it. The issue you won't confront is the one you are afraid will defeat you.

Puzzler

Should you use a comma after "premises" in the following sentence?

The tenant could either maintain possession of the premises, or find another retailer and enter into a sublease.

Generally, you should not place a comma between subject and verb. The subject is "tenant," and the compound verb is "could . . . maintain . . . [or] find . . . [and] enter." Do not place a comma between "tenant" and any of the elements of the compound verb. If you restate the subject using the pronoun "he," then you would need a comma:

The tenant could maintain possession of the premises, or he could find another retailer and enter into a sublease.

You Have to Walk a Mile in the Reader's Shoes

To judge your own work, imagine you are the reader

At all stages of the writing process, from pre-writing through proofing, the self-critical faculty is crucial. You may work diligently and in a timely fashion, but if you cannot evaluate your ideas and the words you use to express them, then your effectiveness as an advocate is compromised.

We all evaluate our own writing to some degree, even work that is "dictated but not read." In the manner of the Scientific Method, we formulate hypotheses, test them, reformulate them and test them again.

To some degree for each project, we ask ourselves whether we have a point, and if so, whether we have made it. If we perform this self-checking and self-correcting function relentlessly, we may write well.

Letting Time Pass

An associate asked how she could gain the perspective to evaluate her own work. The easy answer, I said, is to let time pass between drafts. A gap in time provides a fresh view because the mind regroups data.

Like a computer, the mind performs functions on data, which means it sorts data. Unlike a computer, the mind may not recreate the same groups each time it visits a database. Memory degrades, and new ideas emerge. Groupings shift, like crystals in a kaleidoscope.

The more time that elapses between visits to the database, and the more complex the data and the issues, the more the mind may forget or reject its groupings. It may create new groups, new sets and subsets, possibly better than the old. Hence, the easy answer to the question of how to gain the perspective to edit your own work is to set it aside and come back to it.

Finding the Right Mind-Set

The more difficult task is to create a mind-set that fosters regrouping, one that enhances the perspective that comes naturally with the passage of time. If you wish to do more than just give your mind time to regroup data, you must develop a mind-set for self-criticism.

The way to develop this mind-set is to imagine being the reader. Pretend to be receiving, not sending, the message.

By imagining yourself to be the reader, you can evaluate your work dispassionately and, as necessary, reformulate it. As the imagined third-party reader of your own draft, you continually ask yourself three questions:

- Can I understand this?
- What are my concerns?
- Have my concerns been addressed?

The first question addresses an elemental building block of communication: To convey an idea, you must make it understandable. From the reader's perspective, is the piece well-organized? Is the prose dense or convoluted? Are the ideas clear?

The second question addresses the actual or apparent weakness in your case. You may have a strong case with no real weakness, but you can't expect the other side to acknowledge that. They will, at a minimum, allege some reason why your client doesn't deserve to win. You have to anticipate that.

The third question asks if you have addressed the reader's concerns. That, ultimately, is the test of persuasion. It is the hardest question to ask yourself, let alone answer.

In short, if you can put yourself in the place of the reader and take an honest look at your own work, you may be able to sail between the Scylla and Charybdis of self-analysis: insularity—meaning the failure to see your writing as the reader sees it—and self-deception.

During the writing process, your intimacy with the material keeps the data and the relationships among the data in current awareness, making simulation of unfamiliarity more difficult. This fosters insularity.

Though you may see all the connections, the reader may not. In your insularity, you don't realize the reader can't see them as you can. As time weakens the connections in your mind, you become more like the reader—dependent on the printed page.

As for self-deception, sometimes you don't have a point and don't realize it. You state your conclusion three times and think you are making a point. You misread or misinterpret cases. You are in the grip of your own desire to have things be as you want them to be.

Taking a Step Back

All writing instructors agree that to overcome insularity and self-deception, you have to "take a step back" from your work. Putting "distance" between yourself and your writing is another metaphor. The distance you need to establish is the ability to see your writing as others see it. The step you need to take, meaning the function you need to perform, is to imagine yourself as the reader.

You have to ask yourself what questions the reader may be asking and what concerns the reader, such as a judge, may have. Your job isn't just to assert the equities for your client ("My client's ox was gored as follows."). You have to anticipate the court's concern that if it rules for you, it will be negating the equities on the other side. How can you help it resolve that conflict?

The court will wish to do what is fair, and to do what is fair, the court has to figure out which way the scales of justice tip—that is, to determine whose equities weigh more. The court will not ignore the other side's equities, so you can't either. You have to account for them.

Puzzler

How would you tighten and sharpen the following sentence?

At the completion of the hearing, the Chairman moved for a resolution granting petitioner's application, however, the application was denied by a 3-2 vote.

Most "howevers" are unnecessary. Just say the Chairman's motion to grant the application was denied. That eliminates the need to punctuate "however" correctly (preceding it with a semicolon rather than a comma) and knocks out the second "application." Technically, the motion, not the application, was denied.

"Motion to grant" is shorter than "motion for a resolution granting" (the resolution is understood), and "end" (of the hearing) is shorter and more precise than "completion."

The revised version:

At the end of the hearing, the Chairman's motion to grant petitioner's application was denied by a 3-2 vote.

Know When It Is Time To Rewrite Rather Than Edit

Sometimes you have to clean house

> One cannot say anything simply and clearly unless one first understands it clearly.
>
> —Henry Weihofen, *Legal Writing Style* (2d Ed.) (1980) at 61

You have drafted a brief and met with your assigning attorney, who told you the draft, or a good part of it, misses the point. The paragraphs are out of synch, and the argument isn't clear.

Maybe you tried to build a theme around facts that are merely flavor. Perhaps you put the wrong spin on the cases, or you failed to marshal your best facts. When you return to work, your first thought is to salvage the draft.

Don't do it.

The wrong thinking in the draft will control you. You must let your investment in the draft go. You can't recycle the sentences by moving them around, just as you can't unpuzzle a jigsaw if the pieces have been mis-cut.

True, the thought of beginning from scratch is intolerable. If you can save time by reusing sentences and even paragraphs, then your initial efforts won't totally have gone to waste.

Your reluctance to discard product is a formidable impediment to improving the brief, not only because recycling old material doesn't work but because you waste energy trying to force a square peg into a round hole and because your focus on salvaging rather than rethinking keeps you from attacking the real problem—your lack of clarity.

The principal barrier to improving faulty drafts isn't the difficulty of forming sentences and paragraphs. It is the confusion of not knowing precisely what you wish to say. If you are unsure of your point, you will struggle to express it. You can edit until your fingers cramp up, but you will accomplish nothing.

Conversely, if you know your point, the words will probably flow. You write more easily about what you understand.

Think and Talk First; Write Later

To get clear on your point, think about it. This seems extraordinarily obvious, but many writers just plunge ahead, fingers whirring over the keyboard, as if a moment's delay is a moment lost. They spend no time contemplating the problem.

You don't have to rent a room for a weekend to think quietly. Just take fifteen minutes in your office, or pace the halls. Thinking about an issue will pay off not only in the strength of your ideas but in the ease with which you write.

When thinking has taken you as far as it can, and maybe even before, discuss your ideas with someone. Discussion does more than just develop collegiality. It provides a dialectic, the back-and-forth that allows you to explore the validity of an idea and the possibility of new ones. It brings fresh perspective, particularly if your listener doesn't have the same investment in the case as you and isn't constricted or propelled by wishful thinking.

A dialogue also lets you test several ideas in succession—something very difficult to do by yourself unless you take the unusual step of writing out alternative arguments. In a discussion, rejected theories can serve as springboards to viable ones. Under almost all circumstances, talking out an issue is more productive than sitting in front of a blank sheet of paper or an empty screen.

Outlining Also Helps

Outlining has long been touted as an organizational tool, but some writers are suspicious of it. They deem it a diversion from the hard task of developing a dominant theme. The energy used to create an outline, some feel, would be better spent crafting one's core point.

Others fear that if they create an outline, they will have to feed it, that is, fill it in, and they'd rather let their creative juices dictate the direction their writing takes.

I don't reject these concerns out of hand, but outlining has saved my bacon many times. It provides psychological as well as logistical support by introducing order to an otherwise unmanageable mass of material.

If outlining seems more of a barrier to you than a passageway, try reducing its scope. Write some ideas on a page and consider how they can be grouped or rank ordered. Let this be your small concession to regimentation. You can control the outlining process. It needn't control you.

After you think, discuss and outline, you are ready to write. The extra thinking and planning will pay off many times over. Not only will your writing be more to the point and more persuasive, but the task will be easier. Words flow more readily from the pen of a writer who has a clear idea.

Writing Helps Us Think

Suppose you can't seem to find time to think (if so, you aren't looking hard enough), or your thinking bears no fruit. And suppose you can't find someone to join you in a discourse, or you won't ask because you are afraid of looking stupid. You want a reputation as someone who always brings something to the table, not someone who looks for handouts. As for outlining, "passive aggressive" best describes your attitude.

You might try free writing your ideas or free dictating them. Get something down that you can mull over. Think of it as notes, not product. You invest more in product than in notes.

Unless you have the mind of a chess master, chances are you will make more progress with something in writing than something in your head, even if the writing is verbose and disorganized. You may be discouraged by the drivel, but soon enough, a few pieces will fit together; some will drop away or be set aside for later; and an argument will emerge, like a chick from a shell.

Writing and thinking are synergistic. Not only does thinking help us write, but writing helps us think. We can see things on the page that we can't see in our mind, just as we play chess better when we see the board.

As W. Ross Winterowd said in *Contemporary Rhetoric* (1975):

> Writing is not only the exposition of ideas, but also the working out of ideas. Often we really don't know what we want to say until we've said it. [at 33].

Ultimately, the writing process is a subset of the Scientific Method: you gather evidence, form a hypothesis, test the hypothesis, gather more evidence and reformulate the hypothesis. Thinking, talking, outlining and free writing all help you formulate and evaluate your hypothesis. They bring you closer to the truth.

Puzzler

How would you tighten and sharpen the following sentence?

There is simply no support for this position in the December 5 order issued by the Court.

Run as fast as you can from "there is" and "there are," which are almost always useless, and drop "simply" as an unnecessary intensifier. Drop the reference to the Court because the Court's authorship of the order is implicit. End the sentence with "gives this position no support" rather than "does not support this position" to emphasize the lack of support.

The revised version:

The December 5 order gives this position no support.

Seek Feedback on Your Work for a Fresh Perspective

When you give feedback, make sure it is received

One of the most extraordinary phenomena in the writing process is the power of feedback. I'm not speaking of red-lining or of highly specific suggestions such as, "You need a comma there," or, "Don't you think the phrase 'failed to' would be stronger than 'did not'?"

I'm speaking of comments that identify a problem but only hint at a solution, such as, "I felt the writing lagged about the middle of page two"; "The first page didn't get right down to it"; "You lost me in the detail on page three"; or, "I might have said something about X before getting into Y." Even a broad expression of taste such as "I don't like it" can send a resourceful writer back to the drawing board with good results.

If a reader says my draft preliminary statement "bogs down" in the second paragraph, then I ask myself why. Is the first sentence dull? Does the paragraph fade after a good start? Does it stray off message? Re-examination almost always, magically, produces results.

When a reader expresses confusion or doubt, I resist the urge to believe the reader is missing it. Any reader intelligent enough to pass the Bar probably doesn't "miss it." He might not write well (which is a ready excuse for me to pretend he can't read well, either), but he knows what works and what doesn't. I don't like falling short of the mark, and I don't like extra work, but I expect it, plan for it, and as best I can, handle it.

Few writers like being told that a brief or memo could have been better. Those who disavow pride of authorship are probably fooling themselves or just posturing. Generally, we grin and bear it. We endure the discomfort of criticism because it's our job and because responding to criticism is not without its rewards.

A writer who improves a product after feedback receives nearly all the credit for the final version. The positive impression created by the stronger product and by the writer having improved the work in response to criticism—which means he is a functional member of the team—overrides the potentially deflating fact that the writer didn't do it alone. Team members understand team play.

What, then, is the lesson?

Seek feedback. Don't be a hero. Don't try to prove you are Mr. Turnkey and can produce a finished product entirely on your own. Seek another perspective. Sure, it's depressing when you are told, correctly, that you overlooked the significance of a case, put something last that should go first or (hopefully not) missed the point. But as drafter, you are prone to such mistakes. Have someone tell you if you are making them.

In doing the research, analyzing the cases and tooling the sentences, you become expert in the trees. In focusing on the trees, as you must, you sometimes miss the forest. Feedback shows you the forest. The reader, after all, does not have to study the trees.

The value of feedback is magnified when a reader comments on a passage that already troubles the writer. The synergy can be powerful. I make some of my best changes when a single remark, oral or written, calls attention to a passage about which I already had doubts.

Unfortunately, the magic of the critical comment doesn't work for everyone all the time. I have told associates that they didn't write up a case well or that a long paragraph was too hard to follow. The next draft was no better, and the convolutions the associate went through to try to fix it were embarrassing.

I think I know why. The associate didn't understand the point. Not understanding the point, the associate couldn't write it clearly. That may be a truism (a self-evident truth too obvious to mention), but assigning attorneys often lose sight of it.

If we fully understood this truth, would we insist that an associate who wrote a weak draft "try again with more discussion of the case law"? Would we write "unclear" in the margin and leave it at that? Would we tell the associate to rewrite without helping her rethink? How frequently do we spew our analysis as the associate writes furiously, trying to capture the words in the hope of later filling in the thought?

Admit it—showing how smart we are is fun; it takes less time and energy than helping an associate see the point; and it resonates with our sense that if we pay associates so much, they ought to be able to develop the idea once we state it. Join these dubious motivations with the more healthy perspective that an associate needs to be challenged to grow, and we easily persuade ourselves that associates can and should make the quantum leap from frantic scrivener to articulate author.

I remember being afraid to ask for guidance. The fear was a tremendous barrier, and it wasn't imaginary. As one member of my informal polling group says, with only slight exaggeration, "Getting a rep for being 'stupid' is the quickest way out the door in a law firm."

Experienced writers are better trained and less afraid. They have more confidence in their image and their ability to cope, and thus they are more receptive to criticism (except when they become uncritical of their gut response and Go Stubborn, which is another issue). Being less fearful of looking stupid, they are more willing to show ignorance. They understand that ignorance is transient, merely an embryonic phase in the development of a memo or brief.

Experienced writers listen better because they know better; they force themselves to accept criticism; and they make sure they understand it, restating the criticism to confirm it. They are better at testing alternative solutions and getting to the point. They know—from experience—that the point is the only place worth getting to.

The perception of many partners is that some associates can respond to criticism, and some cannot. That is true, but in degree, not in kind. Understanding comes later for some. I have faith that feedback works if received.

But feedback sent isn't feedback received. One way to find out if it has been received is to ask—not merely, "Do you understand?" which almost always generates a nod, but "How would you restate the point we just discussed?"

Try that. Having a listener restate a thought is a powerful way to confirm receipt of a message, to see if the listener has truly embraced it.[1]

Puzzler

How would you improve the following sentence?

He expressed dissatisfaction and disdain for the settlement negotiations.

Dissatisfaction and disdain take different prepositions. We speak of dissatisfaction "with" and disdain "for" negotiations. For clarity or emphasis, you may wish to set off the second phrase with commas.

The revised version:

He expressed dissatisfaction with, and disdain for, the settlement negotiations.

Alternate version:

He expressed dissatisfaction with and disdain for the settlement negotiations.

[1] An attorney I know carries this to an extreme. If I suggest that we argue, for example, that a plume of contamination could not possibly have traveled 200 feet from ABC Co.'s property in one year, he then says, with vigor, "A plume of contamination could not possibly have traveled 200 feet from ABC Co.'s property in one year," as if he'd just had the thought. Depending on my mood, I'll say either, "That's what I just said" or "Good idea."

When Writing a Memo, Keep the Reader in Mind

Dispel preconceptions as quickly as possible

Your most important task in creating a memo is to deal with the substance—to determine, for example, whether your client breached a contract or committed a business tort. You deal with the substance by gathering the law and the facts and applying each to the other. Your research should be thorough and your analysis sharp.

Your second most important task in creating a memo is to get your point across. This is where "the reader" comes in. Your memo is useless unless its message is received.

Because readers aren't robots, you have to account for human factors that can interfere with transmittal of the message, such as attitudes (*e.g.*, impatience), preconceptions and prior knowledge. For every sentence, if not every word, ask yourself, "What does the reader need to know? What do I want the reader to know? What is the reader thinking?"

Suppose your client in a civil case wants to depose a criminal defendant who has entered a plea of *nolo contendere* (no contest) and is out on bail awaiting sentencing. You have been asked whether a defendant who has entered a *nolo* plea is deemed to have waived the Fifth Amendment privilege against self-incrimination. If the defendant retains the privilege pending sentencing, he can quash a civil subpoena because a deposition would place him at risk of self-incrimination.

Your assigning attorney believes that the Fifth Amendment privilege is waived when a guilty plea is entered because the defendant has incriminated himself. The attorney reasons that *nolo* pleas should also waive the privilege because a *nolo* plea functions like a guilty plea, exposing the defendant to incarceration.

The case law does not support his views. Courts have held that persons awaiting sentencing after a guilty plea retain their Fifth Amendment privilege against self-incrimination. The rationale is that anything they say to their detriment pending sentencing could be used against them in the sentencing proceeding. According to the case law, the "incrimination process" isn't over until sentencing.

You find nothing about the effect of *nolo* pleas on the privilege against self-incrimination, but you conclude that the rationale for the privilege surviving a guilty plea should sustain the privilege after a *nolo* plea as well. Both pleas are dispositive.

Let's examine three choices you'll make in drafting the memo: (1) how to formulate the question; (2) how to formulate the Short Answer; and (3) how to shape the discussion. The factual elements are as follows:

(1) defendant
(2) *nolo contendere* plea

(3) Fifth Amendment privilege against self-incrimination

(4) pending sentencing hearing

Listing these elements helps you draft the following question:

Does a defendant who has pled nolo contendere retain the Fifth Amendment privilege against self-incrimination pending sentencing?

The question tracks the facts. First you establish the subject—the defendant. Then you "modify" the subject (describe it) to show the reader that your focus is on defendants who have entered *nolo* pleas. Then you move to the verb "retain," which is particularly efficient. It implies that the defendant has a privilege (you have to have something to retain it), and it primes the reader to receive the temporal information in the phrase "pending sentencing" (the reader asks, "Retain when or how long?" and the answer is "Pending sentencing").

A possible reformulation of the question, favored by several members of my informal polling group, is as follows:

Does a defendant retain the Fifth Amendment privilege against self-incrimination after entering a plea of nolo contendere and prior to sentencing?

This formulation gains by posing the question early (Does a defendant retain the privilege?), but it loses by posing the question before presenting the reason for the question (that the defendant has entered a *nolo* plea). It gains a bit of clarity by highlighting the time frame ("after entering . . . and prior to"), but it loses some fluidity. I prefer the original version. It presents the information in optimum order, and it is more compact.

Your Short Answer also presents a choice. You can begin with the conclusion (that the Fifth Amendment privilege survives) or with the reason why the privilege survives (a defendant could be prejudiced at sentencing by self-incriminating statements made between plea and sentencing). Because of your reader's preconception, begin with the rationale, not the conclusion.

Beginning with your conclusion—that a defendant who has entered a *nolo* plea retains the Fifth Amendment privilege pending sentencing—may trigger a doubting response in a reader who has a preconception to the contrary. Weaken the preconception by beginning with the reason:

Because anything a defendant says before sentencing can be used against him at sentencing, the Fifth Amendment privilege against self-incrimination is not extinguished by a dispositive plea, whether "guilty" or "nolo contendere." The privilege survives until sentencing is complete.

Now the reader is "softened up." By leading with the rationale, you have shown respect for the reader and loosened the grip of his preconception. You can now begin the discussion.

Assume you found no case addressing whether the Fifth Amendment privilege against self-incrimination survives a *nolo* plea. The rationale for survival of the privilege between guilty plea and sentencing should apply to *nolo* pleas as well. A person awaiting sentencing after a *nolo* plea is as vulnerable to self-incrimination as a person awaiting sentencing after a guilty plea.

The logical chain would run as follows:

Defendants who plead guilty retain the Fifth Amendment privilege against self-incrimination pending sentencing.

A nolo plea places a defendant in the same position of vulnerability pending sentencing as does a guilty plea.

Therefore, a defendant who enters a nolo plea retains the Fifth Amendment privilege against self-incrimination pending sentencing.

You always need a logical chain. Outlining it helps confirm its validity.

Puzzler

How would you tighten and sharpen the following sentence?

The court in Smith v. Jones applied a five-part series of factors for consideration in determining whether to permit limited discovery from the ISP of sufficient information to permit service of process on defendant Jones.

Internet service providers (ISPs) can be compelled to reveal the identity of persons who post defamatory material on the Internet if the requesting party satisfies a multipart test. Shorten "series of factors for consideration" to "test."

Change the concept of "permitting" discovery to "compelling" production. Words like "order," "grant" or "compel" more accurately describe the judicial process because the court will order discovery, not merely permit it. Such words are also more assertive. "To determine" is more forceful than "in determining."

"Limited" and "sufficient" cover the same ground, so you don't need both. You can drop "defendant" at the end of the sentence because it is implicit, but you probably need "on Jones."

The revised version:

The court in Smith v. Jones applied a five-part test to determine whether to compel the ISP to produce sufficient information to permit service of process on Jones.

When Editing Time Is Limited, Perform a Triage

Begin by confirming your purpose and your dominant point

A reader asked how to prioritize editing tasks when time is short (or when money is short, which makes time short). The touchstone, as always, is persuasion. Address the elements that will have the greatest impact on the reader.

First, confirm your purpose. This may be easy—*e.g.,* you seek to have a complaint dismissed—or it may not. Perhaps you want to advise a client that the defendant's settlement offer is inadequate but warn the client that trial may bring no recovery at all. Be clear on your goal. To paraphrase Yogi Berra: If you don't know where you're going, you may not get there.

Next, make sure you have a theme—a dominant point that you can express in a sentence or two (*e.g.,* "Plaintiff's claim must be rejected because he sat on his rights for three years."). Test your theme against elemental principles of morality, such as, "Keep your promises"; "Don't lie"; "Be careful"; "Be timely"; and "Don't be greedy." Put yourself in the reader's place. Does the result you advocate seem fair?

The suggestion that you put yourself in the reader's place isn't facile self-help advice, like telling someone to meditate who has never done it before. Identifying with the reader is a subset of "perspective taking"—the ability to see things from another's point of view. This ability is a kind of intelligence, and it is within every lawyer's skill set.

Once you are clear on your purpose and your theme, confirm that your theme has support. Do you have good facts? If not, you will lose. Facts rule. They are the basis on which the court decides how to balance the equities and do the right thing.

Do you have law? Without law, you may lose if the balance of the equities isn't clear. Because rulings in other cases are largely the result of equitable balancings, the absence of favorable law may cause the court to suspect that the balance should be struck against you.

Once you are confident in your theme, ask yourself if you have confronted the other side's best argument. You may already have done so in formulating your theme. If you haven't, do so now. Ultimately, the question is, "Whose dominant point is more dominant?"

When you are confident in the strength of your theme, ask yourself if you have begun powerfully. In a brief, this means a strong preliminary statement. Get the reader on your side early so you benefit from the tendency of readers, like jurors, to reconcile additional information with their first impression. The reader will tend to interpret facts and cases as consistent with your theme if the writing was persuasive from the outset.

Starting strong also gives the reader confidence in your theme because you had the confidence to lead with it. Deep down, the reader wants you to take command and to make the reader's decision easy.

The impact of the preliminary statement was confirmed for me years ago when a senior partner said that my draft brief missed the point. I refocused the first paragraph of the preliminary statement and, knowing my reader, changed almost nothing else. He said the revised brief was "much stronger."

Because your theme is built around your best fact, your first sentence should, if possible, feature that fact. Forget about procedure ("This is a brief opposing summary judgment") and forget the intensifiers and the *ad hominem* attacks ("Without an iota of support in the facts or the law, plaintiff unjustifiably [outrageously, blatantly] blah blah blah"). Go with your best fact (*e.g.,* "A plaintiff who doesn't recognize the duty to mitigate is looking for a free ride.").

When you are confident that you have a clear purpose, a solid theme and a strong beginning, make sure the writing flows. Lather on the headings, subheadings and bullets to break up the text, and make sure your logic is tight. Chances are, it isn't. Check your topic sentences. Any that seem awkward, or that aren't really topic sentences, may signal that you have lost the thread. Sentences within paragraphs should be in proper sequence.

At this point, if circumstances are exigent, you may have run out of time. But you must do one more thing—proofread. It won't make your point, but it will keep you from unmaking it. Because the court has to rely on you for the facts and the law, the court is sensitive to your integrity as an advocate. Lack of physical integrity (typos) suggests lack of intellectual integrity. Sloppiness undermines credibility.

If any time does remain, perform the following tasks, not necessarily in this order:

- Reiterate your best facts. This is different from reiterating conclusions. Facts persuade; conclusions do not.
- Continually guide the reader. Make everything clear, shifting back and forth from your perspective to the reader's. Always ask yourself what the reader needs to know. Introduce quotations; never punt with "As the court said." Use internal summaries. Keep your quotations short or highlight them with underlining.
- Shape your prose with parallel structure, active voice, strong sentence endings and precise words. Trim intensifiers, editorials and excessive words. Bring subjects and verbs close together.
- Finally, check your punctuation or, if you can't punctuate, ask for help.

Even in a short time frame, have someone read the draft. Whether it is the first or fifth draft will depend on your tolerance for criticism, your wish to maintain an image as a good writer and your sense of when the help would do the most good. A fresh view is an asset.

You can sharpen your own "reader's perspective" by placing work aside. Even an hour away from a brief, memo or letter helps. Overnight is better. As time passes, the patterns in your mind weaken, and fresh patterns emerge. The fresh patterns are new ways to see your work, as if you were the reader.

Setting a draft aside and coming back to it is generally less productive than obtaining feedback from an enlightened reader. On the other hand, setting a draft aside and then reviewing it critically yourself may be more productive than giving the piece to an uncritical or unmotivated reader. Use your judgment.

The best way to handle a short time frame is to prepare for it. Be certain of your purpose and your theme. Confirm them in strategy conversations with other lawyers. Have your materials lined up and your ideas outlined so you don't have to sacrifice chunks of time for supplemental research or re-organizing the brief. If you are discomfited by the question "What should I edit in a short time frame?" you may not have fully prepared.

Puzzler

How would you tighten and sharpen the following sentence?

In reaching its conclusion, the court reasoned that plaintiff had instigated the events which led to his termination.

The first four words are a classic delete, just like the phrase "In its opinion" or "In his brief." All are implicit. At the end of the sentence, "which" should be "that."

The revised version:

The court reasoned that plaintiff had instigated the events that led to his termination.

Good Editing Is Important, But Solid Preparation Is Key

Thorough research and analysis reduces work on the back end

The editing process is a word puzzle, the pieces of which are denotations and connotations, tones, rhythms and word order. Good writers shuffle and shape these puzzle pieces until they mesh seamlessly to make a point. They refine the work until it says exactly what the writer means, clearly and compactly, and until they are sure that what is said is correct. Good editing can make writing sing.

Some say the "secret" of good legal writing is good editing. I disagree. Though editing is important—it can make the unclear clear and the dull vigorous—it cannot save a badly conceived piece. It is not a panacea for a poor approach. To the contrary, the possibility of salvaging weak writing through editing traps some lawyers into thinking that their haphazardly recorded thoughts constitute workable drafts.

Some litigators shoot first (type or dictate ideas as a purported draft) and ask questions later (like, "Is this a persuasive approach?" "Do I have facts to support this thesis?"). They don't think the problem through because they are impatient or overworked or because they overvalue their gut instinct.

At the other end of the confidence spectrum, some lawyers are so afraid of "getting a zero"—having nothing to say—that they write prematurely just to get something down. Typical of this category is the isolated associate who has to write a brief in support of a marginal argument and has nobody with whom to brainstorm and nobody from whom to obtain more facts or new ideas for legal research. Both types of writers are out of touch with the more significant "secret" of legal writing—thorough preparation. (It isn't really a secret; it's just crucial.)

The backbone of a good brief develops long before the drafting, let alone the editing. It begins—not strangely—with the goal, the purpose for writing. If the goal is attainable (*e.g.,* a well-grounded motion to dismiss or motion to compel), then the brief may persuade. If the goal is misguided (*e.g.,* too ambitious), then the brief won't persuade, whether well-written or not.

Assuming the goal makes sense, then the person assigned the task of writing the brief must understand the issue. Solving the wrong problem accomplishes nothing. Assigning attorneys know this, but they often fail to confirm that an assignment was correctly received.

Even before the legal research begins, the facts should be "marshaled" (gathered, sorted, presented). Without all the facts, you don't know how the scales of justice should tip (*i.e.,* whether you should win and why), and you can't analogize or distinguish case law very well, which is why assigning attorneys who ask associates to research "the law" but give them only skeletal facts might wish to rethink that approach.

After gathering and grouping the facts, you are ready to do what you were trained to do in law school—find and analyze cases and state the law. If you are resourceful, you will use other attorneys as sounding boards and sources for ideas, accomplishing much more at the hub of a network than you can on your own.

You will also outline your ideas, whether traditionally, with Roman numerals, or nontraditionally, with mini-paragraphs, lines, circles or the like. Outlining helps you order and group, which helps you create the logical thread.

At some point, you will "theme" the case. You will review your facts and your law—mostly your facts—and will determine why you should win, that is, why your client wears the white hat, or the other side wears the black. Your theme is the focal point of the case. If it is strong, you will probably win. (Talk about "secrets" of legal writing!)

A theme will be something like, "The defendant held back a crucial fact," "The plaintiff could have negotiated for a liquidated damages clause but didn't," or "The defendant's actions were the reason the plaintiff could not perform." If the court is persuaded that your client holds the high moral ground (has the best theme), and in some cases, if the court is comfortable that ruling for your client will not weaken the fabric of the law (hard cases make bad law), then you should win.

If you take all these steps before you create your first draft of a brief—that is, formulate a manageable task, marshal the facts, thoroughly research and analyze the legal issues, order your thoughts and theme the case—you will have less need later to move points and paragraphs around, scrap topic sentences and change your spin.

You can then put the editing process to its highest and best use—achieving clarity and punch by beginning powerfully, trimming unnecessary words, reiterating key facts, adding transitions, shaping sentences for emphasis and flow, choosing the right word and supplying internal summaries. Such changes make writing sharp and powerful. But without them, your writing can still be effective.

In contrast, if your goal is foolish, or if you fail to develop the facts, research and analyze the cases, order your ideas and adequately theme the case, then your writing will be ineffective no matter how assiduously you refine your prose.

Ultimately, thinking and writing are synergistic. Thinking is a prerequisite to writing, and writing can aid thinking, as when the flaws in an argument don't become apparent until the argument is written. Though I prefer to test ideas in conversation, I may write an argument just to see how it looks. (Don't get jealous. I don't do it much. Writing is not so easy for me, nor do I have so much time, that I write points experimentally as one would dab paint on a pallet.)

If you write before you have finished gathering, grouping and thinking, don't view what you write as a draft. It is merely the manifestation of your preliminary thoughts. If you treat it as a draft, you'll do several times the editing to get it right, and you may not get it right at all.

Puzzler

How would you tighten and sharpen the following sentence?

Lawyers need to be tenacious in the extraction of facts, and they need to be patient to wait for the information to emerge, thoughtful to ponder the problem and creative to find a theme that will resonate with the court.

Look for opportunities to group. Here, lawyers are performing essentially two functions—extracting facts and shaping a theme. The pondering is part of the shaping. For starters, link the four adjectives (tenacious, patient, thoughtful and creative) to the two sets (extracting facts and shaping a theme), two adjectives to a set. Tenacious and patient relate to extracting facts, and thoughtful and creative relate to shaping a theme.

Look to delete words that are implicit. For example, a person is thoughtful "to ponder the problem." Thus, "to ponder the problem" can be deleted. Similarly, a person is patient "to wait for the information to emerge," so you can delete that phrase, too.

The "-ing" form ("extracting facts") is shorter and generally better than the three-part combination of article ("the"), noun ("extraction") and prepositional phrase ("of facts").

For extra credit, "shape" rather than "find" a theme. Persons who shape are in control, which is where you wish to be. For additional extra credit, drop the concept of thoughtfulness to shorten the sentence and add punch. The concept is implicit.

I prefer the "to be" version here ("Lawyers need to be patient") over the more active version ("Lawyers need patience") because I like the rhythm and because the slow emergence of the thought using the passive verb reflects the deliberateness of the process. For the same reasons, I prefer "in extracting" rather than "to extract."

I like "patient" before "tenacious" because of the sound and because it builds from the passive (patient) to the aggressive (tenacious).

The revised version:

Lawyers need to be patient and tenacious in extracting facts and creative in shaping a theme that will resonate with the court.

Alternate version:

Lawyers need patience and tenacity in extracting facts and creativity in shaping a theme that will resonate with the court.

Misinterpreting Cases Is an Occupational Hazard

Beware of both wishful thinking and defeatism

Doing legal research can be like watching a professional basketball game. When you are finding cases that seem helpful, your team is scoring at will and holds a comfortable lead.

Then you find law that appears to hurt your case, and the momentum shifts. The other team goes on a run, catches up and forges ahead, index fingers jabbing the air as if to say, "We're Number One! We're Number One!"

Be wary of the hope and despair generated by legal research. Your emotions cause you to read too much into judicial opinions, whether the opinions appear helpful or harmful. Precedents are often not as good or bad as they initially seem. Because their facts are almost always different from the facts in your case, the cases are rarely "on all fours."

Falling in Love with Dicta

We tend to interpret cases to support the results we desire. As the saying goes, "Be careful what you seek, for what you seek, you shall find." If you lack support for a proposition, you will be tempted to see a case that is only vaguely relevant as being directly on point, and you will be tempted to suppress your awareness of how the case is materially different from yours. I doubt you do this consciously; few are that cynical. You believe what you think you see.

You overvalue cases where the fight is heaviest, where you are straining to support a position that is only a little better, or a little worse, than the other side's. Driven by the hot blood of the fight and pressed for time, you overlook facts, or you focus on language that appears to support your position but is, by any fair analysis, inconsistent with a governing rule.

For example, counsel looking to defend the rejection of all bids by public entities in New Jersey have latched onto the phrase "good faith" in the following dictum to support the argument that under the bidding statute, a public body can reject all bids for any reason—including nothing more than the desire to force the bidders lower—as long as the public entity's intent is not to direct the contract to a favorite son:

> *When a municipal governing body concludes in good faith that the purposes of the public bidding statute are being violated, it may reject all bids submitted and in its discretion order a re-advertising of the contract.*

Because the "purposes of the public bidding statute" include saving public money, advocates figure that anything done to save public money is acceptable, short of favoritism.

"Good faith" was not a good choice in the above dictum because the actions of public bodies in New Jersey are governed by the "arbitrary and capricious" test, which is objective, not by the good faith test, which is subjective. Rejecting all bids merely because the public body thinks the bids may be lower the next time is considered arbitrary (though rejecting all bids because they exceed the public body's cost estimate or its appropriation for the job is acceptable).

The objective test doesn't stop advocates desperate for support from taking a shot at the subjective test with the "good faith" dictum above even though, earlier in its opinion, the court said that "our courts do not subscribe" to the view that arbitrariness and capriciousness is immaterial provided that bids are rejected in good faith.

Expanding the Rule

Not only do advocates misread dicta, but they may try to create a rule broader than the facts of a case allow. Suppose, for example, that you represent a public entity that gave notice to a bidder that it would be awarded a contract, but now the public entity wants to award the contract to another bidder. As counsel to the public entity, you seek to establish that mere notice of award does not create a binding contract between the bidder and the public entity.

You find a case that appears to state that rule, but the facts are different. Notice of award fell short of creating a contract because the request for bids said negotiation was required before the awarded contract would be deemed final. Though the dictum appears helpful, the facts are materially distinguishable.

You convince yourself that notice of award never creates a contract between bidder and public entity even though the only rule derivable from the holding in the case you cite is that notice of award fails to create a contract if negotiation is required between bidder and public entity before the contract is considered final.

Exalting the Factual Coincidence

In another typical instance of wishful thinking, writers may fix on a factual similarity between a putative precedent and their case even though the fact is collateral to the holding and thus immaterial. Because they are trying to hit a home run with an apparent match, they stretch their analysis of the holding past the breaking point. This could apply, for example, where the same product is at issue in both cases (*e.g.*, PVC pipe) or where the defendant is the same in both cases (*e.g.*, the same insurance company).

Being Intimidated by Bad Dicta

All researchers are discouraged by bad dicta. Some are intimidated and give up. They concede where they should stand firm and give ground that should be defended.

Do not be easily discouraged. Chances are, something in the facts of the case you need to distinguish is materially different from the facts of your case. If you find a case on all fours where the highest court of your state held against the position you espouse, then you lose. But that rarely happens. When it does, your job is to settle the case short of a judicial resolution or, if you are the plaintiff, not to bring an action in the first place.

Read every important case at least twice, better yet three times. Get the gist of the case and then re-read it to examine why it is like, or not like, your case. Then read it again. Some cases may warrant Talmudic study if the amount at risk justifies the cost. I can almost guarantee that your insight will deepen with each reading and that the law of diminishing returns will take far longer than you think to take hold.

Associates complain, reasonably, that they don't have time to examine cases. They are given only a few days, maybe a week or two, to research and write a brief, even as other assignments nag at them for attention. They can feel the assigning attorney hovering, waiting to opine that their brief lacks punch or misses the point. These are legitimate concerns for which I have no easy answer. Personally, I try not to hover or nag.

If you are forced to rush through cases, or if reviewing attorneys are finding mistakes in your analysis, then perhaps you should defend your reading and thinking time with greater vigor. Say "no" to new work and don't overbook. Leave more time for thought.

Puzzler

How would you tighten and sharpen the following sentence?

The charts which appear in the report show the trend.

Proper usage calls for "that" instead of "which" because you are differentiating these charts from other charts, but the demands of brevity obviate that choice. Drop "which appear" altogether.

The revised version:

The charts in the report show the trend.

2

Strategy

Formulating Your Point

Strategy

Formulating Your Point

Like everyone else, judges have personal moral views. In deciding cases, they look, as anyone would, for the good guy and the bad guy, the "white hat" and the "black hat." Judges want to know who deserves to win and who deserves to lose. Within parameters set by the law, they have acres of discretion to decide issues on the basis of their personal moral codes.

This is why a brief writer should show the court that the adversary's client wears the black hat and deserves to lose and that the writer's client wears the white hat and deserves to win. "Deserve" describes the sense that someone should be rewarded or punished. People believe that a person who has done a bad thing, something that would hurt them if it were done to them, deserves punishment. In litigation, that means the wrongdoer should lose the lawsuit. People also believe that if a person has done a good thing, creating a benefit rather than a threat, then the person deserves a reward, that is, to win the lawsuit.

Under most circumstances, judges determine who deserves to win or lose on the basis of one dominant reason. A spray of reasons isn't necessary or even helpful. A litigant wins largely because of a reason that trumps all reasons the other side can present. This dominant idea can be set forth in a sentence or two. It is your "theme."

Footnotes Are Where the Horse Is Buried

Think twice about using substantive footnotes in briefs

In law review articles, footnotes are a sign of scholarship. They enable the author to supply citations and substantive information while maintaining a logical flow. Because law review articles are meant to be studied at the reader's leisure, the footnotes work in synergy with, and are an acceptable adjunct to, the text.

Briefs are a different story. Because a court handles many cases and has piles of paper to read, it is not likely to treat your brief as an academic resource. Your footnotes may not get read, and if they do get read, they will interrupt the smooth, seamless presentation needed for persuasion.

Footnotes Often Hide Weakness

Experienced lawyers know that footnotes hide weakness. "That's where the horse is buried," one of my partners used to say. If you feel the desire to use a footnote, examine your motives.

Ask yourself if you aren't just dodging an unpleasant issue. A good gauge of this is whether you are footnoting in response to one of the adversary's strong points. If so, you are probably using the footnote to avoid confrontation.

Another possibility is that you are pushing aside a thought you can't quite fit in. You sense but cannot articulate its relevance, so you drop a footnote and leave the reader to make the connection.

Some writers place strong arguments in footnotes to create the impression that their position is so powerful that even their footnotes are dispositive. They like the image of tossing off winners at will.

This is wasteful. Footnotes may not even be read because they are interruptive and because they so often contain weak, or at best collateral, arguments. Don't create the risk that a strong argument may be overlooked. Put it in the text, where it will receive more attention.

Exceptions to the Rule

You can and should use footnotes to denote a series of transcript or appendix references (*e.g.,* March 25 is T1; March 26 is T2; and so forth). This is a necessary aid to the court.

You may wish to use a footnote to dismiss an argument that is so bad that it isn't worth a double-spaced response. But do this cautiously because you are vulnerable to two tendencies: (1) underestimating the power of an opposing argument, and (2) leaving your own argument undeveloped. Be sure you are not unjustifiably minimizing the other side's point or missing an opportunity to highlight a fundamental flaw in the other side's case.

If a subject is complex, novel or esoteric, you may wish to provide supplemental authority without interrupting the flow of your argument. Dropping a footnote that contains such authority shows diligence and may help the court buttress an opinion in your favor.

But know that you pay a price for every footnote, like a commission on a securities trade. Footnotes force the reader's eyes to the bottom of the page, interrupting the train of thought. As an advocate, you want to create an argument so tight that everything you say seems to flow naturally, giving the impression of flawless logic. Footnotes interrupt this flow.

Sometimes you have to use footnotes, as when you face a page limitation, and you didn't leave enough time to slice away the fat without cutting muscle as well. As a last resort, you fall back on footnotes to make everything fit.

You may get away with it. In other words, the court may not bounce your brief though you used footnotes to fit everything in. But you will pay for it nevertheless, having created a choppy, bloated "read." The court will likely be annoyed, and it may skip the footnotes altogether.

In sum, a few uses of footnotes may be acceptable as long as you recognize that they come with a price, and as long as you make sure you are not using them to dodge a tough issue or to avoid figuring out how to drive your point home.

Fortunately, the tendency to use footnotes is not physiological ("once a footnoter, always a footnoter"). You can overcome the desire by developing the mindset that the text of the brief is where your battles must be fought.

Puzzler

How would you tighten and sharpen the following sentence?

The use of the word "volunteers" in the statute creates an ambiguity as applied, in resolving whether the word "volunteers" in light of the surrounding circumstances means that to be culpable the actor must take the initiative in giving the false information or whether the actor could be culpable by simply giving the false information in response to a non-compulsive solicitation.

To get to the point that the statute is ambiguous, the revised version states up front that the word "volunteers" is ambiguous. To support the point, the revised version then sets forth the two possible meanings of "volunteers."

Phrases such as "in the statute," "as applied," "in resolving whether," "in light of the surrounding circumstances" and "to be culpable the actor must" are implicit and fall away. The concept of the actor needing to take the initiative also falls away because it is implicit in the word "unsolicited." Finally, the revised version eliminates one use of the phrase "the word 'volunteers.'"

The revised version:

The word "volunteers" is ambiguous because it could mean either that false information must be unsolicited or that it must be given in response to a non-compulsive solicitation.

Which Comes First: The Chicken or the Egg?

Sometimes you lead with your point, and sometimes you lead up to it

Rules of thumb for persuasive writing can conflict. For example, instructors often say, "Begin with your point," which is solid advice. But that rule may be superseded where you need to concede a point to establish credibility.

Suppose you represent a second-low bidder challenging a municipality's waiver of a material defect in the low bid. The municipality contends that it can waive the irregularity because the procurement was conducted under the bidding statute's new "competitive contracting" procedures, which permit public entities to consider factors other than price in selecting a winning bidder.

You contend that material irregularities in bids can never be waived, even under the new, more flexible law.

Looking to comply with the rule of thumb that you should lead with your point, you begin a brief in support of your challenge to the low bid by stating that the new bidding statute does not give the municipality the flexibility it claims. You present that idea first, and then you acknowledge that competitive contracting procedures increase the flexibility of the bidding statute:

> *The competitive contracting process does not, as defendant suggests, give a municipality carte blanche to ignore material defects in bids. Competitive contracting was intended to give municipalities more flexibility than under the traditional lowest responsible bidder test, that is, to allow them to use criteria other than price to evaluate proposals.*

Your point is that even though competitive contracting was intended to give municipalities more flexibility in choosing among bidders, it does not give municipalities "carte blanche" to relax one of the bedrock principles of public bidding—that material irregularities in bids cannot be waived.

But you wrote the sentences out of order. After making a restrictive statement—that the competitive contracting process does not give municipalities carte blanche—you followed with a permissive statement—that competitive contracting was intended to give municipalities more flexibility. The sequence is ineffective because the concept of permission in the second sentence undermines the concept of restriction in the first.

The reader finishing these two sentences should be thinking restrictively, not permissively. Therefore, the second sentence—the one that makes the concession—has to come first:

> *Competitive contracting was intended to give municipalities more flexibility than under the traditional lowest responsible bidder test, that is, to allow them to use criteria other than price to evaluate proposals. But the competitive contracting process does not, as defendant suggests, give a municipality carte blanche to ignore material defects in bids.*

Instead of making your point and then backing away from it, begin by conceding that the new law gives municipalities greater flexibility. Then carve off a portion of that flexibility with the qualification, "but not carte blanche to ignore material defects in bids."

You gain credibility by acknowledging the greater flexibility in the law. By not fighting that fact, you ensure that when the reader sees the point you wish to make—that the greater flexibility given to municipalities in bidding matters does not rise to the level of carte blanche—the reader is not thinking, "I'm not so sure," or "Prove it to me."

It is easy to see why someone would present the material backwards. The mantra of writing instructors is to make the point early, and advocates are eager to come out punching. The writer thinks, "My point is that the competitive contracting process doesn't relax all the rules of public bidding, so I'll state that idea first."

The thought would be fine as a sub-heading:

(1) The Competitive Contracting Process Does Not, as Plaintiff Suggests, Give a Municipality Carte Blanche to Ignore Material Defects in Bids.

Then you could begin the paragraph as discussed above:

Competitive contracting was intended to give municipalities more flexibility than under the traditional lowest responsible bidder test, that is, to allow them to use criteria other than price to evaluate proposals. But . . .

Subheadings and first sentences serve different purposes. The subheading is your point. The first sentence may be your point, or it may lead to your point.

As a subheading, the "carte blanche" sentence works well. Your point is that the flexibility of the competitive contracting process has limits—the process doesn't give municipalities "carte blanche." The reader accepts this as a subheading because a subheading doesn't purport to tell the whole story. It is understood to constitute just the point.

Puzzler

How would you tighten and sharpen the following sentence?

Once the recommendation is presented for consideration, it is the Board that makes the final decision on whether to accept the recommendation or not by majority vote.

The entire opening clause is implicit and can be dropped because the Board cannot vote unless a recommendation is presented. You can reduce "it is the Board that" to "The Board" and "makes the final decision on whether to accept" to "decides" ("final" being implicit), and you can drop "or not" as unnecessary.

The revised version:

The Board decides recommendations by majority vote.

Weak Arguments Are Pellets for the Shotgun Approach

Fight the temptation to include them "just in case"

Some writers will make almost any argument they can think of because they are afraid to lose with cards still in their hand. They fear—not totally without reason—being second-guessed by clients, partners or peers.

Judges sometimes fan this fear with rulings "from out of left field," in other words, on uncertain grounds, to reach what they believe is the right result. Attorneys then justify making weak arguments (once burned, twice shy) on the theory that you never know what will appeal to the court.

You never do know, but you can make a good guess. Weak arguments almost always hurt your case and rarely help it.

Gamblers will continue to gamble even as their stakes dwindle as long as they receive intermittent, unpredictable payoffs. This is how slot machines keep the patrons pulling—random payoffs.

So it is with weak arguments. We have all won something with a weak argument, so we keep using them. We seem to think that persuading a judge is a matter of pushing buttons until we find the right one.

The right argument is, in a sense, a button—if you press it, you persuade. But weak arguments are buttons, too, and unlike the "Close Door" buttons on elevators, they are connected to something. At a minimum, weak arguments hurt your credibility and cast doubt on your belief in your case; they irritate the court because they lengthen the brief; and they may even insult the court's intelligence.

Some lawyers view weak arguments as a negotiation tactic. They expect the court to reject their lesser points, but they figure these shock troops will help "soften the court up." Or they think their strong points will appear stronger by comparison. I have also heard the rationale that judges like to be able to reject something from both sides so the court does not appear partial.

These strategies assume that (1) the court is more likely to be moved by the best argument if it can cast other arguments aside, and (2) the advocate's role is "transparent" to the court, that is, the advocate's credibility is irrelevant.

Not having judged except in moot court, I polled sitting and former judges, state and federal. The consensus was, without dissent, that weak arguments don't work. They don't help the court feel comfortable ruling for one side or the other; they don't make stronger arguments look good by comparison; and they don't soften the court up.

To the contrary, they irritate the court because they waste time, and they may insult the court by suggesting the court is too stupid to see through them. Most of all, they cast doubt on the advocate's judgment for having used them, and thus they cast doubt on the advocate's whole case.

A judge can't help being affected by weak arguments, just as an employer can't help being affected by an employee's weak performance. The weakness of the argument reflects poorly on the advocate.

One judge analogized to the expression, "False in one, false in all." That is, if you lie about one thing, you'll lie about anything. Similarly, if one of your arguments is weak, then the rest of your arguments may be weak as well.

Not only do weak arguments suggest you lack judgment, but they suggest you lack confidence in your strong arguments to carry the day—that you are grasping at straws. Weak arguments mark you as a shotgun advocate and all your points as pellets.

Weak arguments also make easy targets.

For example, courts can develop momentum in their opinions by soundly rejecting a series of feeble contentions. By the time a reader gets to the point in the opinion where the strong arguments face off, the reader is primed to accept that your best argument is just as weak as the rest. Weak arguments thus add length and strength to the court's litany of rejection.

On occasion, courts refute only your weak arguments and ignore your strongest. The court may write, "Plaintiff argues X and Y, which are wrong because . . . ," and the court will be correct. Then the court will stop. "What about Z?" you ask. "That was my best argument."

Figuratively, the court shrugs. To your embarrassment, the newspapers report that you argued X and Y, as if you said nothing about Z. This should come as no surprise—X and Y make better targets and therefore better news. If this happens at the appellate level, all you have left is the possibility of discretionary review by the state's highest court, with the other side arguing, not unreasonably, that substantial justice has been done.

In sum, you don't get to make weak arguments for free.

The time you spend on weak arguments would be better spent on strengthening your best point. When you lose a case—and you usually know when you are going to lose—even your core argument seems to lack an irresistible bite.

Maybe your case is inherently weak, but maybe you just haven't thought your best point through, or you haven't brought your best facts to bear. Maybe you cut the research short and lack good dicta, or you haven't found a good theme. You are spread too thin, and you didn't put enough time into your best argument to craft a winner.

The very sense that you may lose the case seduces you into making arguments you know are inadequate in a desperate attempt to find something that works and to cover yourself so that when you lose, nobody can say you missed an issue.

To serve your client and yourself, consider sharing your briefing strategy with the client. By explaining why you plan to omit arguments—including ones the client may like—you may reduce the likelihood that if you lose, you aren't held more responsible than you should be.

Puzzler

How would you tighten and sharpen the following sentence?

There was no case within the annotations to the statute which addressed the issue.

The construction "there is" or "there was" is rarely needed because it adds nothing. It is easily deleted, usually taking a third word with it (in this case, "which"). "Within" is ponderous and can be replaced by "in." I would drop the phrase "to the statute" for readers who are lawyers or judges because they would find the concept of "statute" implicit in the reference to annotations.

The revised version:

No case in the annotations addressed the issue.

Look Within for the Premise of Your Argument

You can determine what the court is likely to deem fair

> Theme development is the rock upon which all writing and oratory are constructed. It is the most basic and essential concept for planned and structured communications.
>
> —Amy Singer, PhD., *Jury-Validated Trial Themes*

> The court wants above all things to learn what are the facts which give rise to the call upon its energies, for in many, probably in most, cases when the facts are clear there is no great trouble about the law. *Ex facto oritur jus,* and no court ever forgets it.
>
> —"Readings on Oral Advocacy," Harvard Law School (1957) at 6

Describe the facts of a lawsuit to an experienced attorney, and the attorney will quickly tell you, with surprising accuracy, which side will win and why. The scary thing is that in many instances, if you describe the facts of a lawsuit to an intelligent lay person, the lay person will quickly tell you, with surprising accuracy, which side will win and why.

Nonlawyers can do this because the law isn't just a set of rules to be memorized by candidates for the Bar, nor is litigation a game of paper covers rock, rock breaks scissors, and scissors cuts paper, as if winning were a matter of finding a precedent better than the precedent invoked by the other side.

The law is, in essence, what most people agree is fair. Judges know this implicitly. It's their port in the storm. It's the well they dip into in close cases, and it never runs dry.

Judges look to do what is fair, as you would if you were in their shoes. When you judge a dispute between family members or friends, don't you try to do what is fair?

Given that judges look to do what is fair—to do "the right thing"—your diligent presentation of the law will go for naught if the other side can portray your client as seeking relief that would be unfair.

Fair Is in the Facts

For a court to feel it is acting fairly, the court must know the facts, because fairness requires a balancing of interests. To effect a balance, the court must understand the interests, and to understand the interests, the court must know the facts.

Your job is to persuade the court why the facts entitle your client to relief—why, in balance, the scales of justice should tip your client's way. You have to make the relief you seek appear fair or the relief the other side seeks appear unfair.

Good facts can persuade by themselves, without your invoking the law. For example, if you represent X in an action for assault against Y, the court will immediately be on your side if it reads the following at the beginning of your preliminary statement or statement of facts in any brief, for any purpose: "On such and such a date, Y walked up to X on Maple Street and, for no apparent reason, struck him in the face and broke his jaw."

Like any reader, the court would react viscerally to the apparent unfairness in what Y did. The court would identify with X ("What if that happened to me?") and would think about punishing the wrongdoer and deterring such behavior.

How Do You Know What Is Fair?

Undoubtedly, you have heard the expression "Look within." You can look within, for example, for the strength to overcome adversity. You can look within for your true feelings, for the solution to a knotty problem or for inner peace.

One secret to good legal writing, and for that matter, to being a good lawyer, is that dominant arguments are found by looking within for your sense of fairness. Run the facts past your conscience to determine what offends you and what does not.

Do this not as an advocate—that is, don't merely ask how your client was hurt—but as an observer. Ask yourself what offends you about what both sides did.

When you have determined what offends you, you can attack the other side's weakness and deflect attention from yours. Looking inward works because your sense of fairness is like that of most people. What you feel, they feel.

Just as you hate thieves, liars and bullies, they hate thieves, liars and bullies. Nobody likes laziness, and almost everyone believes that promises should be kept.

Because we are living beings, we reject behavior that threatens our survival. Instinctively, we deem it immoral, and we outlaw it. Our reactions are rooted in genetics and reinforced by our environment, which is relatively homogenous.

Americans watch more or less the same shows on TV and read many of the same books, magazines and newspapers. We go to schools having similar curricula, and we support religions that espouse similar guidelines for good behavior. Under such influences, we develop comparable moral codes. What seems right and just to us generally seems that way to others.

Exceptions exist where moral premises conflict, as on the issues of abortion (preserving life vs. preserving the quality of life) or the death penalty (preserving life and rejecting unequal punishment vs. deterrence, revenge and closure). But for the most part, our moral codes are congruent.

Once you realize that you can anticipate the likely response of your audience by consulting your own sense of right and wrong, you will have confidence that when you look within to ask yourself what offends you, you will find the basis for your best argument.

One caveat: You can carry this too far. Because relationships with clients depend in part on lawyers feeling their client's pain, lawyers often perceive only their client's pain, not the pain their client has inflicted on others. Lawyers look within, yes, but in only one direction. As a consequence, they jump too quickly for one-sided arguments and stay with them too long.

Looking within requires a dangerous trip to the netherworld of neutrality. Sometimes, it's best not even to say you've been there. Just bring home the prize—the winning argument—and let others think what they will.

Puzzler

How would you tighten and sharpen the following sentence?

There are a number of variables which will determine the relative accessibility of the data contained in backup files.

Dump "there are," losing "which" in the bargain—three words gone in a flash. Drop "will" as unnecessary and reduce "a number of" to "several." Drop "relative" as implicit, and drop "contained" for the same reason unless you need the connotation of confining data so it can't get away.

Finally, unless you need to mention "files," consider converting the place of storage (backup files) to an adjective.

The revised version:

Several variables determine the accessibility of backup data.

Alternate version:

The accessibility of backup data depends on several variables.

If a Square Peg Won't Fit, Try a Round One

The rationale for a rule may support you though the words do not

Don't give up on a statute or rule that seems to bar the relief your client seeks until you have explored the applicable legislative or judicial rationale, especially if your sense of right and wrong suggests that a literal reading of the stricture would be unfair. Suppose, for example, that you represent the husband in a divorce action where the final judgment covers alimony, custody and equitable distribution. Only the custody ruling is on appeal.

Shortly after the trial, the husband quit his job as a securities analyst and became a math teacher. As a result, his annual income decreased by 75 percent. In response to your application to the trial court for a downward adjustment of alimony, the wife's counsel contends that you can't make such an application while the divorce action is on appeal.

Counsel cites the rule of court that once an appeal is noticed, the case is under the supervision of the Appellate Division, leaving the trial court only with "continuing jurisdiction to enforce judgments and orders," as the rule states. Counsel argues that you aren't looking to enforce the final judgment; you are looking to change it.

You cannot believe your client would be denied access to the trial court to seek equitable relief for the duration of the appeal, which could take a year or more. Yet the rule says that litigants can return to the trial court during the appeal only to "enforce" a judgment, not to change it.

Your first instinct is to try to fit your client's situation within the terms of the rule, in other words, to say that in seeking to modify alimony, the husband seeks only to enforce the judgment, not to change it—to enforce alimony, as it were, only less of it. You are also inclined (if not programmed) to say the opposite of whatever the adversary says, fearing that any point you fail to challenge may come back to bite you. Both tendencies may lead you to argue that by seeking a reduction of alimony, you are looking only to enforce the judgment, not to change it.

That, of course, is a stretch. Counsel for the wife is correct. You aren't looking to enforce the judgment; you are looking to change it. And because you are looking to change it, the words of the rule seem to bar your application.

Opposing counsel will illustrate what the rule permits by pointing out that if the wife sought to compel your client to pay alimony, she would be asking the trial court to enforce the judgment. The court has that sort of power while the case is on appeal.

In short, the words of the rule are a barrier, and you have to look elsewhere.

Case law shows the rule to have a prophylactic purpose—to preserve the subject matter on appeal so the appellate court doesn't rule on facts that have changed.

In line with this purpose, cases interpreting the rule say that matters "collateral" to the issues on appeal can be addressed by the trial court while the case is on appeal.

This is an opening. You can argue that the issue you are asking the trial court to address—reduction of alimony—is collateral to the issues on appeal because only custody is on appeal. This is a better approach than the awkward argument that you wish only to enforce the judgment.

Some might apply the cliche "thinking outside the box" to this advice. That is too generous. When contesting the boundaries of a statute, administrative rule or rule of court, you should always look to the rationale.

Lawyers who cannot resist the urge to say the opposite of what the adversary says will make both arguments. They will contend first that they aren't looking to change the judgment, and thus they aren't seeking relief that is facially inconsistent with the rule. Then they will argue that even if they are looking to change the judgment, the change would be collateral to the issue on appeal and thus permissible under the case law interpreting the rule. They will figure that if they lose the first argument (as they will), they can still win the second.

I would not make both arguments. If you are asking the court to change the judgment, don't pretend you aren't. Not only will you lose that argument, but in the process, you will lose credibility. The court will wonder how strong your "collateral issue" argument is if you have to precede it with a weak alternative.

Puzzler

Assuming you retain all the words in the following sentences, which version do you prefer—A, B, C or D:

Version A:

I declare pursuant to the laws of the State of X that the foregoing statements are true under penalty of perjury.

Version B:

I declare that the foregoing statements are true under penalty of perjury pursuant to the laws of the State of X.

Version C:

Pursuant to the laws of the State of X, I declare under penalty of perjury that the foregoing statements are true.

Version D:

I declare under penalty of perjury pursuant to the laws of the State of X that the foregoing statements are true.

I would not say that something is "true under penalty of perjury." It suggests that the statement might not otherwise be true (Versions A and B). I prefer to have affiants "declare under penalty of perjury" (Versions C and D), as the law requires.

I favor Versions C and D for the additional reason that "true" is the key word from the perspective of the authority demanding the swearing. I like to place key words in a position of prominence at the end of a sentence.

Because the laws of the state aren't merely threatening perjury but requiring the affiant to swear, I would begin with the laws of the state (Version C). In Version D, the connection between the declaration and the laws of the state is diluted by distance.

Preferred version:

Pursuant to the laws of the State of X, I declare under penalty of perjury that the foregoing statements are true.

Don't Be Afraid to Make Your Own Dicta

Sometimes you have to declare what the case law merely implies

As researchers and brief writers, we are always seeking to match our facts to the facts in cases with good dicta and, where necessary, to distinguish our facts from the facts in cases with bad dicta. This is one of the challenges of advocacy under *stare decisis*.

Sometimes, we find only bad dicta or no dicta at all. Instinct tells us that our client has a decent case, and we think that some court must have declared that persons in our client's situation deserve relief, but no court has addressed our fact pattern. In such cases, we may need to create our own dicta.

Suppose, for example, that you represent a small specialty food store that has leased space in a shopping center anchored by a department store. Many of your client's food products are also sold by the department store, which has a specialty food section. Nothing in your client's lease says that it can't sell specialty foods, but the "exclusivity clause" in the anchor tenant's recorded lease says that no other store in the shopping center can sell, among other things, specialty foods.

The exclusivity clause is enforceable if your client had notice of it. Your client did not have actual notice, but it had constructive notice by reason of the anchor tenant's lease being recorded.

The custom in the shopping center industry is for non-anchor tenants to rely on the landlord to identify pertinent use restrictions. As a consequence, tenants such as your client almost never perform a title search. No court has addressed whether this customary reliance on the landlord can override the constructive notice provided by a recorded lease.

The anchor tenant has filed a complaint and an Order to Show Cause why your client should not be preliminarily enjoined from selling its specialty food products in the shopping center. The anchor tenant contends that at a minimum, your client had constructive notice of the exclusivity clause. If the court grants a preliminary injunction, your client will go out of business because specialty food accounts for nearly all its sales.

Your research quickly leads to the classic three-part test for preliminary injunctive relief: (1) likelihood of success on the merits; (2) irreparable harm to the moving party; and (3) balancing of the equities. The cases say that the most important criteria for determining whether to grant a preliminary injunction are likelihood of success on the merits and irreparable harm.

Because of the threat to its business, your client is strongest on the third element, the balancing of the equities. But this element is said to be subordinate to success on the merits and irreparable harm, both of which are troublesome.

On the merits, the anchor tenant will have plenty of cases declaring the importance of constructive notice. Unless custom in the industry overrides, you may lose.

As for irreparable harm, exclusivity clauses in shopping center leases can support permanent injunctions in favor of anchor tenants because of the difficulty in calculating damages over the full term of the offending lease. No exclusivity cases have involved preliminary injunctions. As far as you know, no court has opined that the likely destruction of a business precludes preliminary injunctive relief.

You did find an old case that says courts should be cautious in granting a preliminary injunction that would destroy a business, but that court also said the plaintiff "should have a very good case" to obtain the preliminary injunction. The anchor tenant claims to have a very good case because of constructive notice. You are reluctant to invoke the portion of the dictum about being cautious with preliminary injunctions because the rest of the dictum (that plaintiff can obtain a preliminary injunction with a "very good case") could be quoted back at you.

You wish you had a judicial statement that preliminary injunctions aren't intended to create irreparable harm but to prevent it. That would provide nice dictum—well-balanced and on point. But you couldn't find such a statement, reasonable though it may be.

Your client has a very strong equity—it will go out of business if the court preliminarily enjoins its sale of specialty foods. But this threat to the business goes to the balancing of the equities, not to success on the merits or to the anchor tenant's irreparable harm.

Your best course is to accentuate your client's strength. Get past the dictum that the likelihood of success on the merits and irreparable harm are the dominant elements. In your case, they aren't. Balancing the equities is dominant because destruction of your client's business would be dispositive. You needn't find a judicial statement to this effect for your position to be credible.

You may wish to acknowledge the traditional dictum by saying, "Usually the likelihood of success on the merits and irreparable harm are the dominant elements in a preliminary injunctive context, but not where the injunction would destroy the subject matter of the suit." Whether to acknowledge and distinguish the traditional dictum is a judgment call.

On the one hand, you needn't apologize for dictum that doesn't apply, but on the other hand, you may do well to defuse it if the reader may wonder why you didn't.

Whatever your decision, argue that the dominant element in your case is the balancing of the equities because a preliminary injunction would destroy your client's business. You are on solid ground because your position has equitable weight and makes sense. A preliminary injunction that destroys a business is really a permanent injunction, which arguably shouldn't be granted without discovery and a trial.

From your perspective, the absence of dicta to that effect is merely a fortuity.

As for the nice turn of phrase you couldn't find—that preliminary injunctions aren't meant to create irreparable harm but to prevent it—again, just say it. You may ask, "Who am I to say what preliminary injunctions are meant to do? I didn't write a treatise on injunctions. I'm not a Chancery court judge."

If what you say has the ring of truth, you don't have to be anyone special to say it. That's the beauty of persuasion. You don't need a silver tongue, gray hair or gravitas to persuade—just an idea.

Puzzler

How would you tighten and sharpen the following sentence?

Both a TRO and preliminary injunction are required to maintain the status quo and a level playing field, as otherwise, the lack of a preliminary injunction in and of itself will permit a change such that the underlying equities of this matter may be moved away from plaintiff, so that its loss of the TRO and preliminary injunction may well result in its loss of the underlying permanent injunction against defendant's stealing plaintiff's business.

You probably get the point of this sentence: If the court does not grant an injunction now, plaintiff will have trouble obtaining an injunction later because the defendant will have become entrenched. But the sentence is slow-starting and verbose.

Use the "If" construction rather than "as otherwise" for better flow and a tighter connection between the desired action and the consequences of non-action.

"Level playing field" can be dropped as unnecessary and imprecise, and "defendant will build equity" can replace the ponderous sequence, "the lack of a preliminary injunction in and of itself will permit a change such that the underlying equities of this matter may be moved away from plaintiff."

"Plaintiff may ultimately be denied injunctive relief" can replace the much longer and less pointed "so that its loss of the TRO and preliminary injunction may well result in its loss of the underlying permanent injunction."

Finally, "defendant is stealing" is more forceful than "injunction against defendant's stealing."

The revised version:

If the status quo is not maintained by a TRO and preliminary injunction, defendant will build equity, and plaintiff may ultimately be denied injunctive relief even though defendant is stealing his business.

Alternate opening:

If the court does not grant a TRO and preliminary injunction to maintain the status quo, defendant will build equity . . .

Sometimes the Illogical Is Very Logical

Off-point arguments can be persuasive if they address fundamental fairness

We all admire logic, but sometimes we enslave ourselves to it. We narrow our vision by insisting that every argument "go" to the issue before the court.

Suppose you represent a patient whose health insurer reimbursed a ridiculously small portion of huge medical bills. You sue the insurer for breach of contract and breach of fiduciary duty under ERISA. You also sue the insurer's co-venturer, Insurer X, described in an agreement between the co-venturers as a "re-insurer." Insurer X moves for summary judgment on the ground that as a re-insurer (someone who agrees to accept a piece of the underlying risk in return for a fee), it has neither a contractual nor a fiduciary relationship with your client.

You have facts to counter that argument. Insurer X shared 50-50 in the profits and losses of the health insurance business; it set premiums and collected them; and it helped administer claims, all of which in your view makes it a contracting party and a fiduciary.

Your assigning partner wants you to argue as well that Insurer X belongs in the lawsuit because it knowingly used an old and downwardly skewed database to determine how much to reimburse patients for what they pay their doctors. You resist because you think Insurer X's method for paying claims is irrelevant to whether Insurer X has a contractual or fiduciary duty to your client. The method for calculating reimbursement, you say, does not go to the insurer's contractual or fiduciary status. You are so sure of this that figuratively, if not literally, you stamp your foot.

Such scenarios play out between partners and associates every day. The partner is thinking that if Insurer X (the so-called re-insurer) is dismissed from the lawsuit, then Insurer X can continue underpaying claims with impunity. It will never be called to account.

The associate thinks, "I suppose Insurer X deserves to be held liable, but I can't ask the court to rule that Insurer X breached a contractual or fiduciary duty to the insured when I haven't even proved it had such a duty. The issue of breach isn't before the court on this motion."

This is where you have to take your thinking to a different level. By arguing that Insurer X underpaid claims, you aren't looking to prove its contractual or fiduciary status. You are looking to persuade the court that Insurer X's method of calculating reimbursement is flawed and unfair. You are not giving the court an additional ground on which to find a contractual or fiduciary relationship. You are giving the court incentive to be satisfied with the grounds it has.

Underpayment of claims wouldn't be a heading or even a subheading in the argument section of your brief, but you would include a thorough explanation of how the claims process works in your Statement of Facts. Then in the argument, you might write something like, "If Insurer X is dismissed from this suit, it will continue to underpay claims, and persons who paid their premiums thinking they would be meaningfully insured will continue to be devastated by their medical bills."

A sentence that won't work is, "Another reason that Insurer X has a duty to plaintiff is that it underpays claims." That isn't a reason why Insurer X has a duty. It's a reason why it deserves to answer for its actions.

Will targeting Insurer X's claims practices foster that great bugaboo, "result oriented jurisprudence"? Not really. You do want the court to choose a result (keeping Insurer X in the suit) rather than the rule (that re-insurers have no relationship with the insured), but you contend that the "re-insurer" in your case falls within an exception to the rule because of its involvement in profits, premiums and claims. By trying to fit Insurer X within an exception to the rule, you are playing by the rules.

Without reasons why the court should deem Insurer X to have a contractual or fiduciary duty to your client, your black hat argument ("Insurer X underpays claims") will fall flat anyway. It isn't intended to work alone. It's a clincher, a scale-tipper, a source of comfort for the court that by making a call in your favor, the court is doing the right thing.

New lawyers may view such out-of-the-box arguments as street fighting bordering on rule breaking. It isn't. It's just smart tactics. You'll lose points with the court for making such arguments only if you have no support for the premise you must prove to win the motion—here, that Insurer X had a contractual or fiduciary relationship with your client.

The argument that Insurer X underpaid claims is actually "logical," but in support of a premise different from the one you must prove to win the motion. The alternate premise is that Insurer X should remain a defendant in the lawsuit so the court can supervise and, if appropriate, penalize Insurer X.

When you make arguments that can be considered "outside the box," you have to be clear what you are doing. You can't pretend that underpaying claims—as opposed to handling claims—establishes a contractual or fiduciary duty with the insured. That would be illogical. But it does suggest that the court should keep a grip on Insurer X.

At bottom, courts want to do the right thing. If a court can see that Insurer X would be getting away with something if released from the lawsuit, then the court will be inclined to keep Insurer X in the suit if you provide at least arguable reasons why Insurer X has a contractual or fiduciary relationship with your client. If Insurer X underpays claims and thus wears a black hat, the reasons why it has a contractual or fiduciary relationship with the insured may not have to be as strong, especially for purposes of defeating a summary judgment motion.

Most courts are in the business of doing justice, not of throwing up their hands and saying, "I'm sorry; I am powerless." Courts sometimes declare themselves powerless, but it's usually when the defendant's alleged transgression isn't very offensive or when the plaintiff is, for whatever reason, undeserving.

Puzzler

Which is better, Version One or Version Two?

Version One:

Defendants moved to have all inadvertently supplied evidence suppressed and for the return of all attorney-client communications.

Version Two:

Defendants moved to have all inadvertently supplied evidence suppressed and all attorney-client communications returned.

After the word "and," the reader is ready for any of the following: another verb in the position of "moved" (*e.g.,* Defendants moved . . . and sought . . . "); another verb in the position of "to have" (*e.g.,* Defendants moved to have . . . and to compel . . . "); another verb in the position of "suppressed" (*e.g.,* "to have . . . evidence suppressed and returned"); or a new noun-verb combination (*e.g.,* evidence suppressed . . . and . . . communications returned," as in Version Two).

At the word "and," the reader is ready for a verb, for action, or a noun, for something acted upon. The reader is not ready for a prepositional phrase—"for the return of." In Version One, as the reader finishes the thought that a motion was made to have evidence suppressed, the reader is surprised by the new structure.

In Version Two, the second part of the sentence meets the reader's expectations by repeating a structural element from the first part. "All communications returned" echoes "all evidence suppressed." The consistency and rhythm of the repetition carry the reader along.

This recommendation falls under the rubric "parallelism." Version Two is better because it uses parallel construction.

Choose an Approach That Will Appeal to the Court's Conscience

Show that the other side "deserves" to lose

In *The Unforgiven*, Clint Eastwood has the drop on Gene Hackman and is about to discharge his Henry rifle at a range of one foot when Hackman says, plaintively, "I don't deserve this." Eastwood replies, "Deserve ain't got nuthin' to do with it."

In litigation, deserve has everything to do with it. Courts feel more comfortable taking something from a litigant (*e.g.,* assessing damages for breach of contract) if the facts show that the litigant took something from someone else. That way, the books are balanced. Courts don't like to inflict pain gratuitously. If they must select a loser, they prefer that the person deserves to lose.

Suppose, for example, that in the dead of night, a drunken man breaks through a locked fence enclosing a construction site, climbs onto a bulldozer and falls off, suffering serious injuries. Would a court grant summary judgment to the contractor because the trespasser got what he deserved? Probably. The court would think the plaintiff brought it on himself. He deserved to lose.

Generally, we believe that people who are careless deserve to lose. People who break promises or deceive others deserve to lose. Even people who fail to make an effort to protect themselves deserve to lose. Almost any moral failing can create the impression that a person deserves to lose.

This is one reason litigation sometimes deteriorates into mud-slinging. In trying to show that the other side deserves to lose, advocates shamelessly seek to portray the opposing party as a bad person, whether the party's alleged bad acts are relevant to the matter at issue or not.

Regrettably, the tactic sometimes works, which is why lawyers keep using it. But it can also backfire. The court may see through it, be sensitized by it, and realize that the balance of the relevant equities tips decidedly against the mudslinger.

Novice litigators' devotion to precedent, their compulsion to try to fit their case within the four corners of a reported opinion, can divert them from the essential task of finding the fact or facts that show where "deserve" lies. (Sooner or later every litigator needs to realize, whether gradually or through an epiphany, that the facts control the law, not vice versa.) The facts are the weights that sit on the scales of justice. If well-presented, they show how the balance tips, *i.e.,* they show what is "fair."

> NOTE: The argument that something is "fair" or "unfair" is, by itself, conclusory. Don't use the words fair or unfair until you have laid out facts that would persuade a trier of fact how the balance should tip. Even then, be careful that you aren't just tapping your gut sense of equity—which may be skewed by your loyalties—instead of doing the hard work of analysis.

Experienced lawyers build their arguments around "deserve." Even where the fight isn't over winning or losing *per se* but over valuing and dividing up assets, as in a divorce, advocates try to portray their side as deserving more, and the other side as deserving less.

To shape an argument, particularly in head-to-head litigation under the common law, where the focus is more personal than institutional, look for a fact or a fact scenario that purports to elevate the moral standing of your client over that of the other side, giving your client the "white hat" or the "high ground."

Show the adverse party to have engaged in morally challenged behavior, such as violence, promise breaking, deception, delay, self-indulgence, laziness or lack of care. If the moral offense "goes to" (is within the confines of) the issue in the case (and sometimes even if it is not—but be careful there), you will give yourself a good chance to persuade the court that your client deserves to win and that the other side deserves to lose.

Suppose that Developers A and B are competing for limited sewage capacity. Developer A invokes a 10-year-old contract with the local sewage authority that reserves most of the available capacity for Developer A in return for a contribution to the construction of the sewage treatment plant.

This apparent lock on capacity purports to block construction of a shopping center for which Developer B is ready to break ground. Developer B sues to free up the sewage capacity, contending that Developer A doesn't need the capacity because it doesn't even have a timetable for breaking ground.

Developer A invokes the sanctity of the contract: "A promise is a promise." Developer B argues that hoarding sewage capacity harms other developers and the community. Because Developer A isn't ready to build, its right to sewage capacity, though explicit, hasn't "ripened."

Developer B's dominant equity—the fact intended to persuade the reader—is "hoarding." Hoarding offends, and because it offends, it may persuade. "Hasn't ripened" is the legal hook on which the court can hang its hat. It is important to the argument, but courts don't hang their hats unless and until the dominant equity (the dominant moral element) makes them feel welcome.

Sometimes the dominant equity may be collateral to the factual core, as in a contract interpretation case where the key clause is so unclear that it is truly opaque to interpretation. The court may then ask whose "fault" it was that the clause wasn't clear. One way or another, the court wants to know who is at fault and therefore who deserves to lose.

Readers react adversely to morally substandard behavior because they identify with the persons who were harmed by it. They imagine themselves being hurt, and they perceive a threat. This is why readers feel that immoral actors deserve what they get. Readers don't like people who do immoral things.

A court's moral views should not be a mystery. If something seems wrong to you, it probably seems wrong to the court. You and the judge were probably exposed to similar religious training, similar school curricula, and similar print and electronic media, all espousing a relatively homogeneous moral code. The court's conscience is likely to be congruent with yours.

The court's conscience is also likely to be congruent with the law. After all, morality is the code of conduct on which people generally agree, and what people agree upon becomes law in a country under the rule of law.

Consequently, when you present the law (what courts did in prior cases), you are usually just confirming what the court already knows instinctively from its sense of right and wrong. The law strengthens the court's resolve and removes any lingering doubt.

In sum, the ultimate arbiter in litigation before a court is the court's conscience—its sense of right and wrong. Judges trust their sense of right and wrong to dictate a result congruent with the law. If the law is unclear, the court's conscience will suggest what the law should provide. Therefore, the theme of your argument should appeal to the court's conscience. This is the playing field on which litigation takes place.

Puzzler

How would you tighten and sharpen the following sentence?

This appeal is the only chance that the parties to this suit have to seek appellate review of all of the decisions that the trial court has made prior to this time.

The possessive can save words, as by changing "the only chance that the parties . . . have" to "the parties' only chance" and by changing "the decisions that the trial court has made" to "the trial court's decisions." The word "appellate" is implicit and therefore unnecessary, as are the phrases "to this suit" and "prior to this time." Never say "all of," and here, don't even say "all."

The revised version:

This appeal is the parties' only chance to seek review of the trial court's decisions.

Look Behind the Quotation for the Rationale

Supply reasons even if your quoted source did not

Brief writers love to quote treatises and judicial opinions because they carry weight. In fact, brief writers who find a credible source stating a conclusion they like may quote a statement even if it isn't backed by a rationale. If you are tempted to do this, think about it first.

Try to deduce the rationale that the source did not supply.

Suppose a contract requires the parties to make "reasonable efforts" to perform but does not define reasonable efforts. Because you contend the other party made no serious effort to perform, you want "reasonable efforts" to be a tough test and the other party's nonperformance to constitute a breach.

A treatise on contract law characterizes the reasonable efforts test as "more onerous than that of good faith." With this statement, you figure you have struck gold. The language is directly on point. You plan to drop the quotation from the treatise right into your brief for the bench trial, adding emphasis to make sure the court doesn't overlook the felicitous phrase "more onerous." This is the excerpt from the treatise as you plan to quote it:

> *The "reasonable efforts" test requires a party to make such efforts as are reasonable in light of that party's ability and the means at its disposal and of the other party's justifiable expectation.* ***Such a duty is "more onerous than that of good faith."*** *[Citation; emphasis added].*

A "more onerous" duty sounds like a tough standard, but the treatise doesn't say why the reasonable efforts test is more onerous than the test for good faith. Initially, you aren't concerned because you have faith in quotations. You have been quoting since the sixth grade. Your sources knew more than you did then, and you suppose they know more than you do now.

This may be true, but sources do not always explain what they know. If the source you wish to quote doesn't give a reason for its conclusion, try to fill the gap. Readers are persuaded more by reasons than by conclusions.

The first place you will probably look for support—because of how you were trained—will be the citations in the footnote to the "more onerous" statement in the treatise. Sometimes the cited cases provide a rationale; sometimes they don't. Assume that in this example, the cases merely repeat the "more onerous" statement, providing no rationale. One or two cases even quote the treatise, but none provides a rationale. Thus, you are left to your own devices.

Let's look at the reasonable efforts test. The treatise says that the test requires a party to make such efforts as are reasonable in light of (a) that party's ability and the means at its disposal and (b) the other party's justifiable expectation. These elements do not seem onerous. They are premised on the relatively benign, very flexible terms "reasonable" and "justifiable." Why, then, would the reasonable efforts test be more onerous than the test for good faith?

Think about it (and cover the next sentence if you wish to test yourself).

The reasonable efforts test is more onerous than the test for good faith because the reasonable efforts test is "objective." It is tied to a minimum level of acceptable behavior (*e.g.,* what is "reasonable") regardless of the actor's intent, whereas good faith is tied to the actor's intent. One can fall short of reasonable efforts even though one acts in good faith.

In the brief, you could follow the statement from the treatise with the following rationale:

> *The reasonable efforts test is more onerous than the good faith test because it is objective, not subjective. One can fall short of reasonable efforts even though one acts in good faith.*

You would then tie that generalization to the facts of your own case, showing how, despite the other party's claimed good intentions, it failed to meet a reasonable standard of performance.

A Second Rationale

Something else is worth noticing about the test—it has two parts. The definition examines not only whether the actor's efforts were reasonable but also whether the non-actor's expectations were justifiable. This gives a person invoking the test "two bites at the apple"—two ways in which the test may not have been met.

You can characterize the test as having dual elements by adding the following sentence after your discussion of objective and subjective:

> *Not only is the reasonable efforts test objective rather than subjective, but it is a function of two variables: what the performing party is reasonably able to do and what the nonperforming party justifiably expects.*

The "not only . . . but also" construction suggests that "reasonable efforts" is a difficult test because the party looking to establish that it made reasonable efforts must not only meet an objective rather than a subjective test, but it may also have to fight on two fronts. The party may have to contend not only that its behavior was reasonable but also that the other party's expectations were unjustified. With this supplementary sentence, you reinforce the reader's view, which you molded a few sentences earlier, that the test is tough.

All you did to get to this point was think. You examined your material—the quotation from the treatise—and you made connections and deductions, just as you would for a set of facts. Your observations added value, just as you would add value by characterizing a time interval and events (*e.g.,* instead of the bland, "On June 15, such and such happened, and on July 15, such and such happened," you would say, "On June 15, such and such happened. Only one month later [thus characterizing the time interval], a similar event took place" [thus characterizing the event, which you then date and describe]).

Look to add value beyond mere hunting and gathering. After you collect material, examine it, understand it, and explain it. Don't ask readers to take anything on faith. Show them the reason.

Puzzler

How would you tighten and sharpen the following sentence?

Differences over valuation will go to arbitration because it is a less expensive way of resolving disputes than litigation.

Shorten "differences over valuation" to "valuation disputes" and reduce "less expensive way of resolving disputes" to "cheaper than." "Resolving disputes" is understood because that is what happens in litigation and arbitration.

The revised version:

Valuation disputes will go to arbitration because it is cheaper than litigation.

If you have any concern that the negative connotations of "cheaper" could reflect poorly on the arbitration or on you, then use "less expensive."

Alternate version:

Valuation disputes will go to arbitration because it is less expensive than litigation.

Jealously Guard Your Credibility with the Court

An untrustworthy act is like ink in the wash—it discolors everything

For a long time, I have resisted the lure of hand-held e-mail devices. I don't want my private time to be invaded by the information explosion any more than it already has, and I don't want to become an e-mail junkie like those poor, immersed souls who poke at miniscule keyboards with their styluses, or thumb them, outside conference rooms, in restaurants, in airport waiting rooms and everywhere else. They usually look harried and always look obsessed.

A lawyer friend of mine recently bought a Blackberry™, was thrilled with it, and urged me to buy one. She said it is very convenient: She can always stay in touch with the office and with her husband and kids, and she can get back to clients immediately. She was exuberant about its virtues.

I was unmoved. With 12-hour workdays, six- or seven-day work weeks, and the relentless pressure of deadlines, who wants to stay in constant touch? Worse, who wants to lead people to expect that you will answer their questions at any hour and from any location? (I know. I know. "If you want to succeed in the fast-paced business world, you have to make yourself available . . . blah, blah, blah." If you do M&A work, I suppose that is true.)

Finally, my friend said something that moved me. She said that paradoxically, a hand-held device allows her more time away from the office because she doesn't have to fear the ire of a client or a colleague who desperately needs to reach her or perceives that they desperately need to reach her. She can attend social and professional events without feeling a steady undertow of stress.

I was immediately persuaded. I practically couldn't wait to jump from my chair, run upstairs to the office manager and order a hand-held device.

This is how persuasion works. When the point hits home, you are moved. It's the same with judges. When your point hits home, the judge is moved. But with judges, you may not have the luxury of running through six or seven arguments until one of them pushes the right button. You could lose the court's attention before you even get to your best point. At a minimum, the unpersuasive arguments will dilute your best argument and undermine your credibility. In litigation, you have to choose your best argument, commit to it, and begin with it, usually in the Preliminary Statement.

But the story continues. My friend sold past the closing, which young attorneys are taught never to do, and suddenly I didn't want a hand-held device anymore. She said, "Candidly, ninety percent of the time, I use my Blackberry™ for personal communications."

Boom! That was it. I didn't want the device anymore. I figured that if only ten percent of the machine's value would be work-related, then I didn't want it. It's just another invasive piece of technology.

I realize the device could still help free me from the office, even if I were to use it only ten percent of the time for business. Nevertheless, the credibility of the advocate was compromised. I was no longer hearing a testimonial from someone who had found an extraordinary business use for it. I was hearing a testimonial from someone who had found an extraordinary personal use for the device. Because my interest in the device was for business purposes only, I lost my desire to have one.

"But that's illogical," she protested. "If the device can help you, why do you care what I use it for? Why cut off your nose to spite your face?"

"I know it's illogical," I said. "But I don't want one."

Ultimately, I may buy the device and not cut off my nose to spite my face. I recognize the illogic of my position. Either the tool will give me more freedom or it won't, and I should be able to make that decision dispassionately and use the equipment responsibly.

But part of me resents the device and looks for reasons not to buy one. And I don't know that the device will help me more than it hurts me. The supposed freedom may carry a serious price if I become addicted to e-mail and can't resist using it to the detriment of my own psyche and the inconvenience of anyone looking to have a personal, as opposed to a business, relationship with me.

The bottom line is that I don't have a sense of what the hand-held device will do for me, or to me. If I don't know the facts, I have to rely on what people tell me. If I can't trust the source, I don't take the advice. It's that simple.

This also applies to brief writing. When you misinterpret or overstate the holding in a case or omit or mischaracterize a key fact, the court will lose faith in you. No matter how good your argument is, the court will think, "Well, that sounds like a good argument, but I don't trust the messenger." This is why you must be trustworthy.

Never say a case stands for a proposition if it doesn't or that a case is inapposite if it is clearly on point. Don't ignore bad facts that are obvious, and don't make facts up. This includes treating ambiguities as if they mean only what you say and can't mean anything else. Never cite a case that has been overruled, even on other grounds, without so indicating. Courts become apoplectic over this.

Don't hide weak arguments in footnotes. Don't restate your conclusions several times in a paragraph because you can't think of enough facts to fill the space. And don't fake your sets, that is, extract subsets from sets to create long lists for apparent weight when you really have only one or two examples.

And be gracious. Never use sarcasm or inflammatory rhetoric. Never impugn the ability or integrity of a lower court. And rarely use intensifiers such as "clearly" and "obviously." Don't embellish, exaggerate or malign.

In short, be well-mannered and honest. You may be tempted to be acerbic because you are worked up, and you may be tempted to say that you didn't break the glass, spill the milk or chop down the cherry tree because you don't ever want to admit you were wrong, but you must resist those tendencies. Your credibility is on the line.

Puzzler

How would you tighten and sharpen the following sentence?

Smith did not participate in the negotiation of any of the terms or conditions of the contract.

"Did not participate in negotiating" would be better than "did not participate in the negotiation of," but "participate" is a weak verb. What mental image do you get of a person who is "participating"? Replace "did not participate in the negotiation of" with "did not negotiate."

"Terms" is a set, and "conditions" is a subset. The set should suffice.

I think the writer meant to emphasize that Smith had absolutely nothing to do with the negotiation, so I would keep "any terms" and not cut muscle by reducing to "Smith did not negotiate the contract." I prefer the "revised version" to the alternate version below because I like the power of "did not negotiate any terms," and I fear the momentary ambiguity in the fortuitous phrase "did not negotiate any contract."

The revised version:

Smith did not negotiate any terms of the contract.

Alternate version:

Smith did not negotiate any contract terms.

3

Primacy

Persuading the Reader as Soon as Possible

Primacy

Persuading the Reader as Soon as Possible

Just as you get one chance to make a first impression in personal relationships, you get one chance to make a first impression in a brief. Maximize the opportunity. Capture the reader's attention quickly and win the reader to your point of view. Begin with your best facts to show the reader how the scales of justice should tip. Don't temporize with "This is a brief in opposition to," and don't pontificate with conclusory statements that have no bite because, by definition, they are conclusions, not rationales (*e.g.,* "Plaintiff misunderstands the frustration of purpose doctrine."). The sooner you bring out the facts, the sooner you will persuade and the sooner the reader will begin to process information through a filter favorable to you.

These are extraordinarily simple truths, obvious to most experienced lawyers but not to beginners, probably because they view judges as high priests and priestesses of logic who take their direction entirely from written rules. They see judges as controlled by the law, not moved, like juries, by human reactions and not vulnerable, like juries, to human tendencies such as looking to choose sides, looking to validate choices once made, and trusting in advocates who show confidence by starting strong.

Don't Give Your Adversaries Free Airtime

Attack their positions as, not after, you restate them

Advocacy is like advertising—if you keep putting the thought out there, sooner or later the consumer may try it on for size. Don't do your opponents' advertising for them. Don't give them "free airtime."

An associate representing a defendant began a preliminary statement by repeating six of the plaintiffs' allegations. I deleted the paragraph. She acknowledged that she was giving plaintiffs "free airtime" by restating their case, but she thought she was obliged to begin by listing the points she would need to refute. She also thought the allegations would be neutralized if she preceded each one with "Plaintiffs allege."

Saying "plaintiffs allege" won't neutralize the allegations unless they are incredible on their face. To the contrary, restating the allegations may fix them in the reader's mind, especially if the reader, whether judge or law clerk, has just finished plaintiffs' brief, which probably cast the allegations in their best light.

Naked reiterations of the other side's position are frequently (actually, just short of invariably) followed by what I call the "no-no statement." You write, "Plaintiff says X," and then you follow with, "Plaintiff is wrong," "misses the point," "falls short of the mark" or "fails to understand the issue." Initially, you provide no "because," just a negation, a "no-no statement."

The no-no statement seems necessary to you, as indeed it might. You've just finished stating plaintiff's position, so every fiber of your advocate's body demands that you say the opposite, fast. So you do. You make a no-no statement.

Sometimes no-no statements are immediately followed by a supporting rationale, which repairs some of the damage, but sometimes they are not. Even if you supply a rationale, you lose a tempo because you spend two "beats," as it were, accomplishing nothing—one beat to restate plaintiff's argument and another to deliver the bare negation, the "no-no statement," which has little value other than to assure the reader you haven't given up yet.

The following no-no statement is accompanied by, but delays, a rationale:

> *Insurer X alleges that ABC Co.'s retention of environmental consultants shows that ABC Co. knew or suspected that its groundwater was contaminated.* ***This is untrue, and Insurer X is unable to muster any evidence to support this contention.*** *Quarterly groundwater testing was mandated by RCRA.*

All the information the writer wishes to convey is in this paragraph, but in the wrong order. First the writer gives the other side free airtime, restating the insurer's contention that the hiring of consultants to test groundwater shows knowledge of contamination. Then the writer makes a no-no statement ("This is untrue and Insurer X is unable to muster . . . blah blah blah"). So far, the score is one to nothing for Insurer X, and ABC Co. is thirty-eight words into the paragraph.

Changing the order of presentation avoids giving the insurer free airtime and eliminates the no-no statement:

> *ABC Co. retained environmental consultants because RCRA mandated quarterly groundwater testing, not because ABC Co. knew of or even suspected groundwater contamination, as Insurer X contends.*

As in the first version, the writer presents the insurer's position and the company's position, but the order is different. In the revised version, the writer provides the explanation first, so when the reader sees the insurer's position, it is with the explanation in mind. Not all no-no statements are this easily eliminated, but many are.

A second example appeared as the opening paragraph of an appellate reply brief:

> *Respondent argues that, for this Court to reverse the trial court, it must repudiate the holding in Smith v. Jones. Respondent is mistaken. Contrary to Respondent's argument, this Court need not challenge the holding in Smith in order to find in Appellant's favor. Smith is silent on federal law. It does not mention ERISA or cite even a single federal case.*

This opening grants free airtime and uses not one but two no-no sentences, beginning with "Respondent is mistaken." We do not learn until the last sentence of the paragraph, forty-three words in, why the Court would not have to repudiate *Smith* to find for Appellant.

Minor adjustments shape up the opening:

> *Respondent incorrectly contends that this Court will have to repudiate Smith v. Jones to reverse. Smith is not an ERISA case and doesn't even mention federal law. Thus, it is inapposite.*

The word "incorrectly" interrupts the free airtime and provides the negation for which the writer previously used a no-no sentence, allowing the writer to get more quickly to the point. Replacing the phrase "to find for Appellant" with the punchier phrase "to reverse" further shortens and sharpens the passage, propelling the reader toward the conclusion.

Puzzler

How would you tighten and sharpen the following sentence?

> *The parties conducted the depositions of the experts for discovery purposes prior to the submission of the trial briefs.*

If you use a non-specific verb like "conducted," you get stuck having to add "the depositions of." See if your principal noun can be converted to a verb. Here, the principal noun is "deposition," which makes the verb "deposed." You can drop the phrase "for discovery purposes" because it is assumed. "Prior to" becomes the more compact "before," and "the submission of" becomes the more compact "submitting." Often, you don't need "the." Here, it can be removed from in front of "trial briefs."

The revised version:

The parties deposed the experts before submitting trial briefs.

Point Headings Should Persuade

Argument summaries advance your case and assist the court

> The wind tore through the bivouac area like a great scythe, slashing the palm fronds from the coconut trees, blasting the rain before it.
>
> —Norman Mailer, *The Naked and the Dead*

You may not wish to accent point headings with Mailer-style metaphors, but you should at least give them punch. Point headings should persuade, not merely serve as topical dividers.

Of the following two versions of a point heading, which would you use?

ABC CO.'S MOTION TO DISMISS PLAINTIFFS' FIRST AMENDED COMPLAINT SHOULD BE GRANTED.

PLAINTIFFS' FIRST AMENDED COMPLAINT SHOULD BE DISMISSED BECAUSE ABC CO. IS NOT SUBJECT TO THE STATUTE ON WHICH THE COMPLAINT IS PREMISED.

The answer is easy. You would use the second version because it provides a reason. It also has more force than the first version because it demands the harsh remedy of dismissal rather than the bland procedural remedy of a motion being granted.

Stating reasons in point headings shows you have confidence in your case; you are not afraid to display your wares. It also suggests your points are strong because they can be stated crisply, within the confines of a point heading. Conversely, omitting reasons from point headings suggests you may have no reasons. Advocacy is subtle that way. If you say nothing, the reader may figure you have nothing to say.

Stating reasons in point headings also helps the court understand the direction of your argument just by reading the table of contents. This is a convenience for which the court will be grateful. With a little skill and a few good facts, you may even begin to move the court toward your side. Brief writers pride themselves on persuading the court in the preliminary statement, but imagine the momentum you could develop by beginning the persuasive process in the table of contents!

Additional examples of effective point headings include:

THE TRIAL COURT PROPERLY ENFORCED THE EXPIRATION DATE OF MR. X'S STOCK OPTIONS BECAUSE TIME IS OF THE ESSENCE FOR THE EXERCISE OF OPTIONS HAVING A SPECIFIED TERM.

THE TRIAL COURT ERRONEOUSLY CERTIFIED A CLASS WITHOUT FINDING THAT THE NAMED PLAINTIFF SATISFIED THE TYPICALITY

REQUIREMENT OF RULE 4:32-1(a) OR THE REQUIREMENT THAT COMMON QUESTIONS OF LAW OR FACT PREDOMINATE.

Not only should point headings state reasons, but they should have vibrancy. Use verbs rather than nouns, and use the active rather than passive voice. Trim excess words. Give your client a name rather than a procedural designation such as "putative intervenor."

The point heading below was transformed by these suggestions. The old version:

PLAINTIFF'S WILLFUL FAILURE TO GIVE THE PUTATIVE INTERVENOR NOTICE OF ITS APPLICATION FOR TEMPORARY RESTRAINTS AND ITS KNOWING MISREPRESENTATION THAT IT COULD NOT IDENTIFY ANY OTHER NECESSARY PARTIES TO THE ACTION PRECLUDE PLAINTIFF FROM OBTAINING EQUITABLE RELIEF.

The new version:

PLAINTIFF IS BARRED FROM RECEIVING EQUITABLE RELIEF BECAUSE IT WILLFULLY FAILED TO NOTIFY ABC CO. OF THE APPLICATION FOR TEMPORARY RESTRAINTS AND KNOWINGLY MISREPRESENTED THAT IT COULD NOT IDENTIFY ANY OTHER NECESSARY PARTIES.

The old version took forever to get from the dual subject (failure and misrepresentation) to the verb (preclude). The reader had to wait nearly four lines to find out what happened. Readers don't like to wait; they become irritated and move on.

In contrast, the revised version hits home. It begins assertively by saying plaintiff is "barred," which is the bottom line. If plaintiff is "barred," then plaintiff gets no relief. Instead of preaching "Plaintiff's willful failure blah blah blah" and making the reader wait to learn the proposed consequences of this failure (preclusion of equitable relief), the point heading gets right to it.

The author of this point heading asked me, "Shouldn't I say first what plaintiff did wrong, that is, failed to give notice and misrepresented? Aren't those the persuasive facts?" Yes, but they are more persuasive if delivered with force, which verbs supply. Verbs portray action, which engages the reader and, in this case, emphasizes the intentionality that you hope will persuade the court that plaintiff deserves to lose ("willfully failed," "knowingly misrepresented"). Embodying key facts in verbs rather than nouns can be worth the grammatical delay.

Puzzler

How would you tighten and sharpen the following sentence?

The vehicles must be removed from the property as it is against regulations to store them there.

That the vehicles must be removed from the property is exactly the point. Therefore, don't change the beginning of the sentence if it flows well with what came before. You would shorten the beginning to "Remove the vehicles . . . "only if the context called for a command. Replace "as" with "because" (the principal connotation of "as" being temporal, not causative) and replace the passive "it" construction with the more direct "regulations prohibit." Finally, substitute "storage" for "store them." The reader will understand from the context that storage refers to the vehicles.

The revised version:

The vehicles must be removed from the property because regulations prohibit storage there.

Begin Paragraphs with Ideas Rather Than Case Names

"In *Smith v. Jones*" is a tempting but weak transition

A writer must retain the attention of the reader just as a speaker must retain the attention of the audience. If you lose the reader's attention, you cannot communicate, and if you cannot communicate, then you cannot persuade.

Think of a child watching television. Does the child hear you when you speak? Not likely. His attention is on the television, not on you. Therefore, he receives no message from you.

It is the same for the reader. Lose his attention, and he receives no message from you. Accordingly, you must judge every sentence and every word by whether it helps you keep the reader's attention.

One place you may lose the reader's attention is between paragraphs, in the change of ideas. It's like the gap between segments of model railroad track—if the gap is wide enough, the train derails.

I asked an associate why she hadn't used a transition between two paragraphs that didn't seem to connect. She said the idea in the second paragraph was different from the idea in the first, and she couldn't think of a transition, so she figured none was better than a bad one. She knew she didn't have a transition, but she didn't think that was so bad.

I told her that without a transition, she would lose the reader's attention. She thought about that and was concerned. I asked if she had considered the reader, and she admitted she hadn't. The associate knew, in theory, that transitions are important, but she hadn't made the connection between transitions and keeping the reader's attention.

To the reader, good transitions are "transparent." They go unnoticed until a missing transition or a weak one calls attention to the prose.

To the writer, transitions are a challenge. They require effort because they depend on overview, which requires thought. Moreover, if you realize you lack a good transition, you may be forced to admit that the ideas you have trouble connecting don't make a set. Now you have the unpleasant task of moving or even rejecting one or both of them. It is no wonder that writers sometimes leave the challenge of transitions unanswered.

One of the most popular ways to avoid the task of writing a good transition is to begin a paragraph with a case name:

> *In Smith v. Jones, [citation], the court held that an insurer was not prejudiced by late notice because it had a full opportunity to investigate the claim.*

The format "In *Smith v. Jones*" seems logical because our legal system is based on *stare decisis*—the invocation of precedent. Since precedent is embodied in case law, we figure we are developing a thesis by beginning a unit of thought—a paragraph—with a case name ("In *Smith v. Jones*").

Notwithstanding the importance of case law, paragraphs should begin with ideas rather than case names. A revision of the above sentence might read as follows:

> *Courts find no prejudice from late notice where the insurer had a full opportunity to investigate the claim. For example, in Smith v. Jones . . .*

The idea for which you cite *Smith v. Jones* is that courts do not find prejudice from late notice of a claim if the insurance company had a full opportunity to investigate. Beginning a paragraph with that idea rather than the case name has several virtues.

The idea can echo something in the previous paragraph, thus tying the new paragraph to the old and maintaining the flow of the argument. In contrast, a case name provides no connection. It is inherently meaningless unless the previous paragraph was about *Smith v. Jones*. The case name thus creates a dead spot, a gap in the flow. If the material is difficult or the reader is inattentive, you may lose the reader's attention.

Second, having to state your point forces you to decide what it is. This is a good self-monitoring device. If you cannot state your point, you may not have one.

Third, stating your point at the beginning of the paragraph shows a willingness to take control of the material, which makes you look confident. If you look confident, the reader is more likely to trust you and your argument.

Finally, stating your point at the beginning of the paragraph sets up a challenge. If the rest of the paragraph supports your point, you have met the challenge, and the reader gains confidence in you and your argument.

In short, beginning paragraphs with ideas rather than case names serves several tactical purposes. It takes more work than "In *Smith v. Jones*," but the work, if done well, pays off.

Puzzler

How would you tighten and sharpen the following sentence?

> *In the event that the court orders a remand for an evidentiary hearing in resolving this appeal, appellant will then have the opportunity to cross-examine the expert and use the transcript of his deposition testimony at that time if he wishes.*

"In the event that" can be shortened to "If." "Orders" is implicit and falls away, as does the phrase "in resolving this appeal." "Will then have the opportunity" can be shortened to "can." Since the point is that counsel will be able to use a deposition transcript to cross-examine the expert, say "cross-examine the expert *using* the deposition transcript" rather than "cross-examine the expert *and use* the deposition transcript."

"The transcript of his deposition testimony" can be shortened to "his deposition transcript," and the rest of the sentence ("at that time if he wishes") can be dropped as unnecessary.

The revised version:

If the court remands for an evidentiary hearing, appellant can cross-examine the expert using his deposition transcript.

Alternate version:

If the court remands for an evidentiary hearing, appellant can use the expert's deposition transcript for cross-examination.

Put Your Openings to Good Use

Use them to persuade, not to mark time

> [M]an is by nature credulous. He is victimized by first impressions, from which he can only escape with great difficulty.
>
> —James Harvey Robinson, *The Mind in the Making* (1921) at 100.

Lawyers often begin preliminary statements by reciting the nature of the case ("This is an action for breach of contract") or the purpose of the brief ("This is a brief in opposition to defendant's motion for summary judgment"). Such openings delay the persuasive process and generally waste time.

If procedure will persuade, then use it. Otherwise, stick to the facts because facts persuade. The sooner you get to the facts, the sooner you begin to persuade.

Moreover, once you get readers on your side, they tend to stay there because readers, like jurors, look to reinforce their first impressions. The sooner you create a good impression, the sooner this dynamic begins working for you.

The following opening to a preliminary statement merely marks time and is therefore ineffectual:

> *Plaintiff ABC Co. submits this brief in support of its motion for summary judgment.*

The cover of the brief already says, "ABC CO.'S BRIEF IN SUPPORT OF ITS MOTION FOR SUMMARY JUDGMENT." Why say it again? The reiteration takes up prime space that should be devoted to persuasion.

You may think you give no ground with a bland opening, but it is like leaving your money under the mattress. Not only do you earn no interest, but you lose to inflation. You miss an opportunity to make your point, and, by failing to persuade, you may create the impression that you have no point worth making.

Here is another way not to begin a preliminary statement:

> *This action began with the filing of a complaint seeking damages for breach of an express covenant and breach of the implied covenant of good faith and fair dealing.*

Reciting how the case began does not persuade. You may feel that reiterating the causes of action is assertive, but it is not persuasive because you provide no supporting facts.

Belief Is Not Proof

One of the classic self-deceptions in the writing process is to believe so intensely in your case that you think, wrongly, that you have made a point just by stating your conclusion, as in the following opening:

Summary judgment should be granted against Plaintiff's wrongful dismissal claim because the undisputed facts indicate that Plaintiff failed to supply adequate prior notice to Defendant regarding his leave from work.

What are the "undisputed facts"? You may know them, but the reader doesn't. Even if the facts follow immediately (and they usually don't), you'll spend precious time trying to fill the gap left by the conclusory opening.

Optimally, the opening sentence will tell the court why your client should win, as in the following example:

This is an action to enjoin the award of the contract to repave a section of Route One in Sprawlville because the low bidder omitted a bid bond from its bid package.

Any judge assigned a public bidding case will know that the omission of a bid bond, which guarantees a penalty amount if the low bidder withdraws, is fatal to a bid. Thus, the bid bond opening not only claims victory—it justifies it.

But suppose you cannot encapsulate your key point in one sentence. Then you have to prepare the reader.

Rather than recite procedure (*e.g.,* "This brief is submitted in support of defendant's motion to dismiss Counts III, IV and V of plaintiff's complaint") or even say what the case is about (*e.g.,* "This case involves a contract to distribute perfume products in Argentina, Brazil and Peru"), look for something that begins to color the case against the other side (*e.g.,* "This litigation arose from the decision by defendant John Doe to abandon his contractual and fiduciary obligations to his business partner Richard Roe and sell his services to a competing firm.").

Maybe you don't have one controlling fact, like the omission of a bid bond, but you can begin to cast the departure of John Doe in a bad light. You say that Doe "abandoned" contractual and fiduciary obligations (shows fickleness and disloyalty) to his "partner" (thus abandoning family) to "sell his services" to a competing firm (shows he's an opportunistic hired gun).

Naturally, you need more than just spin. You need good facts. But in most litigations, both sides have some good facts. Your job is to highlight yours so the reader will see the case through the prism of your good facts, not the other side's.

One of my partners says he begins the preliminary statement as if he had thirty seconds on the evening news to pitch his case. He shapes his opening like the lead sentence in a news article—focused and factual. He says that because he needs to know the case well enough to reduce the opening to a sound bite, he writes the preliminary statement last.

In sum, look to begin a preliminary statement with your best facts, not with a statement of what the brief is for, when the action was filed, or even what the case is about. Begin at the center and radiate out. If you choose your facts well, you will radiate power.

Puzzler

How would you tighten and sharpen the following sentence?

It is the duty of the reviewing court to adjudicate the controversy in the light of the applicable law in order that a manifest denial of justice be avoided.

"It is the duty" can be reduced to "must." "Adjudicate the controversy in the light of the applicable law" can be reduced to "apply the law." "In order" can generally be replaced by "to," and "denial of justice" can be replaced here by "injustice." Make "avoid" active rather than passive.

The revised version:

The reviewing court must apply the law to avoid manifest injustice.

In a Memo, the Short Answer Should Get Immediately to the Point

Busy lawyers appreciate brevity and directness

Your job as a persuasive writer is to get to the point. If you don't, the reader may become impatient and possibly confused. Though you ultimately resolve the confusion and make a point, you will lose a tempo and, with it, some of the reader's confidence in you as a source of information and analysis.

In the memo format, this principle applies with greatest force in the Short Answer.

For example, a senior attorney asked an associate to research whether a 100-year lease of municipal property is subject to a realty transfer fee when the municipality, as lessor, records the lease. The answer was "no." Long-term leases involving a municipality as lessor or lessee are exempt from the realty transfer fee that would otherwise be due. But the Short Answer at the beginning of the memo appeared, momentarily, to come to the opposite conclusion:

> *A lease of ninety-nine (99) years or more is subject to a realty transfer fee paid by the lessor upon recording. However, a lease by or to a municipality is exempt from the fee.*

The statement that a lessor recording a lease of 99 years or more must pay a realty transfer fee is true but inappropriate as a beginning for the Short Answer because the municipality is exempt from the fee. On the basis of the first sentence in the example above, a reader would deduce, incorrectly, that the municipality has to pay the fee.

The writer quickly changed direction with "However" (the reversal would have been quicker, and the punctuation better, had "however" been preceded by a semicolon), but the damage, more to the writer's standing than to the reader's understanding, was done.

As usual, the writer had a rationale. It was the serviceable principle that a general rule (that fees are required) should be stated before a specific application of the rule (that municipalities don't have to pay the fee). But in the Short Answer, where a reader wants the bottom line quickly, this approach did not work.

The problem is easily fixed by beginning with what the reader wishes to know—whether municipalities have to pay the realty transfer fee:

> *Leases by or to a municipality are exempt from the realty transfer fee that lessors must pay upon recording a lease of ninety-nine (99) years or more.*

The key word is "exempt." It signals that the municipality won't have to pay the fee. Where you know the reader wants a quick answer, as in the Short Answer in a memo, consider placing the key word as close to the beginning of the sentence as possible.

The sentence could also begin with "Although" to alert the reader that an exception exists to the principle the writer is about to state:

> *Although a lease of ninety-nine (99) years or more is subject to a realty transfer fee paid by the lessor upon recording, a lease by or to a municipality is exempt from a fee.*

I favor the construction beginning "Leases" because it gets more quickly to the point. In the first eight words ("Leases by or to a municipality are exempt"), the reader learns not only that a fee is imposed on 99-year municipal leases but that lessors don't have to pay it.

Did the memo writer commit a serious offense? No. The reader would not be confused for long. But readers of memos can be impatient. They preside over many matters and have many issues to resolve. Every second that they have to wait for an answer makes their job harder. For this reason, they not only appreciate but demand brevity and directness.

A crisp, immediate response to a question suggests that the author has confidence in the answer and is willing to take control of the material. In contrast, a slow-developing response suggests the author is shuffling to some drummer other than the principle of getting quickly to the point. A reader will sense inexperience.

Good writing requires a mindset that the reader must be well-served to be persuaded. To serve the reader, the writer must provide what the reader needs or wants to know when the reader needs or wants to know it. A memo reader wants a definitive answer promptly and wants to know that the writer will make every effort to provide one.

Puzzler

How would you tighten and sharpen the following sentence?

> *As a consequence of its status as a Subchapter S corporation, all tax liability resulting from ABC Co.'s operations flows through the company to its record shareholders for all profits the company earns, irrespective of whether ABC Co. actually distributes those profits to its shareholders.*

Like most Puzzlers, this is an exercise in deleting the implicit and shortening the essential. For example, "resulting from . . . operations" is implicit because tax liability results from operations. The same is true for "all profits the company earns" because tax liability results from profits. The phrase "to its shareholders" is implicit because only shareholders receive distributions of profits.

"Because" is shorter than "As a consequence of" (yes, you may begin a sentence with "because"); "is" is shorter than "its status as"; and "whether or not" is shorter and smoother than "irrespective of whether." "Actually" is unnecessary.

The concept of tax liability flowing "through the company" is discretionary. If your audience is naive in tax matters, you may wish to embellish the flow metaphor so that tax liability not only flows to the record shareholders but flows through the company on its way there.

Some may prefer the revised version because of its no-nonsense "shareholders are liable" and the tight link between clauses created by the principal noun ("corporation") being followed immediately by a pronoun ("its") to begin the second clause.

The revised version:

Because ABC Co. is a Subchapter S corporation, tax liability flows to its record shareholders whether or not the company distributes profits.

Alternate version:

Because ABC Co. is a Subchapter S corporation, its record shareholders are liable for taxes whether or not the company distributes profits.

In Case Write-Ups, Get Quickly to the Holding

Then decide how much of the court's reasoning to present

The American legal system is based on *stare decisis*, the doctrine that when a court has laid down a principle of law as applicable to a certain state of facts, that court and courts inferior to it will apply that principle to all future cases where the facts are substantially the same. This makes the case write-up a litigator's meat and potatoes. Because rulings in prior cases control the matter before the court, the advocate's job is to gather and explain prior rulings, which are found in judicial opinions.

Courts' opinions generally follow a format. They state the facts and the law; sometimes they state what both sides argue; and then they apply the law to the facts. This application results in the "holding."

Several approaches are available for encapsulating judicial rulings in briefs or memos, assuming you wish to do more than just cite the case and follow it with a parenthetical: (1) go straight to the holding and then summarize the facts and the court's reasoning; (2) summarize the facts and then present the holding, followed by the court's reasoning; or (3) summarize the facts, recount the court's analysis—"The court observed this . . . Then the court reasoned that . . ."—and then present the holding.

The best approach is usually to go straight to the holding. Not only does the holding quickly provide what the reader needs to know, but it conveys the impression that you have enough confidence in your characterization of the holding and in the value of the holding to your case to state it up front.

Conveying confidence is a benefit of the direct approach, as when you state your point early in a preliminary statement, begin a paragraph with a topic sentence or introduce a quoted passage with a statement of its central idea. With the direct approach, you achieve not only efficiency, but command.

You also force yourself to decide what the court held. If you can't state the holding, then you have more thinking to do. Once you've clarified the holding, the rest of your write-up can flow from and support it.

Beginning a case write-up with the holding is not an immutable rule; it is a rule-of-thumb. The touchstone for determining how to begin a case write-up is to ask what the reader needs to know and when. Generally, your answer will be, "The reader needs to know that I have support for the proposition that under a certain set of facts, the law is such and such." This answer usually directs you to the court's holding.

Depending on your needs, you may add that the court reiterated black letter law, or you may present some of the court's reasoning. Possibly, you will note that the court took the trouble to express any reasoning at all where other courts did not.

One trap in drafting case write-ups is the tendency to present each element of the court's analysis in the order presented by the court —"The court began . . .

The court continued . . . The court further stated . . . Then the court concluded." If you find yourself doing this, consider whether you forgot to consider what the reader needs to know and when. The reader probably needs to know what the court concluded first, not last. By dutifully reporting the court's reasoning process, you take too long getting to the point.

Another mistake in case write-ups is the repetition of principles already stated elsewhere in your memo or brief. For example, in a memo where you have previously cited the principle that an employer will be liable for the torts of employees only when the employee was acting within the scope of employment, the following sentence in a case write-up would be unnecessary:

> *The District Court began its analysis by noting that the doctrine of respondeat superior will hold an employer liable for the torts of its employees only when the employee was acting within the scope of his employment.*

Though the District Court did begin its analysis that way, you already stated the rule and need not use this case to confirm it. Moreover, you don't have to supply the court's entire chain of logic. That approach generally reflects the mindset of a reporter rather than an advocate. Instead of taking control of the material and shaping it, the writer takes refuge—not an unfair characterization—in finding and reporting.

On the other hand, you may wish to discuss the court's reasoning process, or part of it, if you wish to give a blockbuster case center stage, keeping it in the reader's mind and highlighting its importance. Similarly, if you have only one good case, it may achieve prominence by default. In either situation, you still present the holding first. Otherwise, the reader may become impatient.

One uses a case write-up to make a point. Usually, the quickest and best way to make the point is to state the holding first, but this is not always true. Ask yourself why you are using the case and what you should do to impress the case upon the reader or defend the case from attack. If you answer the question "Why am I using this case?" you will know what to say first and where to go from there.

Puzzler

How would you tighten and sharpen the following sentence?

> *Plaintiff did not come forward with a single shred of evidence which even remotely suggested that defendant had agreed to the disputed terms.*

"Did not come forward with" can be shortened to "presented no." Emphasis is supplied by the reversal from the positive "presented" to the negative "no." "Single shred," though temptingly alliterative, is a cliché. If you must use an emphatic (as you sometimes must, politically, to satisfy clients and assigning attorneys), try either "failed to present any" (alternate version) or "presented absolutely no" (second alternate). The phrase "Which even remotely suggested" duplicates the first emphatic—if you use one—and is overdramatic and overlong.

Preferred version:

Plaintiff presented no evidence that defendant had agreed to the disputed terms.

Alternate version:

Plaintiff failed to present any evidence that defendant had agreed to the disputed terms.

Second alternate:

Plaintiff presented absolutely no evidence that defendant had agreed to the disputed terms.

Lead with Good Facts if the Law Is Unsettled

You aren't required to begin an argument with a rule

An associate asked whether the argument section of a brief should begin with law or facts. The answer is that it depends.

If the law is favorable, you can follow the traditional though not exclusive format for argument: state the law; state the facts; and apply the law to the facts. If the law is thin or unsettled, you may wish to open with good facts. Your goal is to begin to persuade the reader as soon as possible.

Suppose you represent a person who is looking to hold an employer liable for the negligence of an employee who caused an auto accident while returning to work from a coffee break at a nearby restaurant. The employer can be held vicariously liable for the employee's negligence only if the employee is deemed to have been on the job while returning from the coffee break.

Generally, commuting to and from work is not within the scope of employment. This is the "coming and going rule." To establish the employer's liability for the tort of its employee, you have to show that the employee's travel to and from the coffee break does not fall within the coming and going rule.

You have two good facts: (1) the employer did not make coffee available on-site, and (2) the employer encouraged employees to go off-site for coffee so they would stay alert on the job.

You also have two helpful though not dispositive cases. An appellate opinion in your jurisdiction in a third-party liability case (not a worker's compensation case, where the standard is more liberal) deems a coffee break to be work-related because it benefits the employer as well as the employee. The case says nothing about coffee breaks off-site.

An appellate opinion in another jurisdiction, also in a third-party liability case, is more on point. It holds that travel to and from a coffee break does not fall within the coming and going rule because the coffee break benefits the employer, just as a business trip benefits the employer. You found no such holding in your own jurisdiction.

You decide to move for summary judgment. The draft brief opens the argument by stating the coming and going rule:

> *An employee's commute to and from work is generally not within the scope of his or her employment. See Smith v. Jones [citation]. In Smith, the Appellate Division noted that traveling to and from work does not render a service to the employer.*

This correctly states the law but seems to have been written by your adversary. Not only does it exclude commutes from the scope of employment, but it states the rationale for the rule. After two sentences, you've given the reader no basis on which to favor your cause. To the contrary, you've begun to make the case for the other side.

Perhaps you felt you couldn't begin the argument with an exception to the coming and going rule because the exception has not been recognized in your jurisdiction. The solution is to open with facts instead of law. Let's consider the possibilities.

Your first instinct may be to say that the employee was acting within the scope of his employment when he caused the accident "because he was on a coffee break and on his way back to work." This mentions "work," which is good, but being on the way back to work smacks of coming and going, which is bad. If the employee was "coming" or "going," he was not acting within the scope of his employment.

You could say the employee was acting within the scope of his employment on break "because no coffee was available on-site." This helps, but the employee could have brought coffee in a thermos, and we have no evidence that the employer denied any requests for a coffee machine on-site. Going off-site is still an independent decision by the employee. The absence of coffee on-site helps, but it is not your best fact.

You could add that the employer encouraged the employee to go off-site for coffee so he would perk up on the job. Now the employer is cast in an active role, having encouraged the employee to do something for the company. It's your best fact. If the employer encouraged the employee to travel for the benefit of the company, then the employer should bear some responsibility for what happened during that travel.

If you combine your good facts, you can say the employee was acting within the scope of his employment on the coffee break "because no coffee was available on-site, and the employer encouraged him to go off-site to obtain it." Even better, say the employer "provided no coffee on-site," further portraying the employer in an active role.

These facts are persuasive, but they can be offset by facts that cut the other way. The employer could argue that the employee chose to go off-site for coffee rather than bring coffee to work and that the employee took the same route to the same restaurant as he did for lunch, which does not fall within the scope of his employment. The employer would argue that the employee was commuting on break just as he commuted in the morning and evening and at lunch.

To overcome the standoff between opposing facts, you invoke higher authority—judicial opinion. First, you cite the local case holding that coffee breaks are work-related because they benefit the employer. Then you look to the out-of-state holding that travel to and from off-site coffee breaks doesn't fall within the coming and going rule The local court isn't bound by out-of-state law, but it may take comfort from the holding and may be guided by the court's reasoning, if any.

Knowing that you have helpful though not dispositive case law to back you up, you begin the argument with your good facts, pointing out that the employee had to go off-site for coffee and was encouraged to do so by the employer:

> *Smith was acting within the scope of employment when he had his accident even though he was driving back from a coffee break because the employer provided no coffee on-site and encouraged the employees to travel off-site for coffee so they would be more alert on the job.*

Because Smith was acting not only for his own benefit but for the benefit of his employer, his off-site trip for coffee falls within the scope of his employment.

Now you are ready to discuss the law, having used good facts to incline the reader against an application of the coming and going rule even before you mention it.

Puzzler

How would you tighten and sharpen the following sentence?

Defendant filed a motion to dismiss the claims against it and filed a separate motion for sanctions pursuant to Rule 11 of the Federal Rules of Civil Procedure.

Shorten "filed a motion" to "moved" and drop "the claims against it" as implicit. Would a party move to dismiss anything other than the claims against it?

If Rule 11 is mentioned, a motion for sanctions is implicit, as are the federal rules. All you have to say is "sought sanctions under Rule 11."

The revised version:

Defendant moved to dismiss and sought sanctions under Rule 11.

Preliminary Statements Should Focus on the Facts

Be selective rather than comprehensive

> Although the order in which information is received should be irrelevant to decisions that rely on that information, the mind does not work this way. First impressions are powerful influences on judgments and seem to provide the prism through which subsequent information is filtered. Even when first impressions are erroneous, they continue to affect judgment long after they have been discredited.
>
> —Prentice and Koehler, "A Normality Bias in Legal Decision Making," 88 Cornell L. Rev. 583, 603 (2003)

An associate asked about writing preliminary statements when moving for summary judgment against a multicount complaint. He asked how to do better than "Plaintiff's Count One fails because . . . Plaintiff's Count Two fails because . . . " and so forth.

The associate correctly deduced that recitation by the numbers is not an effective opening for a brief. It bores the reader and wastes prime space, and it is unlikely to have any positive effect because a preliminary statement is too short to provide back-up for a litany of conclusions. True, one can declare opposition to each count, but one can't make a strong impression while covering too much ground.

This tactical issue arose in a whistleblower suit where a terminated employee alleged a violation of the state whistleblower statute and several common law causes of action: breach of contract, breach of the implied covenant of good faith and fair dealing, tortious interference with existing and future economic advantage, intentional infliction of emotional distress, and defamation.

Representing the defendant employer, the associate initially considered beginning the preliminary statement to our summary judgment brief with, "Plaintiff's cause of action for X must fail because . . . " and continuing in that mode for each count, including not only the whistleblower count but all the common law claims. Because he knew the approach would be tedious, he rejected it.

But instead of drafting an opening based on facts, he defaulted to: "Defendant, through its undersigned counsel, respectfully submits this brief in support of its motion for summary judgment." Toward the end of the first paragraph, he dutifully assured the court, "There are no genuine issues of material fact."

The associate acknowledged that this approach was duller than a tent peg, and he was frustrated—a good sign—not to have done better. We talked about it and decided that the facts in support of our proximate cause defense, that is, that the employee was fired not in retaliation for whistleblowing but because of bad behavior, could open the preliminary statement. The facts were relevant to the defense and, more importantly, they were the reason the plaintiff deserved to lose. The plaintiff was fired because he did a bad job.

The revised preliminary statement began by saying that the plaintiff was terminated after botching one assignment, refusing to perform another and causing such acrimony among the employees that management had to intervene. Only then did we acknowledge that plaintiff claimed his termination was a consequence of having blown the whistle on illegal behavior by a co-employee. First we made our point; then we addressed plaintiff's.

Look First to Persuade

The preliminary statement isn't a procedural history by another name. Nor is it a condensation of your entire brief into two or three pages. It doesn't have to cover the field; it has to persuade. It should show the court why your client deserves to win, why the other side deserves to lose, or both. Having accomplished that, you can turn, as we did in this preliminary statement, to individual causes of action. Chances are, they can be grouped.

Because a person bringing a statutory whistleblower claim in New Jersey waives common law claims, we could say that all causes of action except the whistleblower claim were waived. We didn't have to discuss them individually.

We believed the common law claims would fail anyway because their elements could not be satisfied on the facts of our case, regardless of waiver, but we gave that only passing reference. After presenting our key facts, we said that the common law claims failed not only because of waiver but also because their elements could not be satisfied, "as discussed in Point III."

We made a tactical decision to focus the preliminary statement on the reasons for plaintiff's discharge because those reasons countered the whistleblower claim—plaintiff's only viable cause of action, the others having been waived—and because a good set of facts will defeat most any cause of action, whatever name you give it. Discussion of the individual common law claims would produce only diminishing returns and would dilute the main message.

Lawyers may be concerned that if they fail to address an issue in the preliminary statement, the other side will argue, and the court may conclude, that their position on that issue must be weak. They fear that anything unaddressed will be deemed evaded.

Though confronting or deflecting all the other side's points is important, that task does not have to be accomplished in the preliminary statement. By addressing everything up front, you weaken your primary message.

In this case, the primary message is that the employee was fired not for whistleblowing but for doing a bad job. Your aim is to persuade the court to reach this conclusion before the court heads into the rest of the brief.

If you accomplish this, you develop "momentum," which in the lingo of persuasive writing is shorthand for, among other things, the tendency for a reader to interpret new information to support the reader's initial hypothesis. In other words, if the court is with you after the first paragraph, the court will look to stay with you for the rest of the brief, partly because readers (people) find changing their opinions unpleasant and partly because they have a tendency to root for one side in a contest. If your facts are good, the reader's initial hypothesis will be that the plaintiff was fired not for whistleblowing but for bad behavior.

Good facts will persuade the reader to view the case favorably to your side. The default approach of "Defendants respectfully submit this brief in support of their motion for summary judgment" will not. Besides, you already said that on the cover and in the notice of motion.

Begin the preliminary statement by encapsulating your most persuasive point in a sentence or two. If you can't do that, then take a slower-developing tack (not "tact," though you need that, too), and get to the point as quickly as possible, always focusing on the facts.

Puzzler

How would you tighten and sharpen the following sentence?

The defendant certainly had constructive notice by reason of the recording of the documents.

Drop "certainly." If you don't persuade with your facts, you won't persuade with your intensifiers. Substitute "because" for "by reason of." It is shorter and more direct. Finally, end the sentence with the important fact—the recording. Alternate versions may work better in context.

The revised version:

The defendant had constructive notice because the documents were recorded.

First alternate:

Recording the documents gave the defendant constructive notice.

Second alternate:

The recorded documents gave the defendant constructive notice.

Develop Momentum by Tapping the Reader's Emotions

Among other things, seek agreement with the reader early on

For a change, I will analyze my own work. The goal, as always, is to uncover some truth about persuasive writing. The subject matter is my column entitled "To Get to the Point, Get to the Verb" [reprinted in Chapter 8].

The point of the article was that writers should not test readers' patience by interposing long phrases between nouns and verbs. Once a noun appears, the reader demands action and is annoyed and even confused if the verb is delayed.

A draft of the article began:

> *The amount of information lawyers have to impart in a single sentence can be substantial and the task of organizing it imposing.*

The final version began:

> *Lawyers write long sentences, which isn't necessarily bad. We write for an intelligent audience that can handle large chunks of information, and we want our prose to seem smooth and sophisticated, not choppy and adolescent. But the longer the sentence, the tougher the task of organizing it.*

The article went through many drafts, but the expansion of the opening occurred in one burst halfway through the process. It was not a matter of accretion to, or deletion from, earlier drafts. It was a wholesale change. In my judgment, the change was good.

"Lawyers write long sentences" creates common ground with the reader because the reader knows, and at some level probably resents, that lawyers write long sentences. The opening also alliterates ("Lawyers write long . . ."), creating rhythmic appeal. Together, the sound and the sense engage the reader.

The sentence then changes direction. It says that writing long sentences "isn't necessarily bad." This reversal creates tension between the quasi-critical observation that lawyers write long sentences and the supportive comment that long sentences may not be so bad. To see how the tension is resolved, readers will probably continue reading.

I resolved the tension by explaining why long sentences aren't necessarily bad: A lawyer's audience can handle complex thoughts, and a well-crafted long sentence often makes a better impression than two or three shorter ones.

Let's look again at the original opening:

> *The amount of information lawyers have to impart in a single sentence can be substantial and the task of organizing it imposing.*

The first four words, "The amount of information," say nothing interesting. Can you envision "an amount of information"?

Add the next seven words ("have to impart in a single sentence"), and you still have nothing. You can't agree or disagree with it, and it isn't likely to inform you or make you angry, sympathetic or curious.

The sentence hardly improves when you characterize the amount of information as "substantial" and the task of organizing it as "imposing." The thought is obvious, and it isn't entirely accurate. Lawyers don't have to impart a substantial amount of information in a single sentence. They can write short sentences.

The Creative Process

The first version of the opening remained unchanged through several drafts. Then I wrote, "Lawyers write long sentences," and the rest followed. I didn't derive the new version from text already written. I simply observed it. For all I know, the alliteration of "lawyers" and "long" triggered it.

In some respects, the creative process is a mystery. It's unpredictable, like answers from the Magic 8-Ball™, a grapefruit-sized black sphere that looks like the 8-ball in pool. You ask the device a question ("Will I pass the Bar?"); you shake it; and an answer floats up in a little window (e.g., "It is certain"). Disturbingly often, our minds provide answers with what seems like the same fortuity as the Magic 8-Ball™.

Can we glean practical truths about writing from that column? Yes.

Concepts don't engage readers. Details do. The original version of the opening said that lawyers have trouble organizing their sentences because they have to put substantial information in them. This is true, but "information" is vague, and so is "substantial." Say instead, "Lawyers write long sentences." It paints a picture.

Highlight actions, not obligations. Rather than discuss what lawyers have to do (put information into their sentences), say how they do it (they write long sentences).

Make statements with which the reader agrees. If you cause the reader's head to nod in affirmation, literally or figuratively, you create a sympathetic vibration and develop momentum for your version of the story.

Make statements with which the reader disagrees if you are confident you can change the reader's mind. Contention can be a hook to draw the reader in.

Make statements to which the reader is likely to have some affect (emotion) attached. If you connect with the reader's emotions, you tap an energy source. The energy propels the reader through your piece and, if your point is solid, inclines the reader to your side.

You can tap this energy by, for example, provoking anger at an opposing party, generating sympathy for your client, or stimulating curiosity. Or you can tap the energy through nothing more than the comforting rhythm of the communication contract, in which the writer performs by being clear and direct, and the reader performs by absorbing the message. Clarity can energize a reader, partly because a "good read" is energizing and partly because a reader is likely to be pleasantly surprised by clarity because it is so rare.

The revised opening to the article began with an idea with which the reader would probably agree and about which the reader might well have strong feelings—that lawyers write long sentences. Then the opening said this isn't necessarily bad, setting up a point of contention. When I gave reasons why long sentences aren't necessarily bad, the reader hopefully agreed, and momentum developed as the reader shifted from skepticism or disagreement to agreement.

The purpose of the opening for that column was to engage, not to begin an argument. The subject of the column was not whether long sentences are defensible, but whether subject and verb should be separated. In a brief, you would go directly to your point, but you would still look to engage.

Puzzler

How would you tighten and sharpen the following sentence?

The Court rejected creating a general rule with respect to the applicability of marketability discounts.

Instead of "rejected creating," try "declined to create." It's more direct. "Creating" is amorphous, and "rejected creating" is ambiguous. Did the court reject the idea of the court creating a general rule or did the court reject the idea of anyone creating a general rule?

Replace "with respect to" with "for" and reduce "the applicability of" to "applying." You need a version of "apply" to distinguish the idea from, say, "quantifying" marketability discounts. For extra credit, substitute the metaphorical "blanket" for "general."

The revised version:

The court declined to create a blanket rule for applying marketability discounts.

Focus on the Essential Flaw in Your Opponent's Argument

Begin a response or a reply with a point, not merely a declaration of disagreement

Briefs written in response to an opponent's brief, whether as a "responding brief" (*e.g.,* opposing a motion) or a "reply brief" (in further support of a motion) often begin with a statement that the other side missed the boat, as in the following opening to a reply brief in support of a motion to dismiss:

> *Plaintiff's brief in opposition to defendant's motion to dismiss the complaint distorts the arguments in defendant's brief and misinterprets the case law relevant to plaintiff's claims.*

This opening has no grip because it is abstract and conclusory. Except for the accusations of distortion and misinterpretation, the words have no visceral appeal: "Plaintiff's brief in opposition," "defendant's motion to dismiss," "complaint," "arguments," "defendant's brief," "case law" and "plaintiff's claims." They are conceptual and sterile.

The accusations of distortion and misinterpretation, though serious and presumably heartfelt, are only name-calling when presented without factual support, as here. To break bones (persuade), you need sticks and stones (facts).

Some briefs compound the sluggishness of a conclusory opening by restating the conclusion from another perspective. For example, the following was the second sentence in the same reply brief:

> *An accurate reading of defendant's arguments and defendant's incorrect interpretation of the case law demonstrates that plaintiff's claims should be dismissed.*

After accusing the adversary of distortion and misinterpretation, the writer says that a careful reader will see through the deception. That's not a point; it's a prediction.

Language like this merely marks time; it does not persuade. It tells the court what you think of the other side's arguments, but the court already knows what you think. The court rarely reads a brief that says, "We agree with the adversary and concede."

The opening sentences in a brief receive special attention because they come first, when the reader is alert, interested, and ready to tip one way or the other, depending on the strength of your message. If you begin well, you build momentum. Conversely, if you open flat, as with unsupported negation ("Plaintiff misses the point") or neutral procedure ("This is a brief in opposition to . . ."), you waste an excellent opportunity to win the reader over.

I am not surprised that writers default to naked negation. It is a natural though misguided outlet for the anger and indignation stimulated by the adversary system.

Puffing up and declaring that the other side is "simply wrong" seems as if it should move the reader—but it doesn't. A conclusory accusation is like a blank cartridge—full of powder and good for a bang, but nothing comes out.

On the other hand, I am surprised that so many experienced lawyers embrace the conclusory approach. When their associates dare to use the opening to jump into the facts or encapsulate the key flaw in the other side's position, the supervising attorney pushes the facts deeper into the opening and inserts a conclusory statement up front. They seem to be under the misimpression that postures persuade.

Some reply openings unnecessarily restate the procedural posture of the case, as in the following from a reply brief in support of a minor's appeal from an adjudication of delinquency:

> *AZ appeals from an Order of the Superior court, Family Part, adjudicating him delinquent on various sexual offenses.*

The opening continued with a naked negation of the other side's position:

> *As demonstrated herein in this reply brief, the arguments of the State in its brief lack merit. Several errors of constitutional dimension occurred in AZ's case and his adjudication as a delinquent should be reversed.*

At that point, the appellate judges probably shrugged, figured "Whatever," and turned to the first page of the reply argument.

A common tactic in responding briefs is to attack the other side's apparent motive:

> *Defendant's response to plaintiff's motion for summary judgment is merely an attempt to stall a simple collection case.*

Maybe defendant was attempting to stall, but motives aren't merits. The kernel of persuasion in this brief actually appeared about 20 lines down the page:

> *Although defendant opposes this motion on the basis that discovery is incomplete, it has made no discovery request for nearly a year.*

That fact has weight and speaks for itself. The writer should have given it prominence at the beginning of the reply brief.

In contrast to the foregoing, the following opening from a reply brief in support of an application for a preliminary injunction gets right down to brass tacks:

> *Defendants acknowledge that they failed to make good on their promise to operate a men's clothing store at the Plaza Shopping Center. Without notice, they emptied their store of goods, transferred employees, and closed up shop. Two weeks later, just as suddenly, their demolition crews returned to tear out the walls and lighting, leaving a scarred and pockmarked space.*

This opening tells a story. It presents the facts and lets the reader draw the conclusion, which, given the facts, will be unfavorable to the defendant. It doesn't tell the reader what to think.

The following opening from an appellate reply brief uses the same technique:

Plaintiff's responding brief fails to explain how the jury could determine without expert support that light from a hooded doorway fixture with a 60-watt bulb—had the bulb been functioning—could have prevented a trip-and-fall in a parking lot more than 70 feet away.

A judge knows from experience that hooded light fixtures above doorways aren't intended to, and don't, illuminate parking lots 70 feet away. The fact speaks for itself. That is your goal — to have your facts speak directly to the reader. Once the message is delivered, you can sum up.

Puzzler

How would you improve the following sentence?

Some states either impose no franchise tax at all or it is very minimal.

This is a run-on sentence because independent clauses are connected without a comma (the second independent clause is "or it is very minimal"). But that isn't the sentence's only problem.

The word "either" in front of the verb "impose" prepares the reader for another verb after "or," but the sentence supplies a pronoun instead ("it"), disappointing the reader's expectations.

Also, the natural progression in this sentence about the absence of franchise tax is from minimal tax to none at all, not from no tax to minimal tax. Once the reader sees "no franchise tax at all," the reader senses closure, only to have the sense of closure disturbed by the reference to minimal tax. Again, the reader's expectations are disappointed.

In a close call, I would retain "either" as a signal that the unit of thought will continue past "minimal franchise tax."

The new version:

Some states impose either minimal franchise tax or none at all.

The Need for Clarity May Override the Risk of Exaggeration

Don't be afraid to make an overstatement that you quickly qualify

I caution writers not to overstate their case because exaggeration hurts credibility. But clarity may require that you overstate a point and then qualify it (modify it) rather than try to squeeze the point and its qualifier into the same sentence.

This challenge arose in a letter to a client who proposed to make a campaign contribution to a "joint candidates committee," which raises funds for a group of political candidates. In New Jersey, a person wishing to make a contribution to a joint candidates committee is not limited to the $2,600 that is allowed per candidate in each election cycle (calendar year).

A person may contribute $2,600 times the number of candidates supported by a joint candidates committee. For example, if a joint candidates committee supports three candidates for city council, then a person can contribute three times $2,600, or $7,800, to that committee.

But nothing is easy.

If a candidate who is supported by a joint candidates committee is also supported by an "individual candidate committee" (a fund-raising committee specific to that candidate), then the amount you can give to the joint candidates committee will be reduced by a multiple of what you give to the individual candidate committee.

Suppose you give $1,000 to an individual candidate committee supporting candidate A. Because the maximum you can give to a candidate is $2,600 per election cycle, you are limited to giving $1,600 more to candidate A.

Now suppose you wish to contribute to a joint candidates committee supporting candidates A, B and C. If you were to give $7,800 to the committee supporting candidates A, B and C, $2,600 would be attributed to candidate A.

But you have already contributed $1,000 to candidate A, so you can't give the joint candidates committee $7,800. You can give it only $4,800, $1,600 of which would be attributed to candidate A. With that $1,600, and the $1,000 you already gave candidate A, you "max out" at $2,600 as to candidate A.

The practical effect of making a campaign contribution to an individual who is also supported by a joint candidates committee is that the amount you can subsequently give to the joint candidates committee is reduced not merely by the amount you gave the individual but by that amount times the number of candidates supported by the joint candidates committee.

If you try to fit all that into one sentence, you might end up with the following, taken from a draft letter:

> *A joint candidates committee established by candidates who have not established any individual candidates committees to which you have contributed in an election cycle may accept a contribution from you of up to $2,600 multiplied by the number of candidates supported by the joint candidates committee. This amount could be reduced if any of the candidates supported by the joint candidates committee were to form an individual candidates committee to which you contribute.*

I had to read the first sentence several times to understand it because I kept tripping over the embedded qualifier ("established by candidates who have not established any individual candidates committees to which you have contributed in an election cycle"). The second sentence sought to clarify, but by the time I reached it, I had already expended substantial effort trying to make sense of the first sentence.

The writer told me that he tried to fit the concept and the qualifier into one sentence because he didn't feel he was entitled to overstate his case. He thought he couldn't say the following because it isn't always true:

> *A joint candidates committee may accept a contribution from you of up to $2,600 multiplied by the number of candidates supported by the committee.*

The statement becomes false if you have already contributed individually to any of the candidates supported by the joint candidates committee. Because you aren't warning the reader about that contingency, your sentence in a sense is an overstatement. But the overstatement works if you qualify it immediately:

> *A joint candidates committee may accept a contribution from you of up to $2,600 multiplied by the number of candidates supported by the committee. This amount could be reduced if you were to contribute to an individual candidate committee supporting any of those candidates.*

Even though the first sentence is an overstatement, it is defensible because it conveys a significant concept (that a contributor can give three times the maximum to a committee supporting three candidates); the alternative structure is not viable (setting forth the qualification within the statement itself); and you quickly supply the qualifier, thus disavowing deceptive intent.

When the reader sees the qualification—that the amount one can contribute to a joint candidates committee will be reduced by amounts given to individual candidate committees—the reader won't think, "But you said . . . ." The reader will think, at worst, "Uh oh; this can get complicated."

The writing process often presents choices between competing principles. Here, you serve the principle of clarity at the cost of an overstatement that could, theoretically, affect your credibility.

Initially, clarity and credibility may seem to be at odds, placing you between a rock and a hard place. But this is a false conflict. Because of the importance of being able to give multiples of $2,600 to a joint candidates committee; because of the confusion that would result from trying to qualify this concept even as you present it; and because you promptly set the record straight, you pay less for the overstatement than you might think, and you gain back more.

Puzzler

How would you tighten and sharpen the following sentence?

In September, a motion for partial summary judgment was filed on behalf of the Company seeking dismissal of Plaintiff's specific performance claim, the lis pendens and fixing damages.

Change passive to active. Instead of "a motion for partial summary judgment was filed on behalf of the Company," say "the Company moved for partial summary judgment." To create parallel structure, say "*to dismiss* the specific performance claim and the *lis pendens* and to fix damages" (emphasis added) or use three verbs if you prefer the greater precision of "discharging" the *lis pendens.*

In the alternate version, I use a comma before the last item in the series to slow the pace, emphasizing the importance of the three separate requests for relief and encouraging the reader to take the time to digest the three concepts.

The revised version needs no comma after *lis pendens.*

The revised version:

In September, the Company moved for partial summary judgment to dismiss the specific performance claim and the lis pendens and to fix damages.

Alternate version:

In September, the Company moved for partial summary judgment to dismiss the specific performance claim, discharge the lis pendens, and fix damages.

4

Logic

Maintaining the Flow of Ideas

Logic

Maintaining the Flow of Ideas

A good argument is a logical chain, each link well-conceived and well-defended. Adversaries instinctively seek out and attack the weakest link in the chain.

In part, logic is about connecting the links in the chain. The connections, usually called "transitions," guide the reader from link to link, developing momentum and maintaining flow.

Logic is also about grouping—forming sets and subsets. Some writers proffer subsets as if they were sets and pad their sets with unrelated or repetitive data to make the sets appear more impressive. Carefully review your groupings, especially after bursts of creativity fueled by righteous indignation.

Transition by Repetition: Take One Step Back to Go Two Steps Forward

Transitions are transparent to the reader but good for the flow

> You will be tempted to believe that because a connection between ideas is perfectly clear to you as a writer it is also perfectly clear to the reader. It isn't.
>
> —Lucile Vaughn Payne, *The Lively Art of Writing* (1965) at 96-97

A Zen proverb says that "a good craftsman leaves no traces." In good legal writing, the prose moves along so well that the reader never stops to admire the writer's skill. That is the ultimate goal—to focus the reader on the argument, not the writing.

One device that keeps the prose moving and "transparent" to the reader is the transition, one form of which is the repetition of words from a prior sentence or paragraph. The repeated words are, in effect, a step backward to move two steps forward. Below is an example of words carried from the end of one paragraph to the beginning of the next.

[Last sentence in paragraph:]

For all these reasons, the slow-down of ***traffic*** *at* ***that interchange*** *constitutes a* ***safety hazard*** *and must be alleviated as soon as possible.*

[First sentence in new paragraph:]

Not only do ***traffic*** *conditions at* ***that interchange*** *constitute a* ***safety hazard,*** *but they increase air pollution as well.*

The transition by repetition is in the words "traffic," "that interchange" and "safety hazard."

As suggested by the summational phrase "For all these reasons," the reader beginning the second paragraph probably has a visual, intellectual and emotional matrix regarding traffic conditions at the interchange. By restimulating this matrix with the trigger words "traffic," "that interchange" and "safety hazard," the writer can hook the second paragraph into the first. This not only achieves continuity—which holds the reader's attention—but it adds emphasis through repetition.

In the above example, the paragraphs are linked not only by the repetition of key words but also by the "Not only . . . but also" construction, which is used in conjunction with, and intensifies, the repetition of key words. "Not only . . . . but also" is inherently transitional, like "first," "next," "in addition," "for example," "consequently," "therefore" and "thus."

A Second Example

In the following example, the second sentence does not flow smoothly from the first:

> *To gain access to public records under the Right to Know Law or the common law, a person must pass through several screens. Standing is required under both the Right to Know Law and the common law.*

The paragraph begins by telling the reader that a person needs to pass through several "screens" to gain access to public records. Thus, the reader expects to be told what a person must do (how he must pass through screens), what the several screens are, or both. In effect, the reader experiences the first sentence as the beginning of a story about a person and about screens, and the reader assumes the story will continue to be about a person and about screens.

But the second sentence seems to be about something called "standing," which could be a screen, but the reader does not automatically know that. When the reader sees the word "standing" at the beginning of the second sentence after not having seen it in the first, the reader may wonder, "Standing. Hmmm. How does 'standing' fit in here? It isn't a person. Is it one of the 'screens'? I thought this story was about persons and screens."

When neither word appears at the beginning of the second sentence, the reader is momentarily disoriented. Ultimately, the reader will deduce that standing is one of the screens, but at the cost of time and energy.

In the following versions, the relationship between the two sentences is improved.

Better:

> *To gain access to public records under the Right to Know Law or the common law, a person must pass through several screens. First, the person seeking disclosure must establish standing.*

Alternate:

> *To gain access to public records under the Right to Know Law or the common law, a person must pass through several screens. One such screen is the requirement that the person seeking disclosure establish standing.*

In the improved versions, the immediate repetition of the words "person" or "screen" propels the reader from the first sentence into the second by tapping the expectation energy developed around the terms "person" and "screen."

Readers take transitions for granted until they are omitted; then suddenly the prose is no longer transparent. The reader becomes confused and loses your point. Worse, the reader's confusion, together with his or her resentment at having to work hard to grasp your meaning, may cause the reader to lose faith in you and your presentation. The more this happens, the more the reader will doubt what you say, even to the point of not reading it. In an unfortunate but inexorable progression, serious consequences can flow from an accumulation of small mistakes.

Puzzler

How would you tighten and sharpen the following sentence?

Exclusion of evidence at trial is only warranted where there is a design to mislead which causes unfair surprise and undue prejudice to the other party due to the late amendment of interrogatories.

The point of the sentence—that evidence can be excluded if late amendment of interrogatories causes prejudice—is buried in the middle rather than featured at the end, where it belongs. Therefore, move the concept of prejudice to the end of the sentence.

Delete "at trial" as implicit and "surprise" because it is implicit in prejudice (though if you weren't trying to reduce the number of words, you might like "surprise" for its emotional appeal).

Drop the phrase "to the other party" as implicit; drop "due to" as improper usage and put "only" in the right place (as close as possible to what it modifies). Get rid of the ponderous "which" clause tacked to a "where" clause, which also takes care of a "which" that should have been a "that." Finally, avoid the "there is" construction.

If you were looking to portray the test as broader and tougher rather than limited, you might choose the more active "Evidence will be excluded . . . if," deleting the "only."

The revised version:

Exclusion of evidence for late amendment of interrogatories is warranted only if the delay was intended to mislead and caused undue prejudice.

Grouping and Subordination Help Guide and Persuade the Reader

Use bags and baskets to present your facts and arguments

Facts and arguments are like eggs, tomatoes, marbles or anything else best conveyed in bags or baskets, not loose in your arms. You should group them. After you group them, you can compare, contrast and rank order the groups, creating additional relationships. The more relationships you create, the easier it is for the reader to grasp your meaning, and the more powerful is your point.

Suppose you have a point and five reasons to support it. You could list them ("X is true for five reasons"), or you could look for relationships among the reasons to see if grouping and rank ordering may help you persuade.

For example, suppose your point is that a company should not have to be licensed by state gaming regulators to provide record-keeping services to the trustee of a casino retirement plan because regulation of retirement plans under the Employee Retirement Income Security Act (ERISA) is already vigorous and encompasses companies that serve the plans.

You are writing a brief to the regulators, and you have five principal facts to support your contention: (1) ERISA imposes elaborate reporting and disclosure requirements on retirement plan trustees and others who service covered plans; (2) ERISA prohibits transactions between the trustee and the plan, thus precluding conflicts of interest; (3) ERISA prohibits the employment of convicted felons by persons servicing the plan; (4) ERISA provides remedies and sanctions for violating its provisions; and (5) ERISA provides ready access to the federal courts.

These reasons aren't grouped or rank ordered.

The five reasons actually fit into three categories: (1) reporting and disclosure; (2) standards of conduct (no conflicts or felons allowed); and (3) enforcement, including ready access to the federal courts. Grouping the five reasons into three categories might look like this:

> *Not only does ERISA (1) establish elaborate reporting and disclosure requirements, but it (2) establishes standards of conduct for plan fiduciaries and their agents and (3) provides appropriate remedies and sanctions with ready access to the federal courts. Among other things, ERISA prohibits transactions between the trustee and the plan, and it prohibits the employment of convicted felons by persons servicing the plan.*

You have strengthened the presentation of your original list in several ways. First, you reduced five categories to three, which is easier to remember and understand. The first category is reporting and disclosure. The second is standards of conduct, consisting of the two kinds of prohibition (no conflicts, no felons), and the third is enforcement, consisting of (i) remedies and sanctions and (ii) ready access to the federal courts.

Access to the courts is necessary to enforce the remedies and sanctions. Thus, access to the courts is grouped with remedies and sanctions.

You also created a rank order in which you subordinated the first category (reporting and disclosure) to the other two categories (standards of conduct and enforcement), using a "not only . . . but also" construction. Subordination makes the list easier to remember and emphasizes the most important facts.

In this case, grouping and subordination address the reader's likely concerns. A state gaming regulator is likely to be more concerned with prohibited behavior and enforcement than with the kind of reporting and disclosure required by the Securities and Exchange Commission. State gaming regulators may view reporting and disclosure as less rigorous than, and not an adequate substitute for, regulation that seeks to ensure good character and conduct.

To respond to this concern, you write that "not only" does ERISA provide the kind of scrutiny with which gaming regulators are less concerned (financial reporting and disclosure), but it also provides the kind of scrutiny they consider crucial (standards of conduct and enforcement). You place the elements they consider more important at the end of the sentence, in a featured position. It is featured because you lead up to it and because it concludes the thought. Through the "not only . . . but also" construction, you acknowledge the lesser importance of the element in which the gaming regulators are less interested.

Finally, you conclude the paragraph with your two standards of conduct—no conflicts, no felons—thus giving shape to and emphasizing your most important thought: that ERISA seeks to ensure good character and appropriate conduct just as gaming regulators do. The "not only . . . but also" construction and the transition "Among other things" sufficiently tie the examples to the second element (standards of conduct) without your having to say, "Here are two examples of standards of conduct."

Experienced legal writers group and rank order thoughts naturally, but beginners tend not to. Even the experienced sometimes settle for the additive list, for example, "The court should rule this way for three reasons (four reasons, five reasons)." Listing facts and arguments takes less work than grouping them and finding relationships among the groups, but the extra effort usually pays off. Grouping and rank ordering help the reader understand your point and guide the reader toward the resolution you propose.

Puzzler

How would you tighten and sharpen the following sentence?

The Annual Ethics Statement is circulated on an annual basis to all company personnel to remind them of the basic legal and ethical obligations attending their responsibilities.

"On an annual basis" can be dropped because of the name of the document. "Company" can be dropped because it is implicit in "personnel," and "attending their responsibilities" can likewise be dropped as implicit. "Is circulated . . . to remind" can be replaced by "reminds," which is punchier and focuses on repetition of the message. In contrast, the phrase "is circulated . . . to remind" is passive and suggests the document is passed from hand to hand or department to department.

The revised version:

The Annual Ethics Statement reminds all personnel of their legal and ethical obligations.

If You Have More Than One Dispositive Point, Let the Reader Know Up Front

An overview provides power and aids comprehension

Sometimes you have two or more points of relatively equal strength, each of which would win for you if accepted by the court. Generally, you should give the reader an overview of both points before elaborating on the first. Don't just jump in and leave the reader to find out later that you have more than one arrow in your quiver.[1]

Consider the following two paragraphs that opened a brief opposing a motion to enforce a foreign default judgment:

The Pennsylvania default judgment that plaintiff seeks to enforce is void because plaintiff failed to properly serve defendant with the summons and complaint. Plaintiff mailed rather than delivered the summons and complaint to defendant's statutory agent.

[Further discussion of service is omitted.]

Even assuming service was proper, the Pennsylvania court was without jurisdiction to enter a default judgment because defendant did not enter into a contract with plaintiff in Pennsylvania. Plaintiff's claims arise only from contacts outside Pennsylvania.

[Further discussion of contacts is omitted.]

The writer has two grounds on which to claim the Pennsylvania court lacked personal jurisdiction over his client: improper service and insufficient contacts. Instead of completing the discussion of the first ground before mentioning the second, the writer should tell the reader that two grounds exist on which to void the default judgment and that both grounds are jurisdictional:

The Pennsylvania default judgment that plaintiff seeks to enforce is void because the court lacked personal jurisdiction over defendant in two respects: improper service and insufficient contacts.

In the alternative:

The Pennsylvania default judgment that plaintiff seeks to enforce is void on two jurisdictional grounds: improper service and insufficient contacts with the State.

Then the writer can elaborate on the first point:

Service of process was deficient because . . .

Having established why service of process was deficient, the writer can begin another paragraph by reiterating the first point. The repetition achieves emphasis and provides a transition:

---

[1] I use this metaphor in lieu of the mysterious "another string to your bow." *Brewer's Dictionary of Phrase and Fable* says the allusion is to the custom of British bowmen carrying a reserve string in case of accident. If so, shouldn't the metaphor be "another string *for* your bow"?

Not only did the Pennsylvania court lack personal jurisdiction over the defendant because service was improper, but the court lacked personal jurisdiction for the additional reason that defendant did not have minimum contacts with the State.

The writer can then explain why Pennsylvania lacked minimum contacts, *e.g.*, the defendant did not visit Pennsylvania; the transaction did not affect Pennsylvania, and so forth.

Having two points provides an opportunity for grouping, which aids comprehension and adds force. You "group" here in two ways: You announce that you have not one point but two, and you explain that both points fall into the same category—jurisdictional.

The technique of identifying and characterizing multiple points before launching into the first one has several virtues. It shows the reader you are in control, like a doctor who diagnoses with assurance, a repair person who explains how the igniter in your furnace works, or a person who knows computers. By providing overview, you show that you have "got your arms around" the matter and are worthy of the reader's confidence.

The overview also serves as a roadmap. Like tourists about to set out for a day of sightseeing, readers like to know where they are going. The summary gives the reader a sense of how large the unit of argument will be so the reader can reserve energy for it, and it shows the reader the direction the argument will take so the reader can feel in control.

Finally, the summary is a show of strength. You claim victory not just on one ground but on two. By showing strength, you begin to create the sense that the day belongs to you.

Take the Aggressive Approach

Before revision, the second paragraph in the above example began, "Even assuming service was proper . . ." It should have begun, "Not only was service improper, but . . .," a more aggressive approach. Reassert your first point rather than concede it for argument's sake.

Think about it. On the one hand you are saying, "We win for two reasons." On the other, you are saying, "Even if we lose on one ground, at least we win on the other." Do you sell more brushes by saying, "They are good in the kitchen and the bathroom" or by saying, "If they aren't good in the kitchen, you can still use them in the bathroom"?

Puzzler

How would you tighten and sharpen the following sentence?

There are a number of cases in which the participation of the landowner in the project was a lot less than in this case and the courts have held that the duty to provide a safe working place applies to that landowner.

The necessary elements of the sentence are (a) courts imposing a duty (b) on landowners (c) to provide a safe workplace (d) under circumstances where the landowner was less involved in the project than here. Unnecessary verbiage includes, "There are a number of cases in which" and "in this case."

Speak first of the courts to get more quickly to the action (courts imposing a duty) and speak assertively of courts "imposing" rather than courts "holding" or a duty "applying."

Collateral benefits of the restructuring include (a) shortening "the participation of the landowner" to "landowners whose participation"; (b) eliminating the circuitousness and the drone of the run-on sentence; (c) deleting the phrase "applies to that landowner"; and (d) ending the sentence with, and thus emphasizing, an important concept: "less." Micro-editing includes changing the colloquial phrase "a lot" to "much" and shortening "working place" to "workplace."

The revised version:

> *Courts have imposed a duty to provide a safe workplace on landowners whose participation in the project was much less.*

Use "Accordingly," "Thus" and "Therefore" Sparingly

The context usually supplies the connection

Legal writing is premised on logical connections. If one idea doesn't lead to the next, you aren't making a point.

Sometimes you feel a need to announce the connection between ideas with "Thus," "Therefore" or "Accordingly." You want to declare that you are about to make your point.

I asked the lawyers in my informal polling group which of these three connectors they prefer: "thus," "therefore" or "accordingly." The responses were evenly divided.

I also asked if they try to limit their use of these words. Surprisingly, all said yes. They deem them unnecessary (except when they use them).

Consider the function of "accordingly" between the following sentences:

> *Rule 11 attempts to deter litigation abuse while encouraging creativity within the law. Accordingly, the rule imposes sanctions only on attorneys who file frivolous or unreasonable claims.*

The first sentence tells the reader that Rule 11 seeks a balance between deterrence and encouragement. "While" marks the balance. The next sentence tells the reader how the balance is struck—by imposing sanctions only on a certain class of attorneys: those who file frivolous or unreasonable claims. "Only" effects the balance that the first sentence identifies.

Do you need "Accordingly"?

Without it, the sentences read as follows:

> *Rule 11 attempts to deter litigation abuse while encouraging creativity within the law. The rule imposes sanctions only on attorneys who file frivolous or unreasonable claims.*

"Only" is a sufficient connector. The reader has to wait only five words into the second sentence ("The rule imposes sanctions only") to learn how the balance is struck.

"Accordingly" merely delays and sprays. It delays because it is an extra word requiring extra punctuation. It sprays because it may guide the reader down any of several reasonable pathways different from the one you wish the reader to take. For example:

> *Accordingly, the trial court is given great discretion in deciding Rule 11 applications.*
>
> *Accordingly, Rule 11 protects a plaintiff's right to propose reasonable extensions of the law.*
>
> *Accordingly, substantial case law has developed as courts seek to effect the proper balance.*

"Accordingly" is usually unnecessary because it merely tells the reader that you are about to say something that flows from what you just said. But the reader already knows that. If what you are about to say doesn't flow from what you just said, you are in trouble.

Not only do "accordingly," "thus" and "therefore" delay and possibly misdirect the reader, but they may impair your creative process. When you announce a connection with one of those words, you tend to stop testing the relationship for validity. "Accordingly" declares the connection, and you accept it as so. You stop thinking.

An alternative to either using or dropping "thus," "therefore" or "accordingly" is to combine sentences, subordinating one to the other:

> *To encourage creativity within the law while deterring litigation abuse, Rule 11 sanctions only attorneys who file frivolous or unreasonable claims.*

This solution is tighter. The phrase "To encourage creativity" alerts the reader that a second thought will soon flow from the first.

A Second Example

Do you need "Thus" between the following two sentences?

> *The face of the statute does not reveal whether the word "marketing" in the exemption from public bidding for the "marketing of recyclables" includes curbside collection as well as the disposition of recyclables. Thus, the court relied on legislative history to find that public policy requires the bidding of contracts for the curbside collection of recyclables.*

The second sentence follows coherently from the first without "Thus" because relying on legislative history is what courts do when a statute is unclear. The reader accepts the court's reliance on legislative history as a natural result of the statute's being unclear.

The passage flows even better if you subordinate the first sentence to the second with "Because":

> *Because the statute does not reveal whether the word "marketing" in the exemption from public bidding for the "marketing of recyclables" includes curbside collection as well as the disposition of recyclables, the court relied on legislative history to find that public policy requires the bidding of contracts for the curbside collection of recyclables.*

Subordinating the first sentence to the second—that is, turning the first sentence into a "subordinate clause"—enhances the flow because the first word in the sentence ("Because") immediately identifies the first part of the sentence as a prelude to the second.

Puzzler

How would you tighten and sharpen the following sentence?

> *The audit did not disallow the deduction of depreciation from ABC Co.'s income, but rather changed the timing of the deduction by requiring it to be depreciated over a greater number of years.*

The phrase "from . . . income" can be omitted as implicit. "ABC Co." can also be omitted because the sentence is evidently part of a paragraph about the company. The long phrase "changed the timing of the deduction by requiring it to be depreciated over a greater number of years" can be shortened to "extended the depreciation period."

Eliminate "but rather" because it is awkward. "It merely" is more precise, and the tight relationship in the revised version between "The audit did not disallow" and "it merely extended" justifies a semicolon rather than a period. The revisions also eliminate the imprecision of saying that a deduction will be "depreciated."

The revised version:

> *The audit did not disallow the deduction for depreciation; it merely extended the depreciation period.*

"However" Is Usually an Unnecessary Signal

Negation or limitation may be obvious without it

"However" is used more often in legal writing than it should be, usually to signal negation or limitation where the text already does so adequately. Consider the following however that appeared in a brief:

> *Plaintiff alleges that defendant missed a discovery deadline. The only discovery deadline in this case, however, is the April 25 deadline set by the Court, which has not even arrived.*

Having graciously restated the plaintiff's argument and continued seven words into a second sentence without having countered the contention that the defendant missed a discovery deadline, the writer may have felt that too much time had passed without an assertion or even a suggestion that the plaintiff was wrong. Unwilling to wait for the sentence to unfold, the writer inserted "however" to signal an intent to disagree. In this context, "however" meant, in essence, "Plaintiff is wrong. I haven't told you why, but I will. Bear with me."

You don't need the however. Even without it, a reader can easily deduce that the defendant could not have missed a discovery deadline that hasn't arrived. In the revised version below, the second sentence has been restructured to eliminate the ambiguous "Court, which." Otherwise, the reader may momentarily wonder what hasn't arrived—the deadline or the court:

> *Plaintiff alleges that defendant missed a discovery deadline. The only discovery deadline is the one set by the Court—April 25—which hasn't arrived.*

Removing however serves at least two purposes. It eliminates a pause, bringing the reader more quickly to the point, and it eliminates a word of negation having no inherently persuasive value. Such words (and phrases like "plaintiff is wrong") increase the chance that a reader will think, consciously or unconsciously, that negation is being substituted for fact and law.

An even better solution is to combine the sentences to eliminate the flat restatement of the other side's position:

> *Defendant missed no discovery deadline because the only deadline is the one set by the court—April 25—which hasn't arrived.*

Instead of passively acknowledging that the defendant is accused of missing a discovery deadline, the writer pre-empts the accusation by saying the defendant missed no deadline. And by placing the "because" in the same sentence as the proposition, the writer ensures that the reader doesn't reach the end of a sentence without having read something persuasive.

Always look for opportunities to challenge an opposing argument not after you state it but as you state it. You can use simple negation ("Defendant missed no discovery deadline because . . ."), or, if the facts permit, you can state the adversary's position so that its flaw, at least from your point of view, is manifest (*e.g.*, "Plaintiff contends that defendant cannot pursue his profession anywhere on the Eastern Seaboard for the next ten years.").

Unless you truly cannot think of anything better, don't begin a refutation by restating the adversary's position in the adversary's terms.

Additional Examples

However is often rendered unnecessary by a negative (*e.g.*, "no" or "not") or a minimizer (e.g., "mere" or "only"). For example:

> *Rule 11 requires an objective belief that the complaint is based on well-grounded law and fact. This [, however,] does not imply that the rule is intended to abrogate an attorney's pursuit of novel legal theories.*

However is unnecessary because the phrase "does not imply" supplies the limiting parameter. In the following sentence, "no" suffices without however:

> *An individual must report direct campaign contributions exceeding $100; [however,] no requirement exists to report direct expenditures of less than $100.*

In the next sentence, "only" performs a limiting function just as "no" and "not" did in the previous examples, making however unnecessary:

> *Plaintiff filed separate charges alleging racial and sexual discrimination; [however,] only the sexual discrimination charge was filed with the EEOC.*

A better formulation might be:

> *Though plaintiff filed separate charges alleging racial and sexual discrimination, she filed only the sexual discrimination charge with the EEOC.*

"Though" lets the reader know that a limitation is coming and helps the writer achieve pace and balance by using the active voice and the same subject in both parts of the sentence ("plaintiff filed" and "she filed").

"Mere" can also make however unnecessary:

> *Plaintiff argued that his complaint satisfied Rule 11 because he disagreed with existing precedent. The court ruled [, however,] that mere disagreement with existing precedent constituted neither an objectively reasonable nor a good faith basis for filing the complaint.*

Punctuating However

If you use however, either precede it with a semicolon or set it off with commas:

For many years, he owned a store on the block; however, he never joined the retailers' association.

For many years, he owned a store on the block. He did not, however, join the retailers' association.

Never use however to splice independent clauses and create a run-on sentence:

For many years, he owned a store on the block, however, he did not join the retailers' association.

Nothing is grammatically wrong with beginning a sentence with however, but do it sparingly. Teachers of English have long considered it improper, and presumably they imbued some future judges with that belief. If a court deems the practice substandard, the court may, to some degree, deem your argument substandard as well.

Puzzler

How would you tighten and sharpen the following sentence?

Termination of the contract by ABC Corp. would not amount to a violation of the Telecom Act.

Conceptual nouns such as "termination" and "violation" have little grip because they create no images and convey no sense of action. Replace "amount to a violation of" with "violate" to shorten the sentence and provide more punch. Turn the sentence around to eliminate the other conceptual noun (termination). In the new structure, the alliteration of "Telecom" and "terminating" generates additional power.

The revised version:

ABC Corp. would not violate the Telecom Act by terminating the contract.

Reasons Persuade: Conclusions Do Not

Give reasons to back up your positional statements

Statements of one's conclusions are like violets—expressive if well-tended but congestive, like weeds, if permitted to spread.

Consider the following paragraph from a draft of an appellate brief challenging a trial court's ruling on the value of property. The issue addressed in this paragraph is whether the trial court's valuation findings based on expert reports rather than live testimony are protected on appeal by the abuse of discretion standard notwithstanding the court's failure to hold a hearing.

> *Nothing can hide the fact that the trial court judged the various approaches taken by the experts without a hearing. Plaintiff attempts to protect the trial judge's departures from the law by limiting this Court's review to the "abuse of discretion" standard. He claims incorrectly that the judge's decision not to hold a hearing was within the court's discretion. In truth, the trial court's "findings" in setting a value on the property without holding a hearing are entitled to no deference by this Court, but rather a plenary review.*

The abuse of discretion standard provides that an appellate court should not substitute its judgment for that of the trial court in the absence of a clear abuse of discretion. The rule is based on the trial court's having an opportunity to gauge the credibility of the witnesses and develop a feel for the case. Without a hearing, a trial court has no better perspective than a reviewing court.

The above paragraph from the draft brief does have spirit: It accuses, negates, and draws conclusions. It purports to be making a point.

But the paragraph doesn't actually make a point. It merely stretches out the writer's conclusion—that the abuse of discretion standard cannot protect the trial court's findings. It states no rationale.

Let's examine the first sentence:

> *Nothing can hide the fact that the trial court judged the various approaches taken by the experts without a hearing.*

Who is hiding anything?

The other side isn't. They will argue that the trial court's review of expert reports took the place of a hearing. They won't try to hide what the trial court did; they will seek to justify it. So the concept of "hiding" is a straw man.

The second sentence states what the plaintiff is arguing:

> *Plaintiff attempts to protect the trial judge's departures from the law by limiting this Court's review to the "abuse of discretion" standard.*

This is true, but you don't need to devote a full sentence to it. You aren't educating the court, and you aren't exposing a secret strategy. The winner below always invokes a restrictive standard of review. Though you have to mention the abuse of discretion standard, you can refer to it in passing, as shown below.

The reference to the trial court's "departures from the law" is gratuitous and conclusory. The appellate court knows that unless the trial court departed from the law, the judgment will be affirmed. Because you haven't explained any departures as yet, the reference is just conclusory.

Now let's look at the third sentence:

> *He claims incorrectly that the judge's decision not to hold a hearing was within the court's discretion.*

This sentence doesn't even belong in the paragraph. Though it speaks of the trial court's discretion, as did the second sentence, it makes a different point regarding discretion, namely, that the abuse of discretion standard doesn't protect the trial court's decision to forego a hearing. That may be true, but the subject of this particular paragraph is whether the findings the court made without a hearing are protected on appeal.

Deceptively, the sentence flows smoothly from the one before it because of transitional hooks. The pronoun "he" in the third sentence echoes "Plaintiff" in the second, and the trial court's "discretion" is referenced in both. You can read the paragraph several times before realizing the third sentence doesn't fit.

Now consider the last sentence:

> *In truth, the trial court's "findings" in setting a value on the property without holding a hearing are entitled to no deference by this Court, but rather a plenary review.*

This sentence says that plaintiff can't invoke the abuse of discretion standard, but it doesn't say why. It also takes an ungracious swipe at the trial court with ironic quotation marks around "findings." No matter how strongly you feel that the trial court deserves to be criticized, you must hold your tongue, as it were, because name-calling (the ironic quotation marks) makes you look bad.

Now consider what the paragraph accomplished. It took four sentences to say that because the trial court failed to hold a hearing, the plaintiff cannot invoke the abuse of discretion standard to protect the trial court's findings. It doesn't say why the court's failure to hold a hearing negates the abuse of discretion standard.

Explaining why the standard doesn't apply takes little space:

> *The abuse of discretion standard does not protect the trial court's findings because the court held no hearing, thus forfeiting the opportunity to evaluate the credibility of the witnesses and develop a feel for the case.*

Writers seem to know instinctively when they haven't presented a reason. Sometimes they have a reason but don't state it, and sometimes they have no reason at all. Their makeshift solution in either case—with which they almost always deceive themselves but not the reader—is to reiterate their conclusion or draw it out.

Writers are particularly prone to doing this where they have a partial "because." The writer can say, for example, "The abuse of discretion standard does not apply because the trial court held no hearing." That's true, but it's only the beginning of the explanation. The writer still needs to say why the failure to hold a hearing makes a difference.

Puzzler

How would you tighten and sharpen the following sentence?

It is important to keep in mind that typically it is the responding party that pays for the production of documents requested in discovery.

Drop the warm-up phrase "It is important to keep in mind." Ideally, everything you write is important. Don't suggest that some things you write are not. The construction "It is . . . that" can be eliminated in the same way that the construction "there are . . . that" can be eliminated. Just delete the words.

Reduce "production of documents" to "document production" and drop "requested in discovery" as implicit.

The revised version:

Typically, the responding party pays for document production.

Check Your Lists for Logical Structure

Lists may not emerge from your brain fully formed

Lists are a staple of legal writing. You list elements of a cause of action or a legal test. You list controlling precedents, supportive reasons and dispositive facts. Lists can be powerful.

But lists can also be numbing and ultimately useless if they make the reader work too hard. After you create a list, check it for manageable length and make sure the items are appropriately ordered and grouped.

Consider the following list from an article on electronic discovery:

> *To comprehend the company's computer system fully, counsel must have a basic knowledge of the hardware and peripherals the company uses, such as terminals, printers, modems, and data storage devices, as well as the software and the type of network, operating system, back-up procedures and protocols that the company employs.*

The sentence is more difficult than it needs to be because the grouping is imprecise. Some readers may reject rather than absorb the information, especially if they are unfamiliar with computers or impatient with detail.

The first set of items in the list—hardware and peripherals—is potentially confusing because peripherals are a kind of hardware. Normally, the "and" between two nouns indicates coordinate sets (*e.g.*, "dogs and cats"), not one set that fits within another (*e.g.*, "dogs and Dobermans").

The writer probably intended "hardware" to refer to the computer box and its microprocessor, memory chips and data paths, as distinguished from the software that runs the computer. But some readers might not view it this way, partly because the category "hardware" includes peripherals and partly because the proffered examples of hardware and peripherals give weak support to this limited meaning of hardware.

All but one of the examples are peripherals (printers, modems and data storage devices). The one nonperipheral item—terminals—is at the periphery, as it were, rather than the core of the computer.

A "terminal," in computer lingo, is an "end-use device," usually accompanied by a monitor and keyboard, that relies on another computer for its intelligence.[1] It is not the best representative of a category intended to include computing devices rather than peripherals.

You can improve the presentation of hardware and peripherals by clarifying the dichotomy between core computing hardware, such as processors and memory chips, and peripherals:

---

1 This definition of "terminal" is taken from http://whatis.techtarget.com (last visited January 21, 2007).

> *To comprehend the company's computer system fully, counsel should have a basic knowledge of the core computing hardware, including microprocessors and memory chips, and the peripherals, such as printers, modems and data storage devices.*

I would then begin a new sentence. Otherwise, the reader will have to digest too much at once. This obviates the need for a connector such as the phrase "as well as," which joined the principal segments of the original sentence. That phrase often signals that something isn't well organized.

Lawyers frequently use "as well as" when they mean, "I have something to add here, and I don't feel like figuring out how it should be grouped or subordinated, or I'd rather not know, so I'll just say 'as well as' and toss it into the mix." In more cases than not (test it for yourself), the phrase marks a failure to group or subordinate.

A flaw in the treatment of software in the original sentence is the presentation of "software" and "operating system" as coordinate sets even though an operating system is a kind of software. It's the same mistake as before—mixing sets and subsets.

Software is divided into two broad categories: operating systems, which manage other software, and application software, which performs a specific function, such as processing words. Operating systems include Microsoft Windows, Linux, Mac OS X and DOS. Application software includes word processing, spreadsheet and database management programs.

Perhaps the writer of the original sentence was thinking "application software" but wrote "software." A computer savvy reader may deduce that meaning of software by working backwards from operating system, but the writer doesn't make it easy, separating "software" from its putative sister set "operating system" by a five-word phrase ("and the type of network").

The problem can be corrected by adding "application" to qualify software, by presenting "operating system" before "application software," and by using examples of each. To give the list balance and greater substance, you should also provide examples of networks.

A two-sentence revision of the original sentence might look like this:

> *To comprehend the company computer system fully, counsel must have a basic knowledge of the core computing hardware, including microprocessors and memory chips, and the peripherals, such as printers, modems and data storage devices. Counsel should also understand the type of network—client/server (centralized processing) or peer-to-peer (processing at independent stations); the operating system, such as Windows, Mac OS X or DOS; the application software, such as word processing and spreadsheet programs; and the back-up procedures and protocols.*

The categories in the second sentence now move from broad view to narrow, from system-wide structure (network) to managing software (operating system) to task-oriented tools (application software). Readers are generally comfortable focusing from the outside in.

As categories expand and contract, the mind has to expand and contract with them, from large to small and back again. Each shift takes energy. Consider how fast you wear out the battery in your video camera as you move the lens in and out to change magnification. You can exhaust a reader in similar fashion, moving the lens in and out as you shift unpredictably from large category to small, from set to subset and back again.

A good list can win a case for you; a bad one can lose the reader. Don't deem your list done with the enumeration. Pay attention to the shaping as well.

Puzzler

Which is best and why—Version A, B or C?

Version A:

The regulators found that the firm had inadequate procedures for retaining and making accessible e-mails.

Version B:

The regulators found that the firm had inadequate procedures for retaining e-mails and making them accessible.

Version C:

The regulators found that the firm had inadequate procedures for retaining and making e-mails accessible.

You may think that for efficiency, you should group the objects of the word "for" (retaining and making) as close to that word as possible, as in Version A, but the reader is likely to see "making accessible e-mails" as a unit. You are referring to making e-mails accessible, not to "making accessible e-mails," whatever an accessible e-mail might be.

The third option does not work, either, because the reader will tie both "retaining" and "making" to "e-mails accessible." "Retaining . . . e-mails accessible" makes no sense. The best option is B.

Misusing Sets and Subsets

Don't try to make two facts seem like three

Persuasion requires factual support. You need facts to establish why a contract is ambiguous; why conduct falls short of reasonable care; why an insurance company acted in bad faith; why documents are relevant or may lead to the discovery of relevant evidence; or why a litigant has sufficient contacts with a state to be subject to personal jurisdiction in its courts.

One or two good facts never seem quite enough, particularly when the other side has a strong argument. You may be tempted to lengthen your list of supporting facts by giving equal billing to a lesser included fact taken from a set already stated. Or you may do the reverse: give equal billing to a set of facts that encompasses a single fact already stated—again, to pad your list.

The motivation to create the appearance of more support than you have is compelling. You are afraid that your factual presentation, if short, will look weak, and you will lose. So you try to conjure additional facts from the ones you have—a kind of rhetorical magic act.

Readers know when you've got the goods and when you haven't.

In the following example, counsel for a plaintiff injured in a highway accident allegedly caused by a defective highway repair is trying to persuade the court that the highway authority's motion to dismiss on the basis of plan or design immunity should be denied because discovery is incomplete. The authority acknowledged that its motion to dismiss should be treated as a motion for summary judgment because the authority relies on facts outside the pleadings.

Plaintiff's counsel writes as follows:

> *The Authority concedes in its brief that this motion to dismiss for failure to state a claim, should more properly be considered by the Court as a motion for summary judgment, as facts outside the pleadings in this case must be considered. The Authority's motion, therefore, is premature in that discovery of numerous facts concerning the Authority's decision-making process, the level of involvement of the decision-making personnel who have submitted certifications, and numerous facts regarding this highway repair project are far from completion.*

The paragraph seeks to create the impression that many fact issues have to be explored before the case will be ready for a dispositive motion. Plaintiff proffers three sets of facts allegedly requiring discovery: (i) numerous facts concerning the Authority's decision-making process; (ii) the level of involvement of the decision-making personnel who have submitted certifications; and (iii) numerous facts regarding this highway repair project.

The first set overlaps the second. Facts concerning the authority's decision-making process include the level of involvement of decision-making personnel. Because the second set is merely a subset of the first, exemplifying rather than adding to the first set, the writer appears to be trying to make one set look like two. A better formulation would be to subordinate the second set to the first:

> *The Authority's motion is premature because numerous facts concerning the Authority's decision-making process have yet to be discovered, including the level of involvement of the decision-making personnel who have submitted certifications.*

I don't suggest that "numerous facts" is persuasive, but at least the sentence no longer presents one set of facts as two. With more thought, the writer might have realized that "numerous facts concerning the Authority's decision-making process" includes other subsets, such as the need to balance cost and durability in designing a highway repair. When you sense a need for more facts, either analyze further what you know about the case or find more facts outside your existing record.

The third category, "numerous facts regarding this highway repair project," encompasses and thus duplicates the first two categories. It is broader than facts regarding decision-making (category [i]), which in turn is broader than facts regarding the involvement of decision-making personnel (category [ii]). Though "numerous facts" covers much ground, it is shapeless and therefore powerless. You can't persuade a court with "numerous facts."

The artifice of conjuring facts from other facts is alluring not only because of the support that facts provide but also because of the power of three (facts, not witches). Three is a strong sequence. It has good rhythm and is neither too long nor too short.

Because it has a beginning, a middle and an end, you can shape a series of three to hit hard early and then ease off, to start slowly and build, or to hit hard first and last. The three-element series is such a formidable tool that you may fake your sets just so you can have three of them rather than two.

Faking anything insults the reader's intelligence by suggesting the reader isn't alert enough to notice that one plus one doesn't make three. It injures your credibility, your "ethos," because you are advertising "three-for-a-dollar" but delivering only two. The dollar is the reader's time and energy. For the effort expended in reading your product, the reader expects fair return.

Puzzler

How would you tighten and sharpen the following sentence?

> *The Authority concedes in its brief that this motion to dismiss for failure to state a claim, should more properly be considered by the Court as a motion for summary judgment, as facts outside the pleadings in this case must be considered.*

Delete "in its brief," "by the Court" and "in this case" as implicit, and delete "more properly" as useless. Delete "for failure to state a claim" because the court knows the basis for the motion.

Remove the comma after claim because it separates subject (motion) from verb (should be considered), and remove the comma after judgment because it precedes a dependent clause. Change "as" to "because." Use "treated as" because it is more precise than "considered as."

The concluding dependent clause ("as [because] facts outside the pleadings must be considered") offers options. You could leave it as is—accurate but bland—or you could ask yourself (a) "What are my purposes in writing this sentence?" and then (b) "What can I draw from the facts of my case that will serve these purposes?" After you choose an approach and write the sentence, ask yourself the same questions again.

Here is one possible solution, in which "relies on," "affidavits," "detail" and "decision-making process" all suggest factual substance, and thus possible grounds for factual dispute, with a view to precluding summary judgment:

The revised version:

The Authority concedes that this motion to dismiss should be treated as a motion for summary judgment because the Authority relies on affidavits that detail the Authority's decision-making process.

Be Wary of the "In Order to" or "To" Construction

It is a common source of non sequiturs

The need to recite what the law requires often leads to the "In order to" or "To" construction, as in, "In order to begin an action in Superior Court, one must file a complaint with the County Clerk." When such a sentence is written correctly, it sets forth the task ("In order to [accomplish something . . .]") and then says what the person must do to accomplish the task. (Generally, you can delete "in order" as unnecessary, leaving just "to.")

Sometimes, the "In order to" or "To" construction produces a *non sequitur* (grammatically, a "dangling modifier"), as in the following from an appellate brief:

> *In order to persuade a court to overturn the decision of an administrative agency, a heavy burden is placed on the appellant.*

The opening of the sentence ("In order to persuade") signals that the rest of the sentence will explain what an appellant has to do to persuade a court to overturn the decision of an administrative agency. The reader expects the appellant to be the actor in the continuing story.

But the actor in the second part of the sentence is not the appellant; it is the appellant's burden. This appearance of an unexpected subject will frustrate the intended audience—appellate judges and law clerks. Even though these readers will ultimately comprehend the sentence because they know that the discretion of an administrative agency must be respected on appeal, they will initially balk at the grammar.

Why would someone write such a sentence?

The writer's internal monologue probably went something like this: "The goal is to overturn the decision of an administrative agency, so I'll begin with that to establish the context. Then I'll acknowledge the heavy burden of persuading a court to overturn such a decision and thus cover both ideas in one sentence—the need to overturn agency decisions and the heavy burden that a challenger bears."

Writers almost always have a reason for doing what does not work. They are, generally speaking, more insular than ignorant. Though they have a plan, it may not include the reader. Here, the writer addressed both elements of his point but overlooked the reader's likely reaction.

The sentence can be recast as follows:

> *To persuade a court to overturn the decision of an administrative agency, an appellant must overcome a presumption of validity.*

Now the second part of the sentence fulfills the reader's expectation. The appellant is the actor ("To persuade a court . . . an appellant must overcome").

The idea can also be conveyed without the "In order to" or "To" construction:

An appellant challenging the decision of an administrative agency bears a heavy burden.

The decisions of an administrative agency will not be overturned unless arbitrary and capricious.

The decisions of an administrative agency enjoy a presumption of validity.

In most instances, good alternatives are available. You just need to explore them.

A Second Example

The following use of the "In order to" construction appeared in a brief invoking the principle that statutes should not be interpreted in derogation of (as overriding) the common law:

In order to interpret the statute as defendant wishes, the statute must override the common law.

Because the sentence opens with a statement that someone will have to do something to interpret the statute ("In order to interpret the statute"), the reader expects to be told what the person interpreting the statute must do. Instead, the reader is told what the statute must do—it must override the common law.

Presumably, the reader will deduce the meaning, but only after adjusting for the deviation from normal grammar. Because the deviation consumes time and energy unnecessarily, it erodes the reader's patience and weakens the writer-reader relationship.

Dropping "In order to" or "To" is the best fix:

Defendant would have the statute override the common law.

Slightly more explicit is the following:

Defendant would interpret the statute to override the common law.

Keeping the "To" construction could result in this:

To interpret the statute as defendant wishes, one must override the common law.

This solution is imprecise because lawyers don't override the common law; statutes do. A more accurate but longer formulation might be:

To interpret the statute as defendant wishes, one must view it as overriding the common law.

A Third Example

The following is from a gaming commission regulation:

In order to cover the cost of the licensing investigation, each application must be accompanied by a nonrefundable fee of $3,000 per key employee.

The application isn't seeking to cover the cost of the licensing investigation; the commission is. The sentence can be improved as follows, among other ways:

Version A:

As a contribution toward the cost of the licensing investigation, a nonrefundable fee of $3,000 per key employee must accompany each application.

Version B:

To cover the cost of the licensing investigation, the commission requires that a nonrefundable fee of $3,000 per key employee accompany each application.

In each version, the two parts of the sentence match. In Version A, the fee in the second part of the sentence is the contribution in the first, and in Version B, the commission requires the fee to cover the cost.

Beginning sentences with "In order to" or "To" is tempting when describing legal requirements, but it may lead, as above, to *non sequiturs*. If you are about to use this construction, check for continuity and consider alternatives.

Puzzler

How would you combine the following sentences?

Answers to interrogatories and documents have been exchanged by the parties. Depositions of all employees have been taken.

Use the active voice and parallel verbs ("exchanged" and "deposed") and make "interrogatory" an adjective. "Have" is optional.

The revised version:

The parties have exchanged documents and interrogatory answers and have deposed all employees.

Alternate version:

The parties have exchanged documents and interrogatory answers and deposed all employees.

Without "have":

The parties exchanged documents and interrogatory answers and deposed all employees.

"Rather" Is an Unnecessary, Annoying Signal

In most instances, the change in direction is obvious

Many writers who use "however" also use "rather," an equally irritating and unnecessary announcement that the writer is about to change direction, as in the following:

> *The agreement did not provide that Smith had to apply for his commissions. Rather, it stated that he was to be paid automatically based on the computer printout.*

Because the first sentence says the agreement did not provide that Smith had to apply for his commissions, the affirmative phrase "it stated" at the beginning of the second sentence adequately signals that the reader is about to be told what the agreement did provide. "Rather" merely duplicates the change of direction signaled by "it stated."

The passage should read as follows:

> *The agreement did not provide that Smith had to apply for his commissions. It stated that he was to be paid automatically based on the computer printout.*

Like "however," "rather" tries too hard. It announces a change of direction that even inattentive readers will see without the extra help.

In a sense, using "rather" disrespects the reader because it suggests the reader isn't alert enough or smart enough to spot the change in direction without a boost. It also undermines the writer's command and credibility because it suggests that the thought in the second sentence isn't strong enough or clear enough to signal the change of direction without a direction-changing word.

Not only is "rather" unnecessary—it isn't even precise. It says only that something different is coming. Having no content other than negation, it invites the reader to speculate, albeit for a moment, on the change of direction that "rather" signals. For that moment, the writer loses control.

More Examples

The following "rather" appeared in a brief seeking summary judgment against a discrimination claim brought by cabaret waitresses who said they were never assigned to the higher-tipping tables near the stage:

> *Plaintiffs do not allege and cannot establish any meaningful difference in job functions based on the area of the cabaret to which they were assigned. Rather, plaintiffs' claim is premised only on the unsubstantiated speculation that waitresses assigned to tables near the stage earn more in tips.*

By the end of the first sentence, the reader has been told that plaintiffs do not allege and cannot establish a meaningful difference in job functions between areas of the cabaret. The reader then expects to be told what plaintiffs do allege. The phrase "plaintiffs' claim is premised" at the beginning of the second sentence adequately signals that the writer is about to reveal what plaintiffs allege.

"Rather" adds nothing. The reversal of direction is handled by the phrase "plaintiffs' claim is premised," and the weakness in plaintiffs' allegations is signaled by the word "only" and the phrase "unsubstantiated speculation."

The passage should read as follows:

> *Plaintiffs do not allege and cannot establish any meaningful difference in job functions based on the area of the cabaret to which they were assigned. Plaintiffs' claim is premised only on the unsubstantiated speculation that waitresses assigned to tables near the stage earn more in tips.*

Consider the following comment on Rule 11 of the Federal Rules of Civil Procedure, which creates a mechanism for punishing counsel who bring baseless claims:

> *This does not imply that Rule 11 is intended to abrogate an attorney's pursuit of novel legal or factual theories. Rather, it merely reflects how the rule attempts to deter litigation while encouraging creativity within the law.*

The affirmative phrase "it . . . reflects," contrasted with the negative phrase "does not imply," is enough to signal the change in direction. "Merely" intensifies the change; "rather" is excess.

In the following passage, the writer not only uses an unnecessary "rather" but shows a taste for what I call the "no-no statement":

> *Jones is not seeking to elevate his position in the company over that of Smith. He is doing no such thing. Rather, he seeks recognition that his position as President is entitled to pay equal to that of Smith as CEO.*

I am not sure why writers insert gratuitous negations like, "He is doing no such thing." Perhaps they fear that unless they intensify the negation in "Jones is not seeking," the reader may think the writer doesn't really believe that "Jones is not seeking." Maybe writers reason that anyone can say "not," but six more words of negation ("He is doing no such thing") will persuade the reader that the writer is sincere.

In any case, "rather" is unnecessary. The statement in the first sentence that Jones does not seek to elevate his position in the company leads the reader to expect that the second sentence will reveal what Jones does seek. When the second sentence predictably makes the affirmative statement that Jones "seeks recognition," the contrast is adequately drawn. "Rather" is not missed in the re-write:

> *Jones is not seeking to elevate his position in the company over that of Smith. He seeks recognition that his position as President is entitled to pay equal to that of Smith as CEO.*

Puzzler

How would you tighten and sharpen the following sentence?

A fee agreement is always advisable, as it will usually clear up misunderstandings that may arise.

"As" is substandard in a causative role. Use because. Delete the comma because subordinate clauses generally are not preceded by commas. Here, the comma would slow the pace, making the reader wait to learn why fee agreements are advisable.

The concluding phrase "that may arise" may seem implicit and therefore expendable, but it differentiates later misunderstandings from pre-agreement misunderstandings. I would retain the concept but shorten "that may arise" to "later." If you use "later," then use "resolve" rather than "clear up" to avoid the ambiguous combination "clear up later" (like weather) in the phrase "clear up later misunderstandings."

If you wish to include misunderstandings that precede the fee agreement as well as those that follow it, then drop "later." In either case, drop "usually." Though the appearance of "always advisable " and "usually resolve" in the same sentence is not illogical, the apparent inconsistency may bring the reader up short.

The revised version:

Fee agreements are always advisable because they resolve later misunderstandings.

Alternate version:

Fee agreements are always advisable because they clear up [resolve] misunderstandings.

Carefully Craft Your Sets and Subsets

Make sure the items in a list are of the same kind and size

A topic worth revisiting is sets and subsets—categories, big and small; groups; lists. Items in a list should generally be coordinate to, not more or less inclusive than, other items in the list.

Take a statement of reasons why similar cases before the same court should be consolidated:

> *Consolidation is appropriate because it will encourage the orderly and expeditious adjudication of this controversy, conserve judicial resources, save witnesses' time and expense and avoid duplicative trials.*

Sounds pretty good, doesn't it? It's strong on emphasis because it uses active verbs and invokes efficiency five times (orderly, expeditious, conserve, save and avoid duplicative). It also uses parallel construction well—four consecutive verbs of the same form: encourage, conserve, save and avoid.

Parallel construction lulls readers because the good grammar disturbs no patterns and inspires confidence. Many writers have trouble creating a fluid structure for such a long sequence.

Yet the list is not precise because the writer mixes sets and subsets, causing overlap and thus duplication. This compromises the communication, leaving the reader to puzzle it out or miss part of the message.

The first item in the sequence, the "orderly and expeditious adjudication of this controversy," is essentially the purpose of consolidation. It is a very broad category. The next item, "conserve judicial resources," is a subset. It is one effect of an orderly and expeditious result.

Already, the list has a problem. It begins with a set and continues with a subset without alerting the reader to the switch, as by saying "for example." This suggests that the list is padded, as if the writer were claiming two categories while providing only one.

The next item in the sequence—saving witnesses' time and expense—is also a subset. Like the subset of saving judicial resources, it is another effect of an orderly and expeditious adjudication.

The fourth and last element in the sequence, "avoid duplicative trials," is a subset of the second and third items in the list, "conserve judicial resources" and "save witnesses' time." Avoiding duplicative trials is one way to conserve judicial resources and save witnesses' time. Thus, the fourth item is a subset of the preceding two subsets. The list does not include saving parties' time and expense, which is an omission.

To shape up the list, we could use the broadest category as a controlling set (orderly and expeditious adjudication) and limit the list to subsets—resource-saving items. We already have two such items: "conserve judicial resources" and "save witnesses' time and expense." We could replace "duplicative trials" with "saving time and expense for the litigants," correcting the omission of the parties' time and expense. We would then write the one sentence as two:

> *Consolidation is appropriate because it will encourage the orderly and expeditious adjudication of this controversy. It will conserve judicial resources, save time and expense for witnesses, and save time and expense for the parties.*

Now the sets and subsets work together. The set is presented first, and the subsets follow. The reader knows which is the set and which are the subsets, and the writer does not appear to be faking sets. Because "time and expense" is duplicated, we can trim further:

> *Consolidation is appropriate because it will encourage the orderly and expeditious adjudication of this controversy: It will conserve judicial resources and will save time and expense for the witnesses and the parties.*

This is pretty good, but we sacrificed something to tighten the list. We gave up an example of how to save time and expense—avoid duplicative trials. Our current version of the list speaks of conserving resources but does not say how we'll do it. If we resurrect our reference to avoiding duplicative trials and add a reference to discovery, thus covering pretrial activities as well as trial, we can improve the presentation.

We can group witnesses and parties as "private" interests, create a set called "private and judicial resources," and say that resources for both elements of this set—private and judicial —will be conserved by eliminating duplicative discovery and trial. The reformulation would read as follows:

> *Consolidation is appropriate because it will encourage the orderly and expeditious adjudication of this controversy: It will conserve both private and judicial resources, eliminating duplicative discovery and trials.*

The above reformulation of the second sentence has better pace and in some respects stronger impact. It not only states the conclusion (save resources), but it provides examples (eliminate duplicative discovery and trials). It adds balance in that the elements "private and judicial" parallel the elements of discovery (private) and trial (judicial).

One final concern. We lost our reference to the convenience of witnesses. A court may be sympathetic to third-party witnesses drawn into a fight not of their making. By moving the elimination of duplicative discovery and trials to the beginning of the second sentence, we have a solution:

> *Consolidation is appropriate because it will encourage the orderly and expeditious adjudication of this controversy. Eliminating duplicative discovery and trials will conserve both private and judicial resources, reducing the burden not only on the parties and the court but on third-party witnesses as well.*

Reduced burden is a function of (a consequence of) resources being conserved. By adding the concept of burden to the concept of conservation, we can add back the witnesses.

Much work goes into reformulating sets and subsets to find the optimum way to articulate what is essentially the same group of related facts. We consider the scope of the sets and subsets, the grammatical flow—including, among other things, parallel construction—the sound, including assonance (successive vowels) and alliteration (successive consonants), and the placement of words for impact.

In a consolidation motion, the court probably knows the arguments by heart, so the main virtue of coordinating sets and subsets is defensive—to avoid sending the signal that you fake your sets, which suggests you may fake other things, or that you just don't think things through. You get some offensive credit as well because the reader will instinctively respect a rigorous treatment of sets and subsets.

Close editing like this is a fascinating and sometimes frustrating puzzle. Many writers consider the puzzle solved when they have rattled off several items that seem to relate reasonably well. Some writers don't notice alternatives; others don't care. Readers care, though they sometimes don't realize it.

Few attorneys who review draft briefs challenge a list. At most, a writer might be told, "I think the point could have been a little tighter." Then the dedicated writer will go back to the drawing board to see what could have been tighter. Often, it is the list.

Puzzler

Which is better, Version A or Version B?

Version A:

He utilized all the resources at his command.

Version B:

He used all the resources at his command.

This one is a "gimme." You know the answer. But how often are you tempted to use the longer of those two words in an attempt to make your presentation sound more impressive?

OK. Maybe you cured yourself of "utilize," but have you cured yourself of "commence?" Experienced readers know what you are up to, so don't posture. Use "use" and use "begin."

Be Cautious Using "And" as a Connector

Look for relationships beyond the additive

"And" is one of the most useful words in the English language. It connects just about anything. If water is the universal solvent, "and" is the universal connector.

But the virtue of "and" is also its vice. The connective power of "and" is seductive to legal writers because they have so many facts and arguments to shape, sort and join, and it is insidious because writers often stop looking for relationships between thoughts when they have made a connection with "and."

The writer's job is to show how facts interact, not merely to join them. Connecting thoughts with "and" can be like laying out the materials to build something but never building it.

Consider the following classic misuse of "and":

Smith v. Jones concerned a petition for a writ of habeas corpus and whether the petitioner failed to exhaust his remedies to challenge his conviction under state law.

This sentence says that *Smith v. Jones* addressed two subjects: a petition for writ of *habeas corpus* and exhaustion of remedies under state law, but the sentence does not show the relationship between the two subjects. (Also, "petition" and the "whether" clause violate the rules of parallel construction, but we'll ignore that for this discussion.)

If you do *habeas corpus* work—challenging convictions on federal constitutional grounds—you will understand the connection. A defendant incarcerated in a state facility has to exhaust all remedies under state law before challenging his conviction by means of a *habeas corpus* petition in federal court.

If you don't do *habeas* work, you may be confused. You won't know what the exhaustion of remedies under state law has to do with a *habeas* petition. The sample sentence connects the concepts only with "and," leaving the relationship unclear to everyone except readers who already know of the relationship or can deduce it.

The issue in *Smith v. Jones* was whether a petition for a writ of *habeas corpus* brought in federal court by a person convicted under state law should be denied because the petitioner failed to exhaust all possible state law remedies first. The relationship between the two parts of the sentence is causative. Failure to exhaust remedies under state law can result in the petition for a writ of *habeas corpus* being denied.

The relationship can be expressed as follows:

Smith v. Jones concerns whether a petition for a writ of habeas corpus should be denied because the petitioner failed to exhaust all possible state law remedies for challenging his conviction.

The writer who wrote that *Smith v. Jones* concerns a petition for a writ of *habeas corpus* "and" whether the petitioner exhausted remedies under state law was thinking in steps and writing as each step was completed rather than thinking through all steps and then writing.

The writer focused first on the broad subject of *habeas corpus*, the "set," and then on the subset of exhausting state law remedies. This is a natural progression—thinkers tend to focus from the broad to the narrow—but it is not the best template for writing. The writer did not show the causative relationship between failure to exhaust state law remedies and denial of a petition for a writ of *habeas corpus*.

Other examples of misusing "and" by means of the "and whether" construction include:

> *The case involved a requirements contract and whether the defendant failed to fulfill its obligations thereunder.*

> *The court was concerned about the possibility of forfeiture and whether plaintiff had missed the deadline for exercising his option.*

A Related Misuse of "And"

Understanding the relationship between thoughts is likely to require extra effort where the writer fails to subordinate one thought to the other. In the following example, the writer defaulted to "and" rather than figure out how to show the relationship between two ideas:

> *Parcel A is closer to the highway, and Parcel B benefits from an access agreement over Parcel A.*

Neither of the foregoing thoughts is subordinated to the other. The reader is told that Parcel A is closer to the highway, but initially, the reader is not told why that matters. Parcel A's proximity to the highway is just a floating fact. That Parcel B benefits from an easement over Parcel A (an access agreement) should be featured as follows:

> *Parcel B benefits from an access agreement over Parcel A, which is closer to the highway.*

The idea is easier to understand as revised because the reader is first given the core fact (that Parcel B benefits from an access agreement) and then the explanation (an access agreement is necessary because Parcel A is closer to the highway). Also, you have eliminated one mention of "Parcel A," which saves words.

An associate reports that one of her high school English teachers ran an exercise in which the class had to write a paper without using "and" except to connect two nouns or two verbs, as in "toast and jam" or "ran and jumped." The point was to force the students to show the relationship between thoughts rather than just tack them together with "and," leaving the reader to deduce the relationship.

That was an excellent assignment—subtle but powerful. Writers use "and" more than they realize. It allows them to leave the driving to someone else.

Puzzler

How would you fix the following sentence?

The land, through which the stream runs, was at all times relevant, owned by the defendant.

The sentence suffers sorely from interruptive thoughts and interruptive punctuation. Once a reader sees a subject, the reader expects to find out quickly what the subject did or had done to it. In other words, the reader wants to see a verb. Here, we don't find out what the land is doing or having done to it (it was owned by the defendant) until nearly the end of the sentence.

Writers create these predicaments by recording words as they think of them and then failing to revise. The word "land" evidently came to this writer's mind first because the sentence is about land ownership. Then the writer had a thought about the land (*e.g.*, a stream runs through it) and dutifully recorded the thought as it emerged.

An easy fix is to move the temporal reference—"at all times relevant"—to the beginning. Say "relevant times" rather than "times relevant" because adjectives tend to precede the nouns they modify (describe).

Make the sentence active rather than passive by converting the defendant from the object of a preposition to the subject ("defendant owned"). You could conclude with "through which the stream runs," but one word conveying that concept would be tighter and more graphic.

The revised version:

At all relevant times, defendant owned the land crossed [traversed] by the stream.

5

Perspective

Helping the Reader See It Your Way

Perspective

Helping the Reader See It Your Way

Eventually, we realize that characterizing facts is not over-advocating. We learn that we can call a relationship "acerbic" or accuse a party of being more interested in building market share than in honoring its agreements. Like politicians and advertisers, we can spin. If we look to create a sense of permissiveness, we say, "Plaintiff can do this if," whereas if we look to create a sense of restriction, we say, "Plaintiff cannot do this unless."

To mold the reader's perspective, we color the material, as by introducing a quotation to guide the reader's experience of it. Readers expect us to take control, and they welcome it. Deep down, readers want to be led.

Is the Glass Half Empty or Half Full?

Permissive and restrictive words give different slants to the same rule

One of the classic techniques of persuasive writing is to portray the glass as half full, if full is good for you, or as half empty, if empty is good for you.

For example, if an advocate were looking to characterize a stock exchange rule regarding audit committee membership as permissive, the advocate might write:

> *Subject to a cooling-off period, the rules of the exchange* ***permit*** *former officers to serve on the audit committee of the board of directors* ***as long as*** *the board determines that such person will exercise independent judgment and will materially assist the committee's function.*

If the advocate were looking to characterize the same rule as restrictive, the advocate might write:

> *The rules of the exchange* ***exclude*** *former officers from serving on the audit committee of the board of directors, even after a cooling-off period,* ***unless*** *the board determines that such person will exercise independent judgment and will materially assist the committee's function.*

In the first version, the words "permit" and "as long as" denote permissiveness. In the second version, the words "exclude" and "unless" denote restriction.

Either characterization of the rule—as permissive (half full) or restrictive (half empty)—is correct. They are just "spun" differently.

Another element of spin in the foregoing examples is the placement of the "cooling-off period." The permissive version acknowledges the cooling-off period and quickly leaves it behind, minimizing its restrictive impact.

In contrast, the restrictive version gives the cooling-off period a central position and a major role, suggesting that the test for audit committee membership is so tough that "even after" the cleansing effect of a cooling-off period, former officers will not easily be approved.

A Second Example

Suppose you wish to discover the opinion of a nontestifying expert whom the adversary retained in anticipation of litigation. You would argue as follows:

> *The Rules of Court* ***allow*** *the discovery of the opinion of a nontestifying expert whom the party retained in anticipation of litigation* ***upon a showing*** *of "exceptional circumstances."*

Your right to this discovery is qualified by the need to show exceptional circumstances, but you state the proposition affirmatively ("The Rules of Court *allow* the discovery") because you seek access to the information.

If you oppose discovery, you state it differently:

> *The Rules of Court* **do not allow** *the discovery of the opinion of a nontestifying expert whom the party retained in anticipation of litigation* **without a showing** *of "exceptional circumstances."*

The same proposition has now been stated in the negative ("The Rules of Court *do not allow* the discovery").

Actually, the Rules do allow discovery under exceptional circumstances, but you are not overstating your case to say the rules do not allow discovery "without a showing." To you, the glass is half empty—no discovery should be permitted *unless*. To your adversary, the glass is half full—discovery is allowed if the right circumstances (exceptional) can be shown.

Both statements are true. Neither of you is pushing the envelope.

Don't Say Won't

The antithesis of the "glass-half-full" technique is the self-flagellatory tactic of stating a proposition adversely to one's own case in an attempt to build credibility.

For example, a lawyer seeking a preliminary injunction began his brief as follows: "Courts will not issue a preliminary injunction where all material facts are controverted." Counsel then contended that all material facts weren't controverted, but the damage had been done. The harmful proposition was imprinted on the reader's mind.

Never say that courts won't grant the relief you seek, even if you immediately qualify the statement. Say that courts *will* grant the relief with a proper showing.

The protocol of presenting one's case affirmatively is so deeply embedded in our practice that to do otherwise marks you as a novice, or worse, as injudiciously candid. It may cause a reader to question your judgment—and your point.

Puzzler

How would you tighten and sharpen the following sentence?

> *The combination of steady, well-conceived internal growth and the periodic acquisition of other firms, which fulfilled various needs of the maturing company, created the platform for XYZ Company's growth to its present position as one of the largest investment banking firms in the United States.*

"The combination of" is implicit and therefore unnecessary, as is the phrase "of other firms." "Various" is almost always unnecessary. Here, it drops out anyway because the clause in which it appears—"which fulfilled various needs of the maturing company"—is implicit and can be deleted.

Because internal growth and acquisition weren't really the "platform" for growth—they *were* the growth—you can substitute "became" for the platform metaphor.

Though it is a form of the dreaded "to be" verb, "became" seems better than "evolved into" or "developed into," both of which connote change in nature more than change in size, or "emerged as," which connotes revelation as well as evolution (butterflies emerge). "Became" has no connotational conflicts.

The phrase "present position" is understood and therefore unnecessary.

The revised version begins with a phrase that grows, like the company, and carries the reader to the core thought:

> *Through steady, well-conceived internal growth and periodic acquisition, XYZ Company became one of the largest investment banking firms in the United States.*

Give a Quotation a Good Introduction

A short summary guides the reader and enlists the power of repetition

Just as a moderator introduces a keynote speaker to the crowd, you should introduce quotations to the reader. It is a golden opportunity to engage the reader and drive your point home through repetition.

The quotation below appeared in the appellate brief of a building owner who failed to make a man-lift available to an independent roofer. The roofer was injured when he used an ordinary ladder in high winds and fell. Which introduction to the quotation would you use?

Version One:

A landowner has no duty to protect an employee of an independent contractor from known hazards incidental to the contract work. ***As the court ruled in Smith v. Jones:***

> *The landowner may assume that the worker, or his superiors, are possessed of sufficient skill to recognize the degree of danger involved and to adjust their methods of work accordingly.*

Version Two:

A landowner has no duty to protect an employee of an independent contractor from known hazards incidental to the contract work. ***To the contrary, a landowner is entitled to rely on the employee's ability to protect himself:***

> *[Same quotation; then cite Smith v. Jones.]*

The first version introduces the quotation with the noncommittal "As the court ruled," leaving the reader to interpret the quotation. The second version alerts the reader to the gist of the quotation, which is an embellishment upon, not merely a restatement of, the principle that a landowner has no duty to protect employees of independent contractors from known hazards.

Writers typically use Version One, but Version Two is better. It calls attention to the ability of a contractor's employee to protect himself and the right of the landowner to rely thereon, and it shortens the languid phrase "adjust their methods of work accordingly" to the sharper "protect himself." It is a legitimate rewording for effect.

Previewing quotations serves several rhetorical purposes. It induces the reader to read the quotation—which might otherwise be skipped—by providing a key to its meaning. This proffer not only helps the reader interpret the quotation, which makes the reader's job easier, but it challenges the reader to determine whether the writer's summary is correct.

If the précis is accurate, the reader will deem the writer honest and reliable. Thus, by substantively introducing the quotation, the writer increases the odds of its being read and earns a bonus in the bargain.

A substantive introduction can guide the reader through a quotation in several ways: (i) by directing attention to a particular passage; (ii) by clarifying a difficult thought; (iii) by characterizing something that could but shouldn't be read two ways, making sure the reader reads it the right way; and (iv) if you are aggressive, by characterizing a passage that could legitimately be read either of two ways. All this helps you retain control of the material.

Finally, the introduction drives the point home by repetition. First you say what the quotation will say; then the quotation says it again. If the thought is important enough to illustrate with a quotation, it is important enough to repeat and reinforce.

Not only do substantive introductions to quotations serve a rhetorical purpose, but they serve a creative purpose as well. Having to write such an introduction forces the writer to examine whether the quotation is truly helpful. If the writer cannot summarize the passage in a few words consistent with the writer's position, then the quotation may be off point. Thus, the substantive introduction serves as a self-monitoring device.

A writer may even quote from a quotation to introduce it, as in the following example from a brief on behalf of a public entity appealing an award for injuries from a fall allegedly caused by bad lighting. The public entity claimed that the absence of expert testimony on the subject of adequate lighting was reversible error. It introduced a supportive quotation as follows:

> *In Polyard v. Terry, the Appellate Division observed that an expert's opinion is "undoubtedly admissible, and usually useful" when a condition of public property is not obviously dangerous:*
>
> > *The opinion of an expert is undoubtedly admissible, and usually useful, when, as here, a road-surface characteristic is not so pronounced that its effect upon the control of an automobile is obvious.*

Previewing the phrase "undoubtedly admissible, and usually useful" is a bit repetitious because the quotation is short, but the value of the dictum justifies the duplication.

Writers give several reasons for their reluctance to introduce quotations with more than "As the court said." They feel they can't say it better than the court and might say it wrong; they don't want to bore the reader with repetition, and they don't want to lose credibility by over-advocating. Such concerns are understandable but largely misguided.

You don't have to say it better than the court, merely correctly. You may say it wrong, but if you don't know the point of the quotation well enough to summarize it accurately, then you shouldn't be using the quotation anyway.

As for boredom, repetition in this business is generally a good thing. If you have something useful to say, don't be modest about saying it twice. You would rather the reader think, "Enough already. I get your point," than that the reader ask, "What is your point?"

The fear of over-advocacy is healthy but usually excessive, especially in novice writers. To counter it, think of the service you provide to the reader with a substantive introduction to a quotation. In return for that, the reader will put up with a little advocacy.

Puzzler

How would you tighten and sharpen the following sentence?

After a trial which was heard over a period of seven months, the trial court found a breach of the insurance contract.

The phrases "which was heard" and "a period of" are unnecessary. So is the adjective "trial" in front of "court" because only a trial court would hear a trial. True, the case was "heard," and seven months is a "period," but both those concepts are implicit. The trial does not become any more important because it was heard, and seven months does not become any more impressive because it was a period. Assume the reader knows it was a bench trial. If not, you could say "seven-month bench trial."

The revised version:

After a seven-month trial, the court found a breach of the insurance contract.

Don't Be Afraid to Characterize the Facts

The perspective you supply will assist and persuade the reader

Never forget that you write for a reader who is probably not as familiar with the facts as you are. This unfamiliarity puts the reader at a disadvantage, especially if the case is complex. You can help the reader understand the facts and persuade the reader to see them as you see them by sorting and summarizing.

Suppose that events leading to the execution of a lengthy contract include dozens of letters and e-mails, frequent meetings and multiple drafts. You wonder how to describe the negotiations without bogging down in detail.

One way to handle the glut of information is to warn the reader that it is coming. For example, begin a fact section on the meetings at which the contract was negotiated by saying, "The discussions on April 15 began a hectic series of meetings punctuated by a rapid-fire exchange of drafts."

Now the reader will be prepared to sort out a potentially confusing array of meetings and draft contracts and will have a higher tolerance for detail. By making the reader's job easier, you earn a credit you can eventually cash in.

Not only do you earn the reader's gratitude, but you begin to persuade. By taking control of the facts—sorting and summarizing them—you exude confidence in your material and in turn boost the reader's confidence in you.

Readers know instinctively that writers don't sort and summarize the facts unless they know them well, or purport to. (If it is only "purport," the reader will catch on soon enough.) The reader will trust the writer's characterizations until they are shown to be wrong.

On the strength of this trust and confidence, your characterizations will help persuade the reader to see the facts as you see them. Rather than merely report the facts, you will shape them as you wish the reader to perceive them.

In this instance, you want the reader to view the negotiation of the contract as frenzied, perhaps to lay the groundwork for explaining why memories differ or why a concept not treated explicitly in the contract should nevertheless be implied.

Providing an overview of the negotiations also reduces the need for monotonous transitions such as "another conversation" or "the next draft." The overview provides an implicit connector and increases the usefulness of simple temporal transitions like "On April 23."

Is Advocacy Immoral?

A reluctance to characterize the facts may be rooted, ironically, in too great an adherence to the honorable principle that facts should speak for themselves. Novice writers sense that advocacy is, to a degree, untrustworthy because the writer seeks to direct the reader toward selected facts and away from others. Writers may even deem this aspect of advocacy to be borderline immoral.

Advocacy isn't for the faint of heart or purpose, but it isn't immoral. The brief-writer's job is not to lay out the whole truth and nothing but the truth. It is, among other things, to direct the reader toward good facts and good law—from the writer's perspective—and away from bad facts and bad law.

This goal is attainable because humans are not computers. They have limited attention spans, limited memories and limited powers of deduction, and they are moved by factors other than logic. They can be guided. (As I once heard Yogi Berra say about a hitter, "He could be pitched to.")

Conscious of this seemingly sneaky element of advocacy, novice writers may eschew characterizing the facts and look to establish credibility by remaining studiously neutral, which is a mistake.

Being neutral is not our job. We are hired guns, and as such, we are expected to shoot.

It is all right to characterize the facts as long as you do it accurately and defensibly. Not only will you not be punished, but if you do it well, you will be rewarded. Readers like to take sides (how long can you watch a sporting event without rooting for one side or the other?), and they appreciate your helping them do so.

Though logic must anchor every brief, it is a tool that serves all masters. Logic is of little help if the reader doesn't accept your premise, which consists, essentially, of the vision of the facts you want the reader to embrace.

Risk and Reward

Some courage is required in characterizing facts because you have to make editorial judgments. In the example above, the judgments are in the phrases "hectic series of meetings," "rapid-fire exchange of drafts" and even the word "punctuated." You may be reluctant to commit to those judgments. You may fear that the reader won't see the events as "hectic" or the exchange of drafts as "rapid-fire," or that the adversary will deny those characterizations in his responding brief and quote your words back at you.

When you characterize the facts, you take a risk. The risk is that the reader won't agree with your characterizations, and you will lose credibility.

But you also create the possibility of a reward. By characterizing the facts, you make the reader's job easier—for which you will be appreciated—and you guide the reader toward the view of the case that favors your side. If your characterizations fall within reasonable bounds, the rewards will outweigh the risk.

Puzzler

How would you tighten and sharpen the following sentence?

In reaching its decision, the Court concluded that the relevant facts were not in dispute.

You almost never need to say "in reaching its decision," "in its opinion," "in their brief" or similar formulations. The concepts are implicit. You can further shorten the above sentence by substituting "found" for "concluded that" and "undisputed" for "were not in dispute."

The revised version:

The Court found the relevant facts undisputed.

Characterize Your Time Intervals to Take Control of the Facts

A credible "spin" assists the reader and clarifies your point

Statements of facts are usually arranged chronologically, and they inevitably provide dates. They should also characterize the intervals between dates, for example, "a month later," "after two years" or "less than 10 hours after the meeting." Describing a time interval as long or short, whichever supports the writer's position, is a way to take control of the facts.

Suppose parties negotiating a contract met on June 27 and August 8 but had no communications in between. If you wish to make this interval seem long, you may describe it as "nearly a month and a half" or "six weeks." If you wish to make the interval seem short, you may describe it as "less than a month and a half."

In either case, characterizing the interval aids the reader, who would otherwise have to gauge the gap. Without help, the reader might think, "Let's see—the period runs from June to August, which covers about two months. But June 27 is later in June than August 8 is in August, so it can't be a full two months. It is something less."

Calculating time intervals across months is, for some readers, like trying to add 77 and 17—it has to be reasoned through.

Don't let the reader sink into an internal dialog and drift away. Decide whether you want the time interval to appear long or short and then decide how much leeway you have to "spin" (characterize) the interval. You cannot, after all, sell a donkey as a horse.

You could characterize the June 27 to August 8 interval in strictly neutral fashion, such as "about a month and a half." This has a downside and an upside. The downside is that you forfeit the opportunity to color the facts favorably to your case. Advocates not only gather facts but shape them.

The upside is that you can gain credibility. Like an umpire in a sporting event, you call it fair and square.

The nature of your audience may weigh in the balance. Some judges resent counsel trying to "put one over on them," and they have a hair trigger for spin. Other judges tolerate a more partisan approach. But even they don't want it overdone.

How do you know how much to spin? The answer, like many answers in the law, is that you need to strike a balance between the need to control the facts and the need to maintain credibility. When you spin, you perform your job as advocate by shaping the facts in your favor. But you lose credibility if the reader thinks you are spinning too much. You almost always lose more by overspinning than by not spinning at all because overspinning is a form of deception. If you are caught in a deception, your credibility takes a body blow.

Never exaggerate. If a time interval is about six weeks, and you want to make it seem long, say "almost six weeks," "more than six weeks" or "almost a month and a half." Don't say "almost two months." You gain nothing by exaggeration, and you lose credibility in chunks.

On the other hand, even neutrality can be overdone. If the reader senses that you should be advocating when you are not, the reader may conclude either (a) that you don't have a strong case and are trying, in lieu thereof, to win points through evenhandedness, or (b) that you are less an advocate than an "academic" in the sense that you present not one side in its best light but both sides with equal vigor.

How To Use Dates

You will inevitably have to choose whether to set forth the date before you characterize the time interval, or vice versa. For example, depending on the context, you might begin a sentence, "On June 6, more than two months later," or you might say, "More than two months later, on June 6."

Consider the following example:

> *Smith left XYZ Corp's employment on March 25 to begin working for ABC Co. On June 6, more than two months later, XYZ Corp. sued Smith and ABC Co., claiming breach of a non-compete agreement and seeking injunctive relief.*

You contend that injunctive relief should be denied because the plaintiff waited almost two months after Smith joined another firm before seeking to enforce the non-compete agreement. In other words, the plaintiff sat on its rights.

Because delay weakens the plaintiff's case, you want to bring the time interval to the reader's attention as soon as possible. You accomplish that by saying, "More than two months later, on June 6," rather than "On June 6, more than two months later," as in the example above. The first words the reader sees after learning that Smith left XYZ Corp. on March 25 should be "More than two months later" because you want to emphasize the tardiness of plaintiff XYZ Corp.'s action.

Writers like to begin sentences with dates (not unlike the tendency to begin paragraphs with case names, such as "In *Smith v. Jones* . . ."). Dates are comfortable and concrete. But beginning a sentence with the date may not serve your rhetorical purpose.

In the above example, you characterize the time interval ("More than two months later") before you provide the date ("June 6") so the reader does not have even a short gap in which the significance of June 6 is unclear. The phrase "more than" emphasizes the significant time that passed without XYZ Corp. doing anything about Smith having switched loyalties. If the matter wasn't important enough to XYZ Corp. to take immediate action, then perhaps injunctive relief is inappropriate.

Puzzler

How would you tighten and sharpen the following sentence?

> *There is nothing in the court's opinion to suggest that it found that defendant owed plaintiff any duty whatsoever.*

Drop "There is" because it is passive and ponderous. Drop "it found" because it is implicit. Drop "any" and "whatsoever" because they are exaggerations.

The alternate version below would be viable if the court made an affirmative ruling that the defendant owed the plaintiff no duty.

The revised version:

Nothing in the court's opinion suggests that defendant owed plaintiff a duty.

Alternate version:

The court ruled that defendant owed plaintiff no duty.

Even Procedural Histories Can Be Persuasive

Take any opportunity to highlight good facts

The principal persuasive sections of a brief are the preliminary statement, the statement of facts, the argument, and sometimes a statement of issues, which must be carefully drawn to suggest, or at least permit, a good result. In contrast, the procedural history—a staple of appellate briefs—is typically colorless even though that relatively clinical section of the brief can be used to support your point.

Suppose you represent an electroplating company seeking insurance coverage for the cost of cleaning up a landfill where residue from the company's plating operations, thought to be harmless at the time, was deposited years ago in compliance with state law. The cleanup took place pursuant to a consent order between the Environmental Protection Agency and several generators of waste, including your client.

The first sentence of the procedural history in your appellate brief reads as follows:

> *On April 28, 2006, ABC Corp. ("ABC") filed an action against defendant XYZ Insurance Company ("XYZ"), seeking indemnification for cleanup costs and related expenses incurred in response to a directive of the Environmental Protection Agency ("EPA") to clean up a landfill where residue from ABC's electroplating operations was deposited.*

Even though this is "just" a procedural history, you can add some facts that may begin to shape the reader's view of the merits of the case. For example, instead of saying that cleanup costs were incurred "in response to" an EPA directive, say "in complying" with an EPA directive, casting your client in a cooperative role—less the bad-guy polluter, less the wearer of the black hat.

You can further suggest that your client was cooperative, not a troublemaker, by saying that the expenses were incurred in compliance with an EPA "consent order," which is a subset of "directive." The word "consent" suggests your client cooperated with the government and was a good corporate citizen.

You can also say the deposits of plating residue were made "in compliance with state law" and that the residue was "deemed nonhazardous at the time," showing that your client was law abiding and not an intentional polluter. If your client were an intentional polluter, not only would it have a hard time establishing insurance coverage under standard policy terms, but it would gain little sympathy with the court.

One chooses facts to season the procedural history much as one chooses facts for the statement of facts—to support an element of your claim or defense and to make your side look good or the other side look bad. Procedural histories should not be argumentative or even overtly persuasive, but you do not cross these boundaries merely by choosing words with favorable denotations and connotations. You can advocate without arguing.

The revised opening sentence for the procedural history in your appellate brief would read as follows, with the changes underlined:

> *On April 28, 2006, ABC Corp. ("ABC") filed an action seeking indemnification for cleanup costs and related expenses incurred in* ***complying with a consent order*** *issued by the Environmental Protection Agency ("EPA"), directing the cleanup of a landfill where residue from ABC'S electroplating operations,* ***deemed nonhazardous at the time,*** *was deposited* ***in compliance with state law.***

You don't expect to win the case with the procedural history, but you can echo the theme of the preliminary statement and keep the reader focused on your good facts until you begin the story in the statement of facts.

A Second Example

Suppose you represent a company whose former executive sought to exercise stock options two days after the last permissible date and then sued the company when it declined to honor the options. Would you begin the procedural history with the filing of the complaint or with the missed deadline?

Technically, the first legal procedure in the case was the filing of the complaint, but the case really began when the plaintiff missed the deadline for exercising the options:

> *The expiration date for plaintiff's corporate stock options was April 6, 2006. Plaintiff attempted to exercise the options on April 8, 2006. When ABC Corp. declined to honor the expired options, plaintiff began this action, filing a complaint in the Superior Court on May 4, 2006.*

Note that the first sentence refers to the "expiration date" of the options rather than the "last date for exercising the options." The denotation is the same—time ran out—but the connotations are different. If something has expired, it no longer functions. It is dead.

In contrast, "last dates" can be extended. People often miss deadlines and are granted more time. Because deadlines can be extended, "expiration date" has a stronger connotation of termination than "last date for exercising."

The preliminary statement undoubtedly told the story of the expired options, but the procedural history can repeat key facts to keep the reader focused and to drive the point home.

I would place the missed deadline at the very beginning of the procedural history rather than a sentence later or even several words later as part of a description of the complaint. This way, you direct attention to the missed deadline, and you begin with something the plaintiff failed to do (missed the deadline) rather than with something the plaintiff did (filed the complaint).

Puzzler

How would you tighten and sharpen the following sentence?

Appellant contends that evidence of prior breaches admitted at trial was irrelevant, unduly prejudicial and served to taint the jury verdict.

This sentence has structural and logical flaws. The structural flaw is the absence of parallel construction. The series begins with two adjectives ("irrelevant" and "prejudicial"), leading the reader to expect a third adjective to conclude the series. Instead, the last item is a verb phrase ("served to taint"), disappointing the reader's expectations.

If the final item in the series can't be converted to the same part of speech as the first two items, then the series should be broken up, reducing the number of parallel items to two, as follows:

Appellant contends that evidence of prior breaches admitted at trial was irrelevant and unduly prejudicial and that it served to taint the jury verdict.

Now the two elements of the sentence—the two "that" clauses—are parallel.

But the sentence is not yet right. It contains a logical flaw. Because the third item in the series ("taint") is a consequence of, not coordinate with, the first two items ("irrelevance" and "prejudice"), the three items do not form a set and should not be connected by "and."

Finally, you can trim "jury" and "admitted at trial" as implicit.

Revised version:

Appellant contends that evidence of prior breaches was irrelevant and unduly prejudicial, tainting the verdict.

Be Upbeat But Not Pollyannaish

In memos that deliver bad news, you should spin, not pander

Suppose that after substantial research and analysis, you cannot find support for a proposed transaction, or you conclude that your position in a lawsuit is not as strong as your assigning attorney would like to think. How do you write it up?

Do you let the chips fall where they may, or do you give your message a rose-colored cast, succumbing to the almost palpable pressure to return with good news?

Associates have suffered reversals doing it both ways.

When an associate delivers discouraging news, the assigning attorney or the client may wonder why the associate could not find better law. After all, the transaction or the lawsuit seemed like a good idea. Suspecting that the associate lacks resourcefulness and willpower, the reader may be sorely tempted to wound, if not kill, the messenger.

On the other hand, when the associate invokes ostensibly helpful dicta despite divergent facts or conjures distinctions without a difference in an effort to defuse harmful law, readers are likely to see through the illusion and to be equally disappointed.

In law firm jargon, the bearer of bad news is not "tenacious" enough, and the cheerleader is "sloppy." Both "lack judgment."

Of the two approaches—telling the harsh truth harshly or taking refuge in wishful thinking—the greater offense by far is wishful thinking, which is exemplified by exaggerating or minimizing precedent to support a position. If you are lucky, your effort to tell people what they want to hear will be woefully transparent, and the only harm will be to your reputation.

If you are less lucky, your optimistic presentation may play upon the predisposition of the client and the assigning attorney to believe the client is right, and you may persuade them to enter a battle that should not be fought. When the adversary or the court later reveals the weakness in your client's position, all eyes will turn to you.

As a memo writer, you must deal with bad law (meaning, essentially, bad facts) before the client makes a bad deal or loses a lawsuit. The trick is to soften the blow rather than shade the truth.

Bedside Manner

An associate recently wrote a thoroughly accurate and well-supported analysis of an issue only to be told by the assigning partner that the memo could not go to the client in that form. The memo said, quite unsympathetically, that the client's case was a dead loser.

As it turned out, the case was a dead loser. The associate was right. But writing as if judging rather than advocating wasn't politic, either within the office, where the assigning attorneys are the "clients," or between the office and the client. It wasn't good bedside manner.

As one in-house counsel told me, "You have to give the client the bad news, but you also have to make him feel as if you totally agree that what happened to him was wrong."

Though you must maintain professional distance in addressing a client's problem, you should present your analysis in a style that reassures the client of your unquenchable desire to obtain the best result possible.

I once told a group of summer associates that because clients don't like to hear bad news, lawyers need to accent the good and temper the bad. The associates were astounded if not scandalized. They spoke of pushing things under the rug.

I tried to explain the difference between law as an intellectual exercise and law as a business. To serve the people who pay us—the clients—we must tell them the truth, but with discretion. We shouldn't deceive clients, but we shouldn't smack them in the face, either.

Just as doctors need bedside manner, lawyers need a sensitive touch. If a doctor is gruff, you may go elsewhere the next time you need care, notwithstanding the accuracy of the doctor's diagnosis and even the efficacy of the treatment.

The same is true for lawyers. If a lawyer doesn't make the client feel that the lawyer is sympathetic to the client's cause and entirely on the client's side (delivering bad news can, regrettably, create the appearance that you are not on the client's side), then the client may not return, notwithstanding the comprehensiveness of the research, the strength of the analysis, and sometimes, notwithstanding even a good result.

Questions of Loyalty

If your presentation lacks partisan zest, or at least a sympathetic tone, the assigning attorney and the client may think your first loyalty is to your perception of the law—in which they have uncertain faith—rather than to the client and, secondarily, to the firm.

Clients want to know that the people to whom they are paying hundreds of dollars an hour are vigorous advocates for their cause. A memo that sends a negative message without a tone of positive concern may lead the client to believe that some other lawyer with more enthusiasm, perhaps at another firm, might offer a more satisfying answer.

Assigning attorneys want to know that the associate is making every effort not only to support the client's position but to justify the assurances (of which the associate may not even be aware) that the assigning attorney gave the client when the matter came in.

Rarely should you write a memo to a client that says, "The law is such and such; the facts are thus; and so you lose." Instead, write a memo that says, "These offensive things were done to you, and you wish to bring a claim against the perpetrators. The law creates several hurdles to a claim such as this. The hurdles are as follows."

Again, a word of caution: Just as you shouldn't callously discourage the client, you shouldn't give false hope. If a precedent is harmful, or if a fact is bad, say so. The truth must come out. The art is in how you do it.

You can soften the message with qualifying phrases such as "seems" or "would appear." You can anticipate trouble without appearing to be the author of it by saying, "The other side can be expected to argue," or "The agency will likely be concerned that . . ." You can judiciously insert "may" where your first instinct might be "will." If your analysis is solid, "may" won't be deemed indecisive, merely gracious.

Even though you must deliver a cautionary message, show the client that you sympathize with his problem and that you understand why he has reason to feel angry or betrayed. It is a simple principle that will cost you little.

Your audience can be a client or an assigning attorney. Both need to know that you have faith in the cause and will leave no stone unturned. That is why you are well-advised to acknowledge the client's side of the story, or the assigning attorney's view of the law, before you reluctantly don the robes of the devil's advocate.

Puzzler

How would you tighten and sharpen the following sentence?

The defendant certainly had constructive notice by reason of the recording of the documents.

Drop "certainly." If you don't persuade with your facts, you won't persuade with your intensifier. Substitute "because" for "by reason of." It is shorter and more direct. Finally, end the sentence with an important fact—the recording.

The revised version:

The defendant had constructive notice because the documents were recorded.

Alternate version:

Recording the documents gave the defendant constructive notice.

Be Brief But Not Brusque in Your Shorthand References

Anticipate the reader's likely reaction to your terms

Using shorthand references for names is a universal convention for saving space and maintaining the pace of briefs, memos and letters. After identifying the Department of Environmental Protection, for example, you would call it "the DEP." After identifying the Division of Gaming Enforcement, you would call it "the DGE" or "the Division."

Choosing a shorthand reference is, like everything else in persuasive writing, a matter of strategy. The reference should be unambiguous; it should evoke connotations helpful to your case if possible; and it should be unobtrusive.

The shorthand reference needs no introduction, like "hereinafter" or "hereinafter referred to," as in the following:

> *Consolidated Affiliated Corporation (hereinafter referred to as "Consolidated") objects to Defendant Transglobal Insurance Company's (hereinafter referred as "Transglobal") first request to produce documents as set forth below.*

Limit the parentheses to "Consolidated" and "Transglobal." "Hereinafter referred to" is assumed.

In lieu of creating a shorthand reference by extracting one or two words from a multiword name, you can use the first letters of the name, as in DEP or DGE. I recommend against this method in the above example because the shorthand "CAC" would, for some readers, become an acronym pronounced "kack," a dissonant if not gagging sound that may evoke unattractive images. "Consolidated" has more dignity.

Suppose that in a contract dispute, the parties exchanged memoranda of understanding that, taken together, may constitute an agreement. Assuming you don't want to disparage the documents (a risky tactic), call them "Memoranda," not "MOUs" (memoranda of understanding). Would you want a reader sounding out "Mooz" and thinking of cows each time the memoranda are mentioned?

The second parenthetical in the sample sentence exemplifies a common mistake: creating a shorthand reference to a possessive. It's a no-win situation. The shorthand reference is awkward as a nonpossessive (Transglobal) because it is inconsistent with its antecedent, and it is imprecise as a possessive (Transglobal's) because subsequent references will not be possessive. Rephrase using the preposition "of":

> *Consolidated Affiliated Corporation ("Consolidated") objects to the request of Defendant Transglobal Insurance Company ("Transglobal") to produce . . .*

Suppose you are defending a wrongful discharge action against "PG & C Information Systems," a subsidiary of a hypothetical Fortune 500 communications company named "PG & C." You don't want to clog your brief with the client's full name, so you need a shorthand reference. Would you call your client PG&C, PG&C-IS, Information Systems or just Systems?

I prefer "Information Systems." "PG&C" would confuse the subsidiary (PG&C Information Systems) with the parent (PG&C). Also, you don't want to be viewed as defending Big Communications. PG&C-IS is precise, but it is a drag for readers who sound out letters in shorthand references ("Pee gee and see—eye, ess"), and it is dissonant for readers who treat the shorthand as an acronym and pronounce the letters as a unit ("Pidgick is"). Some lawyers refer to excessive or otherwise inappropriate initials as "alphabet soup."

"Information Systems" is easy to say silently, and it has positive connotations. "Information" is generally considered good (except, perhaps, by those who abhor information glut), and "Systems," though clichéd, is at worst bland. If you find that the flow of your brief requires multiple references to the client, you could use both Information Systems and Systems, whichever sounds best in context. Your initial shorthand identifier would then read as follows:

PG&C Information Systems ("Information Systems" or "Systems")

Gathering Names

You can apply a shorthand reference to more than one individual or entity. Use "together" or "collectively," as in the following:

ABL Life Assurance Corp, as assignee of Associated Benefit Life Insurance Company in Rehabilitation (together, "ABL Life")

XYZ Corp.'s employees, including John Doe, Jane Doe and Richard Roe (collectively, "the XYZ employees")

Showing Respect

Don't try to do too much with your shorthand reference. It should be convenient but not caustic. For example, suppose you are suing the Archdiocese of a large city for breach of contract. Would your shorthand reference be "the Archdiocese" or "the defendant"? You might figure that by referring to the Archdiocese as "the defendant," you could tarnish the adversary's halo, as it were.

The tactic is so obvious that you're better off with "the Archdiocese." You can't overcome the inherent respect for the Church with the demeaning term "defendant." Go with the flow and let the facts of the contract breach speak for themselves.

A Punctuating Note

The shorthand reference goes inside the comma, not outside, where the antecedent is followed by a comma:

Wrong: Because of the negligence of Dr. John Smith, ("Dr. Smith") plaintiff suffered serious injury.

Right: Because of the negligence of Dr. John Smith ("Dr. Smith"), plaintiff suffered serious injury.

Puzzler

How would you tighten and sharpen the following sentence?

XYZ Corp. refused to sign the reservation of rights letter, obtained its own defense counsel and the underlying action was litigated to conclusion.

The comma after "letter" tells the reader that XYZ Corp. took a series of actions, the first two of which were "refused" and "obtained." Because the comma is not an "and," the reader looks for another verb describing action by XYZ Corp.

The sentence then surprises—and it may annoy or confuse—by switching subjects from XYZ Corp. to "the underlying action." Because of the switch, the construction is not "parallel." A collateral benefit of keeping the same subject (XYZ Corp.) is that the passive verb "was litigated" becomes the active verb "litigated," which has the same structure as (is parallel to) "refused" and "obtained."

The sentence also "runs on" by omitting a comma after "counsel," thus joining independent clauses (clauses that are sentences in their own right) without punctuation. In the revised version, the comma after "counsel" is optional because the sentence no longer concludes with an independent clause.

The revised version:

XYZ Corp. refused to sign the reservation of rights letter, obtained its own defense counsel, and litigated the underlying action to conclusion.

A Rose By Any Other Name Might Not Be as Popular

The lawyer's job is to find the optimum spin

Sooner or later, you will call prunes "dried plums." You may resist (maybe you don't think an operation is a "procedure," either), but your children will call them dried plums. Never mind that raisins aren't sold as "dried grapes." Prunes are on the way out.

Prunes connote age and irregularity. They are a metaphor for sour facial expressions ("She screwed up her face like a prune"). Prunes are, potentially, an embarrassment, whereas dried plums are not. To sell more prunes, advertisers have begun to eliminate the word from their marketing vocabulary. The new spin is that prunes are dried plums.

Years ago, the results of a vocational preference test suggested I might be comfortable in one of the professional fields grouped as "law/advertising/author-journalist." At the time, the combination of law and advertising seemed strange. Why would the dignified profession of law be joined with the seemingly slick field of advertising?

Now I know. Lawyers, like advertisers, spin. We use words to cast our client's position in its best light, just as advertisers use words, pictures and sounds to cast products and services in their best light. Our facility with spin is one reason we are paid so much by those who can afford us.

Top lawyers are spin masters. They know when to call a spade a spade, when to call it a club, and—perhaps the greatest test of good judgment—when not to mention it at all.

Consider the following two versions of a sentence stating that a plaintiff looking to recover for injuries suffered on State property must prove that the property was in "dangerous condition" at the time of the injury. A plaintiff suing the state would use the first version, and the state would use the second.

Plaintiff's version:

The provisions of the Tort Claims Act include the requirement of establishing a dangerous condition on public property.

State's version:

The stringent provisions of the Tort Claims Act require a plaintiff to prove that public property was in "dangerous condition" at the time of the injury.

The plaintiff's version acknowledges the act's requirement of proving a dangerous condition on public property, but it does so passively, seeking to be as unobtrusive as possible. The verb "include" is unassuming and nonthreatening. The act doesn't demand anything. It just "includes" it. The plaintiff doesn't have to prove anything, merely "establish" it.

The defendant's version emphasizes the burden of proof in several ways. It characterizes the provisions of the Tort Claims Act as "stringent," suggesting that tough barriers stand in the way of recovery against the state. It states affirmatively that the provisions of the act "require" something; it reminds the reader that plaintiff bears the burden of "prov[ing]" the dangerous condition; and it requires that the dangerous condition have existed "at the time of the injury."

It also places quotation marks around, and thus highlights, "dangerous condition," a statutorily defined term that is chock full of tests the plaintiff has to pass. Under the Tort Claims Act, "dangerous condition" means a condition of property that [1] creates a substantial risk of injury [2] when the property is used with due care [3] in a manner in which it is reasonably foreseeable that it will be used. Each of those elements of the definition is a hurdle for the plaintiff to overcome.

If you represent the plaintiff, you would think twice before saying the Tort Claims Act requires "that a plaintiff prove." You would tend to soft-pedal the plaintiff's burden by referring, perhaps, to "the requirement of establishing a dangerous condition."

Similarly, you would not refer to the "stringent" provisions of the Tort Claims Act. That is a defendant's word because stringency represents a barrier to recovery. You also would not gratuitously place quotation marks around "dangerous condition" because the marks call attention to its being a defined term with elements the plaintiff must satisfy.

Both versions of this sentence are legitimate. They are just spun differently. Spinning is part of the lawyer's job.

Puzzler

Which version is best, A, B or C?

Version A:

The trial judge, applying the test in Smith v. Jones, held that defendant owed plaintiff a duty.

Version B:

The trial judge applied the test in Smith v. Jones and held that defendant owed plaintiff a duty.

Version C:

Applying the test in Smith v. Jones, the trial judge held that defendant owed plaintiff a duty.

One should get to the verb quickly because readers like action. In Version A, the verb is the tenth word and is separated from the subject by two commas and a six-word phrase. In Version B, the verb is the fourth word and follows immediately upon the subject. Version B has better pace and more punch than Version A. Phrases that interrupt the progression from subject to verb annoy readers for whom time is a meaningful parameter. Nearly all legal readers fall into this category.

Arguably, Version C is better than Version B. Version C shows the reader that the relationship between the test and the holding is not merely additive. Version B says only that the judge applied a test and made a holding, leaving the reader to deduce—albeit without much effort—that the holding derived from the test. Version C makes the cause and effect clearer.

Nevertheless, one can make a case for Version B. Suppose, for example, that the writer wishes to create the image of a court having little trouble reaching its decision. The writer reports the court's actions succinctly and in sequence to reflect how easily the court made its decision: "The court applied the test and held . . . "

Though the reader has to deduce cause and effect, the task is easy because legal readers know that when a judge applies a test and makes a holding, the holding is based on the test. The extra work for the reader is minimal, whereas the gain in pace is palpable. In balance, the value of getting to the action immediately, as in Version B, may outweigh the value of guiding the reader by subordination, as in Version C.

When you break a traditional rule of writing, as by failing to subordinate, splitting an infinitive or using a preposition at the end of a sentence, a reader may react poorly simply because you are breaking a rule the reader honors. Here, I don't think many readers would be offended. The failure to subordinate is relatively innocent because you aren't using "and" to suggest cause and effect where it doesn't exist.

Brief Writing Requires a Formal Style

A casual tone may suggest you don't take your case seriously

Brief writing is more formal than conversation. You may say to a colleague that banking regulators are "super sensitive" to issues of integrity because the industry handles so much money, but in a brief, you would not write "super sensitive." If you used any intensifier, you would write that banking regulators are "very" or "extremely" (not "super") sensitive to issues of integrity.

"Super" is too casual. It presumes an intimacy you haven't earned, which may offend the reader. The familiar tone may also suggest you aren't taking your advocacy seriously, which in turn may suggest that the righteousness of your cause isn't manifest enough for you to feel comfortable being formal and indignant. If you can be casual in the face of the wrong done to your client, how serious a wrong could it be?

At bottom, if you don't seem moved by the gravity of your client's situation, then you can't expect the reader to be moved.

Does all this flow from one word or phrase? Perhaps. A colloquial expression stands out like a pimple in the formal context of a brief. It marks you as a rebel, a novice or a narcissist because the reader senses that only rebels, novices and narcissists speak colloquially in briefs, whether from anger, ignorance or self-absorption. Once you are marked, your credibility as an advocate suffers.

But you protest! You feel constricted. You want to add your personal mark to the brief. Surely, after all the effort you put in, you are entitled to one word that reflects your innate creative spark!

Don't do it. Make your mark the old fashioned way—with good facts and good law.

Show Respect for the Court

Avoiding the colloquial is especially important when referring to the actions or attitudes of a judicial or administrative body. Don't write that a court was "feeling its oats" or that a planning board was "hot" for a developer. The casual tone would show disrespect, not only for the court or the administrative body but for the legal system itself.

That brief writers are expected to show great deference to courts and agencies by using an elevated level of prose surprises some newer lawyers. As one member of my informal polling group puts it, "In an age where formality in ordinary life has vanished beyond recall, younger lawyers are unprepared for the dignity with which courts expect to be treated."

One small caveat: The need for a formal tone does not mean you should load your briefs with Latinate mammoths like "commence" instead of begin or arcane legalisms like *vel non*. The pompous is not an antidote for the irreverent.

Cuteness Is Also Taboo

Just as you shouldn't be colloquial, you shouldn't be cute, as in the following:

ABC Telephone is not subject to personal jurisdiction in New York because it provides local telephone service and directory service only in seven western states, none of which, needless to say, is in New York.

As the writer conceded with "needless to say," the comment that seven western states weren't in New York is unnecessary. Worse, it is counterproductive because it shows the writer's inexperience and self-absorption. It suggests the writer isn't taking the matter seriously, being more focused on comedy than on his case. If his case isn't worth his full attention, how good can it be?

The flip comment about the western states also suggests that the writer thinks the reader may actually be stupid enough not to deduce—without help—that the telephone company provides no service in New York. That will doubly irritate the reader, not only insulting the reader's intelligence but also, by reason of the unnecessary explanation, wasting the reader's time.

By being colloquial or cute, writers go off message, and their readers may lose sight of the point. The writers are trying to persuade, but their judgment is poor. They can't get past their anger, naiveté or self-absorption to see the consequences of their ill-chosen words.

Using the Colloquial as a Hook

Members of my informal polling group caution that colloquialisms and clichés can serve a positive role, catching the reader's attention at the beginning of a brief, encapsulating a theme, much as a trial lawyer would use homespun phrases to grab the jury's attention and help them organize and process information.

Fair enough. Using casual or even tired language to capture the reader's attention can work. For example, a plaintiff might contend that a defendant "should have used elbow grease rather than trying to elbow his way to the top." "Elbow grease" is colloquial and possibly a cliché, but it juxtaposes nicely with "elbow his way to the top."

Nevertheless, as a general rule, keep a low profile to preserve the flow. Don't call attention to your prose.

Puzzler

How would you tighten and sharpen the following sentence?

Under state law, there is no annual limit on the amount of contributions an individual may make to a state party committee.

Convert from passive to active by substituting "State law imposes" for "Under state law, there is." Drop "amount of" because the concept of amount is implicit in the word "limit." "By" is shorter than "may make."

I prefer "no annual limit on contributions" to "no annual contribution limit." Though the latter is one word shorter, it leaves the reader momentarily wondering why a phrase that appears to convey a negative ("no annual contribution") is used in a sentence stating a positive—that contributions are not limited.

Retain the phrase "an individual" to distinguish individual contributors from corporate contributors, which may have different contribution limits or may not be permitted to contribute at all.

The revised version:

State law imposes no annual limit on contributions by an individual to a state party committee.

You may wish to eliminate the prepositional phrase "by an individual."

Alternate version:

State law imposes no annual limit on an individual's contributions to a state party committee.

Some writers prefer "does not impose" to "imposes no" because the word "impose" momentarily imparts a restrictive connotation to a permissive message.

Alternate version:

State law does not impose an annual limit on an individual's contributions to a state party committee.

Summarize Statutes and Rules Before Quoting Them

Control your material and thus the reader's perspective

We revere statutes and rules. They have the authority of government and the illusion of permanence. The common law may shift, but statutes and rules appear solid. For these reasons and, frankly, because of our timidity, we often introduce statutes and rules with the bland "As the statute says" or "As the rule says," as if fearful of purporting to speak for the statute or rule rather than allowing it to speak for itself.

The following introduction to a Federal Rule appeared in a draft reply brief in support of a motion for consolidation. It consists of the bland statement that the Rule "provides," followed by the text of the Rule:

> *Fed. R. Civ. P. 42(a) provides:*
>
> *When actions involving a common question of law or fact are pending before the court, it may order a joint hearing or trial of any or all the matters in issue in the actions; it may order all the actions consolidated; and it may make such orders concerning proceedings therein as may tend to avoid unnecessary costs or delay.*

The writer was so fearful of intruding on the Rule that she did not even use underlining to highlight the portions of the rule of greatest interest.

After quoting the Rule, the writer made an argument—that the opponent (ABC Corp.) effectively conceded that the threshold test for consolidation is met merely because two cases involve common questions of law or fact. The argument read as follows:

> *ABC Corp. does not dispute that the threshold test for consolidating two cases is simply that they involve "a common question of law or fact." All that is required is that common questions exist and that consolidation will prove beneficial.*

This is a good thought, but it wasn't used to greatest effect because it was presented after the Rule rather than before. The writer could have taken better control of the material by using the thought to introduce the text of the Rule, as follows:

> *ABC Corp. does not dispute that the threshold test for consolidating two cases under Rule 42(a) is that they involve "a common question of law or fact":*
>
> > ***When actions involving a common question of law or fact are pending before the Court,*** *it may order a joint hearing or trial . . . [Emphasis added].*

The substantive introduction to the Rule induces the reader to read the Rule rather than skip it. It provides a preview that helps the reader understand the Rule, and it challenges the reader to confirm whether the writer has fairly characterized the rule. If the writer's précis of the Rule is correct, the following is accomplished:

- The reader's understanding of the Rule is enhanced.
- The point is reinforced.
- The reader senses that when the writer characterizes a quotation, the writer does so accurately. This builds trust.
- The reader senses that the writer is confident enough to take control of the material, which suggests the writer has confidence in her case. If the writer has confidence in her case, so may the reader.

In the revised version of the excerpt from the brief, we underlined the first clause of the Rule. The underlining provides emphasis, focusing the reader on the portion of the Rule that the writer considers most important. Together, the substantive introduction and the underlining lock in the idea.

A Second Example

Assume you represent a state agency whose power to reject all bids in a procurement has been challenged. The agency's draft brief argues as follows:

> *Government bodies are vested with the inherent power to reject all bids. [Case citations]. As the Authority's regulations provide:*
>
> > *The Authority retains the right to reject any or all bids, to waive informalities and minor irregularities and to rebid the entire contract. [Citation to regulation].*

If an agency has "inherent power," it can enact regulations articulating that power, as the Authority did. But the segue from the invocation of "inherent power" to the text of the regulation is weak. The clause "[a]s the Authority's regulations provide" doesn't show the connection between the power and the regulation, and it doesn't preview the substance of the regulation.

The flow and emphasis can be improved by introducing the text of the regulation as follows:

> *Governmental bodies are vested with the inherent power to reject all bids. [Case citation]. The Authority has explicitly articulated its right to reject all bids and re-advertise any of its contracts in the following regulation:*
>
> > *The Authority retains the right to reject any or all bids, to waive informalities and minor irregularities and to rebid the entire contract. [Citation to regulation].*

This is a simple example—short, with a regulation that needs little explanation. Even so, you can see how the introductory language adds value. It translates the "inherent power" to reject all bids into the "right" to do so—like converting from one form of electric current to another—and it previews the substance of the regulation. This induces the reader to read the text of the regulation, and it emphasizes the point through repetition. It provides the iteration to which the quoted text of the regulation becomes the reiteration.

Ideally, a writer controls the reader's consciousness at every moment, never letting go. One way to control the reader's consciousness is to provide substantive introductions to quotations, whether the quotations come from statutes, rules or judicial opinions. Once you understand this technique, you will rarely pass up an opportunity to use it.

Puzzler

How would you improve the following sentence?

Even assuming that there was improper insulation of the boiler causing it to overheat, there are no competent proofs of causation between the alleged improper insulation and the fire.

Rather than conceding the possibility of defeat on one point and falling back to another, make the argument additive. Say that not only did plaintiff fail to prove that the boiler was improperly insulated, but plaintiff failed to prove causation.

To trim and sharpen, eliminate the always-unnecessary "there was" and "there are" and use verbs rather than nouns. "Failed to prove" is more vigorous than "there are no competent proofs," and "caused" in place of "causation" gets rid of several additional words.

Drop the phrase "causing it to overheat" because, being implicit, it is unnecessary and because the phrase is good for plaintiff, not you. It helps color the picture that plaintiff wishes to paint.

I thought about eliminating "that" after the first "prove," but I decided to keep it for parallel construction because I need "that" after the next "prove" to eliminate the potentially confusing combination "prove improper insulation." A reader wouldn't think "prove the boiler" but might think "prove improper insulation."

The revised version:

Not only did plaintiff fail to prove that the boiler was improperly insulated, but he failed to prove that improper insulation caused the fire.

Take Control of Your Quotations, Don't Let Them Control You

Delete or substitute for words that are awkward or may confuse

When we were sent to the encyclopedias in grade school, we were told that verbatim copying was verboten. Our reports had to contain our own ideas (of which we had none) and "our own words." Nobody thought of quoting from a source because that would only announce the crime. We were years away from being able to synthesize a thought in our own words and use quotations merely as accents.

Teachers spoke of "plagiarizing"—an obscure term (to a nine-year old), reeking of pestilence and intended to intimidate. The gist of the offense as we understood it was the failure to use our own words. As a consequence, those of us afraid of getting caught labored in frustration to rewrite perfectly good sentences crafted by writers far better with words than we on subjects about which we knew essentially nothing.

I am not sure what these trips to the library accomplished other than deeply ingraining a distaste for paraphrasing that took a long time to overcome. Couple this with the reverence I had as a young lawyer for judges' words, and I was prone to quote whatever a court said, whether I fully understood it or not.

If you see this tendency in yourself, give special attention to what you intend to quote.

Suppose, for example, that you wish to establish the principle that a court will fill in gaps in a contract, and thus bind the parties, if the court concludes that the parties truly intended to make a deal. The quotation you like from a judicial opinion reads as follows:

> *Courts will not scruple at filling gaps in a contract or interpreting ambiguous terms if there is evidence of a manifestation of assent to enter into a bargain.*

You believe the quotation makes your point—that courts will fill in gaps in contracts and bind the parties if the parties clearly intended to be bound. You prefer to use the quotation verbatim rather than paraphrase it because you like the word "scruple"—it's firm and sharp, and it smacks of moral rectitude.

You also figure that courts make points more succinctly than you, and even though you aren't 100 percent sure what "will not scruple" means, at least it sounds impressive. You want to invoke morality and take the high ground.

Notwithstanding the connotative virtues of "scruple," "courts will not scruple" is almost certain to lead readers astray. The phrase sounds like, or suggests, "will not have scruples," which would mean, in this context, "will cynically maneuver or manipulate." This is hardly your point.

Eventually, a reader will realize that a court is not likely to state that other courts maneuver and manipulate, and the reader will see from the context that the court must have been using scruple to mean something like "hesitate" ("The court will not hesitate to fill in gaps."). Nevertheless, the reader will be confused, at least for a moment.

In persuasive legal writing, the reader's confusion is a serious concern.

Let's edit the passage. Change the phrase "will not scruple at" to "will not hesitate to," dropping the fancy word to remove the ambiguity. A collateral advantage of this revision is that you substitute strong verbs (fill and interpret) that take direct objects (gaps and terms) for a passive "-ing" approach (will not scruple at filling . . . or interpreting). The revised sentence reads as follows:

> *Courts will not hesitate to fill gaps in a contract or interpret ambiguous terms if there is evidence of a manifestation of assent to enter into a bargain.*

Naturally, you cannot place quotation marks around the entire sentence once you have changed several words. Nor would you place quotation marks ahead of "ambiguous" because it would interrupt the flow:

> *Courts will not hesitate to fill gaps in a contract or interpret "ambiguous terms if there is evidence of a manifestation of assent to enter into a bargain."*

Misplaced quotation marks are like misplaced commas—they interrupt the flow because they disappoint the reader's grammatical expectations. Quotation marks work best around grammatical units, whether words, phrases or clauses, in sympathy with the reader's hard-wired reactions to grammatical forms.

The flow is not interrupted if you place the quotation marks in front of "if":

> *Courts will not hesitate to fill gaps in a contract or interpret ambiguous terms "if there is evidence of a manifestation of assent to enter into a bargain."*

The quotation marks now encompass a grammatical unit—the "if" clause.

You can probably guess what I'll recommend next. I would not quote any portion of this sentence because I don't like the "there is" construction; I don't like the ponderous phrase "evidence of a manifestation of assent"; and I prefer "intent" to "assent." I would rephrase the back end of the sentence to something like this: ". . . if the parties have manifested their intent to enter into a bargain":

> *Courts will not hesitate to fill gaps in a contract or interpret ambiguous terms if the parties have manifested their intent to enter into a bargain.*

I am not concerned about losing the opportunity to quote. The paraphrase is accurate. Not only will it survive scrutiny, but its validity will build trust if the reader checks the source.

Save your quotations for powerful words. Don't quote just to avoid having to reshape the court's language, and don't quote bad or ambiguous writing, even if you are desperate to quote authority. If you feel you must quote something from an opinion as a show of strength or to prove you aren't making it up, reduce the size of the quotation, even down to a word or two, until you are no longer featuring bad prose.

Puzzler

What is wrong with the following sentence?

Lacking expert testimony to make a case regarding causation, the court granted summary judgment against plaintiff.

This sentence includes a "dangling participle." The participle is the word "lacking," which is the "-ing" form of the verb "lack." Participles modify (describe) nouns. The participle dangles because it doesn't clearly describe one particular noun, in this case, either the court or the plaintiff.

Though the plaintiff, not the court, failed to produce expert testimony on the subject of causation, on first look the court appears to be the one lacking expert testimony ("Lacking expert testimony . . . the court granted"). In other words, the court appears to be the "antecedent" of the participle "lacking." (Even though the prefix "ante-" means "prior to," an antecedent can either precede or follow its referent.)

You can't shorten the sentence much because you need a reference to the plaintiff, a verb describing what plaintiff did or didn't do, the concept of summary judgment, the absence of an expert, and a reference to causation. In the alternate version, "establish" is tighter than "make a case regarding."

The new version:

The court granted summary judgment because plaintiff presented no expert on causation.

Alternate version:

Lacking an expert to establish causation, plaintiff lost on summary judgment.

6

Focus

Homing in on the Point

Focus

Homing in on the Point

Focus on a point by using only what you need: the best facts, the most telling words from a judicial opinion, or the controlling words from a statute or regulation. Use exactly the right word; make only one point in a sentence; and don't extend the sentence unnecessarily. Be brief and home in.

Use Smaller Categories to Convey Precise Information

Offering unnecessary alternatives creates ambiguity

Legal thinking is like a telephoto lens—it zooms in and zooms out.

For example, it zooms in when you hunt for just the right word or phrase, and it zooms out when you seek common ground between your case and one you wish to cite as precedent. In the first instance, you narrow your focus and home in on a word or phrase that is unambiguous and accurate. In the latter instance, you widen your focus to find a category broad enough to encompass both your case and the desired precedent, but not so broad that it is meaningless. To invoke *stare decisis*, you may have to zoom out.

This column is about zooming in—choosing words to state exactly what you mean. When you choose the right word, not only do you achieve accuracy, but you eliminate ambiguity by avoiding the alternatives that might be suggested by the wrong word.

In the paragraph below, the writer sought to convey that coverage under a statute regulating the storage of hazardous substances expanded to include smaller facilities. Instead of saying the statute "expanded to include" or "expanded to cover" smaller facilities, the writer said the law "was amended to cover" them, leaving the reader to deduce that "amended" meant "expanded."

> *The original act defined "major facilities" as those having the capacity to store 400,000 gallons of hazardous substances of any kind. Several years later, the law* ***was amended to cover*** *facilities having the capacity to store at least 50,000 gallons if the hazardous substances are other than petroleum. Last year, the law* ***was amended to cover*** *facilities that can store at least 200,000 gallons of petroleum and facilities that can store at least 20,000 gallons of non-petroleum hazardous substances.*

The word "amended" embraces at least three subsets (subcategories): "expanded," "contracted" and "clarified." It forces the reader to ask, "How was the statute amended? Did coverage expand or contract, or was it merely clarified?" Having to identify subcategories, select one and discard the rest makes work for the reader and interrupts the message.

The ambiguity in the word "amended" is compounded in the above paragraph because expansion of regulatory coverage seems at odds with a reduction in gallonage. Expansion denotes increase, whereas reduction denotes decrease. A moment's thought is required to deduce that coverage has expanded because the amended statute now applies to facilities that store fewer gallons.

Thus, the reader of the paragraph faces a dual hurdle—ambiguity in the word "amended" and seeming inconsistency between expanded coverage and reduced gallonage. Merely identifying the lower gallonage threshold—50,000 gallons—does not by itself overcome these hurdles.

Using "expanded" rather than "amended" would reduce the ambiguity and make the paragraph more accessible:

> *The original act defined "major facilities" as those having the capacity to store 400,000 gallons of hazardous substances of any kind. Several years later, the law* ***expanded to include*** *facilities having the capacity to store at least 50,000 gallons if the hazardous substances are other than petroleum. Last year, the law* ***further expanded to include*** *facilities that can store at least 200,000 gallons of petroleum and facilities that can store at least 20,000 gallons of non-petroleum hazardous substances.*

You might also say that "*coverage* expanded to include" (as opposed to "the law expanded to include") or that "the law expanded to *cover*." "Include" connotes a gathering and suggests the statute is "putting its arms around" more. "Cover" connotes a larger regulatory umbrella. Both work. The conventional phrase is "expanded to include."

Even with the foregoing change (including the boost from the active verb "expanded" instead of the passive verb "was amended"), the reduction of the threshold for non-petroleum hazardous substances from 400,000 to 50,000 gallons is difficult to follow because regulatory coverage increases as the gallonage threshold decreases. The paragraph would improve if recast around the central idea—reduction of the gallonage threshold:

> *The original act defined "major facilities" as those having the capacity to store at least 400,000 gallons of any kind of hazardous substance. Several years later,* ***the legislature expanded coverage of non-petroleum facilities by reducing the gallonage threshold*** *for such facilities to 50,000. Last year,* ***the now dual thresholds were further reduced***—*to 200,000 gallons for petroleum facilities and 20,000 gallons for non-petroleum facilities.*

The first and second revised paragraphs illustrate two points about writing:

1. Using subcategories—for example, "expansion" as a subcategory of "amendment"—streamlines the message.
2. If you are having trouble articulating an idea, ask yourself what your point is or what your main fact is. Here, the main fact was the reduction of the gallonage threshold. When the key sentence was recast around that concept, it went directly to the point.

Puzzler

How would you tighten and sharpen the following sentence?

Review with the assistance of your expert the articles and treatises relied on by the opposing expert.

When the reader sees a verb ("review"), the reader wants to know the object of the verb, which in this case is "articles and treatises." The phrase "with the assistance of your own expert" is interruptive and should be moved to the beginning of the sentence.

The revised version:

With the assistance of your expert, review the articles and treatises relied on by the opposing expert.

Alternate version:

Have your expert help you review the articles and treatises relied on by the opposing expert.

When Tracking Statutes and Rules, Use Only What You Need

Verbatim recitation is comforting but often unnecessary

Tracking statutes or rules—repeating them verbatim rather than paraphrasing them or taking excerpts—ensures accuracy. But tracking can be overdone. If you use it as false comfort, you waste time and space.

Suppose you are objecting to counsel's submission of an unreported opinion to the Appellate Division after briefs are filed. The unreported opinion is two years old and should have been submitted with counsel's brief. A Rule of Court permits a late submission only if the case was decided after the brief was filed:

> *No briefs other than those herein specified shall be filed or served without leave of court.* ***A party may, however, without leave, serve and file a letter calling to the court's attention, with a brief indication of their significance, relevant cases decided or legislation enacted subsequent to the filing of the brief.*** *Any other party to the appeal may, without leave, file and serve a short letter in response thereto within 5 days after receipt thereof. [Rule 2:6-11(d); emphasis added].*

You consider tracking the rule in your responding letter, figuring that (a) by tracking the rule, you will invoke its power, and (b) in tracking it, you cannot be accused of misquoting or mischaracterizing it. So you draft the argument as follows:

> *The submission of this unreported opinion was untimely because it was sent to the Court pursuant to Rule 2:6-11(d), which permits parties without leave of court to serve and file a letter calling to the Court's attention and briefly describing any relevant case decided <u>after</u> the filing of the briefs. [Emphasis in original].*

The rule says all that, but you don't have to. You could say less to better effect:

> *The submission of this opinion was untimely because Rule 2:6-11(d) permits reference without leave of court only to cases decided after the briefs are filed.*

Several elements of your first version were unnecessary: (a) that a letter can be used to call a case to the court's attention; (b) that the letter can be "served and filed"; (c) that the letter can briefly describe the case; and (d) that the case must be "relevant."

All those concepts are in the rule, but they don't support your point, which is timeliness. Your response should make the point on timeliness as efficiently as possible.

Note the underlined word "after" in the longer version. This is a signal that you have obscured your main point, timeliness, and feel a need to highlight a temporal word—"after"—as a countermeasure to the clutter. Underlining is often a makeshift means of trying to bring out what verbosity conceals.

A Second Example

Suppose your opponent is petitioning the Supreme Court to review a ruling of the Appellate Division and contends that the case involves a question of general public importance that has not been, but should be, settled by the Supreme Court. This is one of several possible grounds for discretionary review ("certification") set forth in the following Rule of Court:

> *Certification will be granted only if the appeal presents* ***a question of general public importance which has not been but should be settled by the Supreme Court*** *or is similar to a question presented on another appeal to the Supreme Court; if the decision under review is in conflict with any other decision of the same or a higher court or calls for an exercise of the Supreme Court's supervision and in other matters if the interest of justice requires. [Rule 2:12-4; emphasis added].*

Your opponent's petition claims only that the case presents a question of general public importance. It says nothing about the other grounds for discretionary review, that is: (i) similarity to a question presented in another appeal before the Supreme Court; (ii) conflict of the decision with a decision of the same or higher court; (iii) need for Supreme Court supervision; or (iv) "the interest of justice." Therefore, you need not begin your opposing brief by tracking all five factors in the rule. Just say the petitioner invokes only one ground for discretionary review and fails to provide support.

You will not be viewed as evasive if you eschew the irrelevant. The Supreme Court is well aware of its rules. You may find it comforting to list all the reasons why certification may be granted because no one will be able to disagree with you for several lines in your brief. But the measure of a brief isn't how far you can go before someone disagrees with you. It is whether you can persuade the reader to agree with your point, preferably as soon as possible. Therefore, if you have a point, get to it. Don't temporize with unnecessary tracking.

Puzzler

How would you tighten and sharpen the following sentence?

> *The court based its decision to deny defendant's motion to disqualify plaintiff's counsel on the fact that the defendant had acted in bad faith in waiting to file its motion for tactical reasons until a trial was pending in order to force the plaintiff to incur great expense and prejudice in finding new counsel.*

This one might have several good solutions. The phrase "based its decision to deny defendant's motion" can be replaced by "refused," and "on the fact that" becomes "because."

"Had acted in bad faith in waiting to file its motion for tactical reasons" can become "delayed" because "bad faith" and "for tactical reasons" are implicit.

"Until a trial was pending" is acceptable but not as pointed as "on the eve of trial" or "just before trial."

"Great expense" and "prejudice" overlap. Prejudice is the set, and expense and inconvenience are the subsets. "In order to force the plaintiff to incur" becomes the shorter, punchier "to maximize." That the plaintiff will incur expense and inconvenience is understood.

I would not oppose a flourish like "purposely delayed the motion" or delayed the motion "for tactical purposes" though both are redundant. They add flavor at low cost.

The revised version:

The court refused to disqualify plaintiff's counsel on the eve of trial because defendant had delayed the motion to maximize the expense and inconvenience of finding new counsel.

Trim the Facts to Bring Out the Essence of Your Case

You may not need marginal facts to make your point

> [I]n general it is better to pass by not only that which weakens the cause but also that which neither weakens nor helps it.
>
> —Cicero, *Rhetorica Ad Herrenium* I, IX. 14

Candor is essential to persuasion. A reader who doesn't trust you won't trust your argument. Nearly all legal writers sense the need for candor, but they deal with it in different ways.

Some think that candor requires comprehensiveness. They include almost everything lest they be accused of hiding something. Though their concern is sound, their exhaustive approach may force the reader to wade through irrelevancies.

Consider how the comprehensive approach might affect a factual exposition, as in an affidavit, a statement of facts or a preliminary statement. Suppose you represent Smith, a vice president of sales and minority shareholder who has been frozen out of a closely held corporation by Jones, the chief executive officer and majority shareholder.

To demote and embarrass Smith, Jones moved him from his executive office to an office half the size and reassigned all the employees who reported to him. Jones defends the office relocation as incident to a consolidation of facilities and the staff reassignments as part of an internal restructuring.

Your draft of a preliminary statement supporting an application to enjoin the freeze-out includes the following sentence:

> *Jones evicted Smith from the executive office he maintained in a separate company building that also housed the company's accounting offices, closed the building, moved Smith to a much smaller office, and transferred the sales employees who had reported to Smith to a location where they would no longer report to Smith.*

The good facts—not good for Smith but good in the sense that they help make your case—are that Smith was moved from an executive office to a hole-in-the-wall and that his employees were reassigned.

The potentially bad fact is that Smith's office was in a separate company building that was closed down. This supports Jones' point about consolidation. The marginal facts are that the building also housed accounting offices and that the employees who reported to Smith were transferred to a location away from Smith.

The easiest fact to discard is the accounting offices. Because Smith was in sales, your reader doesn't need to know that the building where Smith worked also had accounting offices. Without increasing the egregiousness of what Jones did, the fact diverts attention from your key facts—that Smith's office shrank and that his employees disappeared.

You may have to acknowledge that Smith's office was in a building that was closed down because you expect Jones to argue that the company wasn't picking on Smith; it was just consolidating offices by closing the satellite building. Though this fact is of no use to you, you may have to include it so you don't lose credibility. If Jones brings it up first, he gets to suggest that you omitted the fact because it is bad for your case.

Should you say that Smith's employees were transferred to a location away from Smith? This is a closer call. The connotation you seek by including that fact is that Jones wanted to humiliate Smith so badly that not only did he reassign Smith's employees, but he moved them where Smith couldn't even interact with, let alone supervise them.

This is good flavor, but it may subtract more than it adds. The essence of the humiliation wasn't in the relocation of the employees; it was in the reassignment. Smith would no longer supervise the employees because they were reassigned, not because they were moved away. The employees had to move to another building anyway because their building was closed down.

So the geographic element is merely tangential. Because it elevates a minor fact to major status, it may dilute the fact pattern more than it augments it, and it may suggest to the reader that you gild the lily.

Revised, your original sentence might read as follows:

> *Jones evicted Smith from his executive office, relegated him to a room half the size and reassigned all the sales employees who reported to him.*

This presents the story in a short, vigorous sentence that is energized—after you change the phrase "moved Smith to a much smaller office" to "relegated him to a room half the size"—by the alliteration of four "r's" (relegated, room, reassigned and reported).

If you want to anticipate Jones' argument about consolidation, you can highlight the transparency of his excuse:

> *Claiming that he was just consolidating facilities and restructuring staff, Jones evicted Smith from his executive office, relegated him to a room half the size and reassigned all the sales employees who reported to him.*

No matter what Jones says about consolidation, his intent is clear—to demote and degrade Smith. Jones may have had reasons to close the building, but halving the size of Smith's office cannot be excused.

By juxtaposing Jones' purported rationale against the severe consequences of his acts, you suggest that Jones is not only a bully (by stripping Smith of office and employees) but also a liar (by making a bogus excuse). Parties who deny responsibility for their actions generate little sympathy with the court.

Conclusion

Marginal facts can occlude key facts or bury them. By stripping away the tangential, you improve the odds that your good facts will trigger the reader's outrage.

Compare how you feel about what Jones did to Smith after you read the slow-moving original sentence with how you feel after reading the versions stripped of the accounting offices and the geographical move of the employees. All the versions get to the point, but the shorter ones get there faster and with greater impact.

Puzzler

Which ending to the following sentence do you prefer, A or B, and why?

The dissenting shareholder's accusations had an obvious purpose—to discredit the existing Board so that shareholders would: (A) vote for the dissenter's nominees; or (B) elect the directors nominated by the dissenter.

The shorter version has more speed and grip. "Vote" is stronger than "elect" because vote describes a physical act, which can be visualized. Readers are engaged by what they can see in their mind's eye. "Elect," in contrast, describes not what the shareholder does but what happens as a result of it. You cannot visualize a person "electing," but you can visualize a person voting (*e.g.,* checking a box or pulling a handle).

Everything after vote is denouement and should end as quickly as possible. Prepositional phrases ("by the dissenter") tend to drag. The possessive "dissenter's nominees" also adds the subtle suggestion that the dissenter "owns" the nominees.

Eliminate "There Is" and "There Are"

Though useful in speech, these phrases are rarely needed in legal writing

Oral communication uses the phrases "there is" and "there are" to good effect, not only in English but in other languages. For example, Spanish uses "hay" (pronounced "eye") for "there is," and French uses "il y a" ("ee-lee-ah"). These expressions are useful in conversation because, among other things, they temper the speed of the discourse, allowing both speaker and listener to gather their thoughts, and they soften its tone.

The legal writer, in contrast, has plenty of time to gather thoughts, and both writer and reader understand—and thus are not concerned with giving or taking offense—that the point will be made as directly as possible.

Consider the following:

There is no public interest which precludes the Court from ordering the injunctive relief XYZ Corp. has requested.

"There is" is excess. Just say, "No public interest precludes . . . " This saves three words: "There," "is" and "which." The "which" should have been "that," anyway.

Similarly:

BAD: There is no evidence that supports their claim.

BETTER: No evidence supports their claim.

BAD: There is no provision in the settlement agreement that contemplates arbitration of subsequent disputes.

BETTER: No provision in the settlement agreement contemplates arbitration of subsequent disputes.

BAD: There are two measures of damages that have been deemed appropriate.

BETTER: Two measures of damages have been deemed appropriate.

BAD: There is only one case that has addressed that issue.

BETTER: Only one case has addressed that issue.

BAD: There is no causal link to indicate which products will be successful.

BETTER: No causal link indicates which products will be successful.

In conversation, "there is" or "there are" can also serve as a directive. For example, you say, "There are four apples on the table" to call attention to the table and the apples. The listener looks at the table, and you have accomplished your purpose. The listener does not question where "there" is.

A reader, in contrast, has nowhere to look but the printed page. The reader's natural response to a sentence beginning "There are" is to think, "Where are?" But the where has no physical point of reference in a brief, letter or memo. "There are" is just warm-up language to indicate that something exists. It wastes the reader's time.

In many cases, "there is" and "there are" can simply be deleted with no loss of meaning, but sometimes you have to change the verb:

> *BAD: In a client-server network, there are normally file servers to which users can save documents.*

> *BETTER: A client-server network normally includes file servers to which users can save documents.*

Instead of just saying "there are" file servers in the network, say the network "includes" file servers. It's stronger because it creates an image of the network encompassing (including) the servers.

Sometimes you can eliminate a "there" structure by reversing order. For example, "There are many ways to satisfy the minimum contacts requirement" becomes "Minimum contacts can be established in many ways." Though the construction remains passive, you emphasize the key concept "many ways" by ending with it, and you no longer begin with the temporizing phrase "There are."

Some writers eliminate "there are" by substituting "exist," but this fix is usually weak, as in the following example:

> *BAD: The court reasoned that there was not enough proof of non-compliance in discovery to justify giving plaintiff access to defendant's e-mail system.*

> *HARDLY BETTER: The court reasoned that not enough proof of noncompliance in discovery existed to justify giving plaintiff access to defendant's e-mail system.*

Rephrasing improves the sentence:

> *BETTER: The court reasoned that the shortfalls in defendants' responses were insufficient to justify giving plaintiff access to defendant's e-mail system.*

To say that "there is" is never appropriate in legal writing would overstate the case. It could work, for example, as a softening device.

Suppose you wish to advise a client that a person who violates a regulation may suffer a criminal penalty, but you don't want to alarm the client with the strong, active formulation, "Violation of the regulation is a criminal act." So you say, "There is a criminal penalty for violating the regulation," tempering the message.

"There is/there are" is one of those usage flaws that just won't go away. It's too comfortable and too easy. No matter how many times I cross it out and even ask writers not to use it anymore, it comes back, like pantry moths or the clothes on a teenager's floor. Fortunately, deleting it is relatively easy. Look for opportunities to eliminate this unnecessary phrase from your writing.

Puzzler

How would you tighten and sharpen the following sentence?

The primary policy has liability limits of $2 million per occurrence, $4 million aggregate, and is subject to a $100,000 self-insured retention.

The policy limits and the self-insured retention (the deductible) do not belong in a series of three because they are different sets. Separate them.

For parallel construction, move "self-insured retention" ahead of the number $100,000 just as "limits" precedes the coverage numbers. Drop "liability" and "subject to" as implicit and add "in the" in front of aggregate for a parallel to "per" in front of occurrence.

The revised version:

The primary policy has limits of $2 million per occurrence and $4 million in the aggregate and a self-insured retention of $100,000.

The self-insured retention is a bit of a tack-on. If you don't need to place the coverage limits first for transitional purposes, begin with the self-insured retention so the two-part set ends the sentence.

Alternate version:

The primary policy has a self-insured retention of $100,000 and limits of $2 million per occurrence and $4 million in the aggregate.

Take Control of Statutes by Summarizing Them

You may need to offload much of what the legislators lump in

For the most part, statutes do not even purport to be easy reading. Legislators just load in the material and hope that nothing gets left out. For the convenience of your readers, you almost always need to summarize statutes.

Consider the following statutory bar to high-level government officials owning or working for gaming entities during their tenure in office and for two years thereafter. The example is a composite, but it is representative:

> *No executive-level state employee, head of a principal department, head of an independent state agency or member of the legislature, or their immediate family members, shall have, at or following the effective date of this Act, a financial interest in or be employed, directly or indirectly, by any Licensed Gaming Entity, Licensed Casino Gaming Entity, applicant for such licenses, or any holding, affiliate, intermediary or subsidiary company thereof, during his or her status as an executive-level state employee, head of a principal department, head of an independent state agency or member of the legislature and for two (2) years following termination of such status.*

Suppose your job is to summarize this long-winded statute for a memo or a brief. The approach is straightforward. First determine what you need and what you don't need; then group the elements and place them in proper order.

As the statute must, it names all the persons to whom it applies. Unless you are focusing on a particular type of public official, you don't need to present the entire list, just a category that encompasses all persons on the list. Here, the phrase "high-level public official" can include executive-level state employees, heads of principal departments, heads of independent state agencies and members of the legislature.

You can drop the reference to the effective date of the act because a reader will assume the stricture takes effect when the act takes effect unless you state otherwise. You can also drop the reference to "direct or indirect" employment by a gaming licensee unless you have an issue regarding indirect employment. Similarly, you won't need the reference to "applicants," meaning entities that have sought but haven't received licenses, unless you have an issue involving an applicant.

The statute refers to two classes of gaming entities—"Licensed Gaming Entities" and "Licensed Casino Gaming Entities." Again, unless you have an issue that requires you to call attention to either of those two classes, just use a category that covers both ("gaming entities"). The same reasoning applies to the list of related entities—holding, affiliate, intermediary and subsidiary companies. They are all "affiliates."

The statute concludes by setting forth the period for which public officials are restricted—two years. In typical statutory fashion, it repeats the full list of persons covered. You can skip the repetition. Just refer to the relevant period.

The elements of the statute can be grouped as follows:

- high-level public officials and their immediate family members
- financial interest or employment
- gaming entities and their affiliates
- during employment and for two years thereafter

Once the groups are outlined, the summary almost writes itself. Try it.

Whether you begin with "High-level public officials are barred" or with "While in office and for two years thereafter" may depend on your transitional needs, and it may depend on whether you wish to assign the position of emphasis at the beginning of the sentence to the fact of the bar or its duration. The summary might read, for example:

High-level public officials and their immediate family members are barred from holding an interest in or working for gaming entities and their affiliates while in office and for two years thereafter.

In the alternative:

While in office and for two years thereafter, high-level public officials and immediate family members are barred from holding an interest in or working for gaming entities and their affiliates.

If your focus is one category of public official, such as heads of state agencies, you can follow the above sentences with something like:

Heads of state agencies are covered by the bar.

In the alternative, you could build the reference to heads of state agencies right into your master sentence:

Heads of state agencies and their immediate family members are barred . . .

In the above sentences, we substituted a word that is more vigorous than "employment" but conveys the same concept—"working"—and we substituted "while in office" for "during his or her status as . . .," thus saving words, dropping the awkward "his or her," and avoiding the rank-order connotations of "status."

To write well, you must take control of your material. To take control of a statutory summary, decide what to keep and what to cull; how to group what remains; and how to achieve precision and flow. In short, pull the statute apart, strip and group its elements and put them back together, all with a view to making the reader's job easier and getting your point across.

Puzzler

How would you tighten and sharpen the following sentence?

The way in which the level playing field was tilted is through the agency's making findings that didn't have any support in the record.

Eliminate "The way in which . . . is" and then decide whether to stay with "the playing field was tilted" or go to "the agency tilted the playing field." Unless you badly need the playing field to be the subject, as for transitional purposes, use the active construction.

Shorten the sentence further by dropping "level," which is implicit. "That didn't have any" can be dropped or replaced by "without," depending on how the concept of support in the record is handled.

"Record support" is shorter than support in the record, but "record" carries the unwanted connotation of the superlative, as in "record rainfall" and "record performance." Even better may be "unsupported findings."

The revised version:

The agency tilted the playing field by making findings without support in the record.

Alternate version:

The agency tilted the playing field by making unsupported findings.

Use Quotation Marks to Focus the Reader's Attention

The punctuation should go with the flow rather than interrupt it

We quote judicial opinions, statutes and rules to invoke the authority of our source or to report precisely what it says. These are solid purposes. But sometimes we quote too much.

I have seen a full page of text constructed with quotations alone, as if the trick were to run together as many quotations as possible and still make sense. And I have seen block quotes so large that they make the print on the page look like a distended Roman numeral one. Oddly, some writers think courts will read the entire block.

The motivation for over-quoting varies with the writer and the circumstance, but it is usually some combination of, "If the court said it, it must be well-phrased"; "if I quote the opinion (or the statute), no one can say I mischaracterized it"; "judicial, statutory and regulatory language is authoritative—the more I quote, the more authoritative I'll be"; and last, but not least, "the more I quote, the less I need to write."

Writers who over-quote often lack confidence in their analysis or their ability to express it, and they are looking for someone else to make their point.

The example below involves mild over-quoting of a kind that even an experienced lawyer might produce. The subject matter is a bidding statute that did not make clear whether municipal contracts for curbside collection of recyclable materials had to be publicly bid. The statute made an exception to the bidding requirement for the "marketing of recyclable materials recovered through a recycling program," but the word "marketing" was ambiguous. It could include curbside collection as well as the sale of recyclable materials, or it could cover just the sale.

The court held that in view of the strong pubic policy favoring competitive bidding in the garbage collection industry, the word "marketing" was not intended to include curbside collection. (The statute has since been clarified to that effect.) This meant that contracts for curbside collection of recyclables, unlike contracts for their sale, had to be publicly bid. A memo reporting that result read as follows:

> *The court held that the public bidding exemption for "marketing of recyclable materials recovered through a recycling program" does not relieve a municipality from publicly bidding contracts for the curbside collection of recyclables.*

The length of the quotation ("marketing of recyclable materials recovered through a recycling program") dilutes its impact. The quotation marks should bracket only "marketing," not the full statutory phrase, because that word was the focus of the litigation. Quoting the full phrase masks the essence of the court's ruling. Did the court interpret "marketing," "recyclable materials," the "recycling program" or all three?

As a general rule, the shorter the quotation, the greater the impact. Sophisticated writers tend to quote minimally and to paraphrase or track the rest.

If the words of the statute flow well in context, you can track them. Don't worry about being accused of plagiarizing. You aren't trying to pass off the statute's words as your own.

Don't Quote Yourself

Writers also include too much within quotation marks when they place a piece of what they are saying within the material being quoted, as in the following:

The expert explained "that contaminants spread downhill from the site of deposit."

The quotation marks should be placed before "contaminants," not before "that," even if the expert said, "It is clear that contaminants spread downhill from the site of deposit."

Although the quotation in the above example accurately reports a portion of what the expert said, it is not reader-friendly. The writer, not the expert, is using the word "that." The writer is saying that the expert explained something ("The expert explained that . . ."). Until the reader passes the word "that," which concludes the writer's introduction to what the expert said, the reader isn't ready for what the expert said.

If the expert were speaking, the expert would not begin with "that," which is generally found in the middle of sentences. The expert would begin with a subject, such as "contaminants." Including "that" within the quotation will make the reader's task more difficult, costing you a tempo and possibly, together with other glitches, costing you credibility.

Not only is the inclusion of "that" within the quotation grammatically awkward, but it diminishes the power of the quotation by ceding prime position to a warm-up word. Quotation marks draw the reader's attention. Take advantage of the publicity by placing key words under the spotlight.

Begin at the Beginning

Quotations can also be awkward where the writer fails to quote every word that should be quoted, as in the following:

The psychiatrist concluded that the "incident has had an indelible and permanent effect on her."

As in the previous example, the reader expects the quoted material to follow the word "that" because the writer says the psychiatrist "concluded that . . . " The reader wants to know what "that" is.

The word that begins to satisfy the reader's curiosity is "the," not "incident," because the psychiatrist's conclusion begins with "the incident," not "incident." The article "the" belongs to what the psychiatrist said, not to what the writer says the psychiatrist said.

In sum, the touchstone for placing quotation marks is a combination of the reader's expectations and the writer's focus. The writer serves both needs by quoting the essence of the material, neither more nor less.

Puzzler

How would you tighten and sharpen the following sentence?

Defendant attempts to dispute Plaintiff's standing but does not cite a single decision that abrogates Plaintiff's taxpayer standing or negates the case law cited by Plaintiff, which recognizes that a taxpayer's standing is undiminished by his personal interest in the outcome of the litigation.

The sentence makes two points: (1) a plaintiff's personal interest in a litigation does not diminish the plaintiff's standing as a taxpayer, and (2) the defendant fails to cite any law challenging this rule. Because the rule is helpful, present it up front.

Don't temporize with "Defendant attempts to dispute Plaintiff's standing." That is understood. Focus on the defendant's failure and reduce the ponderous "Defendant . . . does not cite a single decision that abrogates Plaintiff's taxpayer standing or negates the case law cited by Plaintiff" to "Defendant cites no law challenging the well-established rule."

"Well-established rule" is better than "case law cited by the plaintiff, which recognizes . . ." You can characterize what several cases say as a rule, and you can call the rule well-established because no case law holds to the contrary.

The revised version:

Defendant cites no law challenging the well-established rule that a taxpayer's standing is undiminished by his personal interest in the outcome of the litigation.

Precision Begets Persuasion

The more precise you are in support of your point, the greater the chance you will persuade

One of the less heralded challenges of persuasive writing is the search for a better word when you already have one that seems adequate. Paradoxically, one of the most fascinating insights about persuasive writing—and for that matter, about any writing—is that fixing your attention directly on a word or phrase inevitably generates alternatives.

In the following sentence, the word "had" suffices, but you can do better.

XYZ Corp. had about forty salespersons.

"Employed" would be more precise. "Had" covers not only employees but independent contractors, leaving the legal relationship unclear. If you said in the next sentence that half the sales persons were employees, and half were independent contractors, then "had" might work. Still, it is so general that it is almost passive.

The mix of (a) facts and (b) words to describe the facts in most cases is so complex that we make our word choices instinctively, barely conscious of the selection. In a sense, we are out of control. But our mind is a willing machine, and if we ask it to consider alternatives, it will. Good writers continually ask their minds to find better words.

Our success in this endeavor is partly a function of the speed with which our brain sorts data and partly a function of other factors, such as love of language, exposure to good prose, and a broad vocabulary. Good judgment helps, too.

At bottom, I suspect that the most important factor is the will to seek the best word, challenging everything.

Let's focus again on converting a minimally descriptive word, such as "have" or "give," to something more specific—a classic edit. Suppose, for example, that you wish to challenge the conclusions of a court-appointed expert. You begin as follows:

The Court gave its expert another task—to evaluate the strength of the relationship between the child and his grandparents.

The court did give its expert another task. But give has connotations of conferring, benefiting or endowing. Here, the court told its expert to perform a job. The court imposed, directed, commanded. A word whose connotations align better with the court's mandate (I almost said, blandly, "the court's action") is "assigned":

The court assigned its expert another task—

Because you are challenging the expert's conclusions, you want to emphasize that the expert failed at something. So you don't say the trial court gave (*i.e.,* conferred upon) the expert a task. You say the court assigned the expert a task (imposed it on him). Then you can say the expert failed to fulfill his assignment.

You might even say the court "entrusted" the expert with the task, which would allow you to suggest, though it might be overdramatic to say outright, that the expert breached that trust.

Whatever word you choose, be precise for a purpose. You aren't paid by the Institute for Greater Precision in Legal Writing, if one exists. You are paid by a client. Everything you write should benefit the client, within the boundaries of ethics and law. If "assigned" is good for your client, then use it. If "give" is better, then use that.

Finding better words may seem easy, but it isn't. The difficulty is brought home to you each time an assigning attorney lines out your words (you wish the edits were in blue instead of red) and supplies language of greater precision, making you wonder, "Why didn't I think of that?"

You didn't think of it partly because you didn't challenge yourself. Rarely if ever is the better word so esoteric that it would fall outside your normal vocabulary.

Granted, your principal concerns in writing a brief or memo are theme, content and organization. Only in later drafts do you feel comfortable turning to specific word choice, and by that time, you are pressured to move on to something else.

Fair enough. But know that you make a good impression when you are precise and a lesser impression when you are not. Also know—and this is a piece of gratuitous advice addressed more to your attitude than to your writing skills—assigning attorneys don't want to play the Essay Fairy, as your father and/or mother did for you in high school, when you could set aside a draft at bedtime and find it magically edited the next morning. Though every brief is, theoretically, a team effort, it is also a showcase for individual performance.

Catch yourself if you begin to rationalize that further effort is unnecessary, that the reader will basically get your point, and that time is short. The reader may get your point, but at a cost, the extent of which you'll never know. Find time to put your writing through at least one precision check, asking yourself at every turn, "Have I used the best word for my purpose here?"

Puzzler

Which is better, Version A or Version B?

Version A: The directors were willing to compromise the interests of the corporation in favor of the competing interests of the CEO.

Version B: The directors were willing to subordinate the interests of the corporation to the competing interests of the CEO.

The alliteration in the first sentence (compromise, corporation, competing) is tempting, but the word "compromise" has positive connotations, which is inconsistent with the directors' breach of duty to the corporation. The first six words of Version A cast the directors in a favorable light, albeit briefly: "The directors were willing to compromise."

To avoid sending a mixed message, even momentarily, use the neutrally connoted "subordinate," whose role is quickly given shape by the phrase "the interests of the corporation."

Also, "subordinate the interests of the corporation" is more precise than "compromise the interests of the corporation." "Subordinate" accurately states that something else will be given priority. "Compromise" could mean "weaken" or "make vulnerable"—connotations that are only partially dispelled by the phrase "in favor of."

Skip the Generalities and Go Straight to the Specifics

Don't make the reader wait as you home in on your point

We think first in larger categories, or "sets," and then, usually with imperceptible effort, we focus on smaller categories, or "subsets." For example, we think "interference" and then "interference with prospective economic advantage." We think "operating system" and then "Windows" or "Mac OS X."

Sometimes we reveal this thinking process in our writing, as in the following excerpt from a brief making the argument that even though an applicant for a gaming license may have to forfeit a nonrefundable application fee upon withdrawing its application, the applicant should not also have to contribute to an industry-wide assessment to cover a shortfall in regulatory funds:

> *The constitutional test for the validity of a license fee or assessment is based on the relationship between the services provided and the charge imposed. Specifically, the charge should be proportional to the licensing entity's costs.*

The statement in each sentence is true. The test for the validity of a license fee or assessment is "based on the relationship" between the services and the charge, and such charges should be "proportional to the licensing entity's costs." If an applicant withdraws an application, the licensing agency can provide the applicant no services. If it can provide no services, it should not assess a supplemental fee for services.

Though both statements are true (relationship and proportionality), making both statements is unnecessary. The better approach is to go straight to proportionality, which is your point:

> *The constitutional test for the validity of a license fee or assessment is whether the services provided are proportional to the charge imposed.*

The statement that the test for the constitutionality of a fee is based on a "relationship" represents only the first step of the thinking process. You think first that a relationship exists between services provided and fees charged, and then you think that the relationship should be proportional.

The possible relationships between services and fee can be considered a "set," and the relationship of proportionality can be considered a subset. Only the subset—that fees and assessments should be proportional to services provided—is your point.

Showing how you reason a problem through can be helpful to a reader, but showing the set from which you draw a subset may be a waste of time. Save the reader work and add pace to your writing by going straight to the point.

A Second Example

Possibly drawing on the otherwise sound advice that one should reason from the general to the specific, memo writers sometimes circle before landing, as this writer did when restating an assignment:

> *You asked me to research the potential ramifications of Mr. X's taking bets on the recent presidential election on his application for qualification under the State Gaming Control Act. Specifically, my research focused on the issue of whether Mr. X's activities would be grounds for automatic disqualification under the Act.*

"Potential ramifications" hints at an array of consequences that could result from Mr. X having taken bets on the presidential election, but the only relevant ramification for this writer is Mr. X's being denied a gaming license.

You can see the writer's mind homing in on automatic disqualification as the writer says "my research focused," which means, essentially, "Here is the ramification with which I will deal."

The writer should have skipped the extra step and gone straight to the point:

> *You asked me to research whether Mr. X's taking bets on the recent presidential election is grounds for automatic disqualification under the State Gaming Control Act.*

With few exceptions, the word "specifically"—and its first cousin "in particular"—are indicators that you can eliminate unnecessary words by combining sentences. When you catch yourself using "specifically," consider whether you are gratuitously showing the reader how you developed a thought. Unless your argument will be strengthened by showing how you focused from set to subset, don't recount the entire journey, just the destination.

Puzzler

How would you tighten and sharpen the following sentence?

> *Special protection is afforded under the Sarbanes-Oxley Act to security analysts employed by brokers or dealers who present adverse, negative or otherwise unfavorable research reports that may adversely affect an investment banking relationship.*

The Sarbanes-Oxley Act is intended to increase corporate responsibility. Because the above sentence will be embedded in a discussion of the Act, the phrase "under the Sarbanes-Oxley Act" is likely to be implicit and can probably be dropped.

"Employed by brokers or dealers" can also be dropped because readers will know that securities analysts are so employed. Not only does this deletion save words, but it solves the ambiguity created by the separation of "who" from its antecedent (security analysts). The sentence could refer to analysts who present adverse research reports or to brokers and dealers who do so.

The writer must acknowledge the potential conflict of interest—that the analyst's employer (the broker or dealer) may pressure the analyst for a positive report because the employer does not want to embarrass its investment banking client. This can be handled by a reference to the analyst's "firm."

Finally, the statute may refer to "adverse, negative or otherwise unfavorable research reports," but "adverse" is enough here, and one use of "adverse" is enough as well. If the report is adverse to the client, implicitly it is adverse to the relationship with the client.

The revised version:

Special protection is afforded to security analysts who present research reports adverse to their firm's investment banking clients.

You could trim more and add a little punch by deleting "security" and "research" as implicit and converting "report" to a verb.

Alternate version:

Special protection is afforded to analysts who report adversely on their firm's investment banking clients.

Though Detail Is Usually Helpful, It Can Be Overdone

Include what the reader needs to know and trim the rest

The porridge that Goldilocks ate was neither too hot nor too cold; it was just right. Persuasive writing is like the porridge—it should convey just enough information and not too much. If the information falls short, the reader will be confused. If it exceeds what the reader needs to know, the reader will become impatient. Too little information sends the reader on a quest without a map, and too much information throws obstacles in the reader's path.

Generally, detail is good. It fills out the story, and it helps show the court which way the scales of justice should tip. But details can get in the way. They can retard the pace, and they can create the appearance that you are using detail to obscure the point.

Suppose, for example, that you have to explain to gaming regulators why the compliance committee of a parent company of a casino licensee failed to uncover a mob affiliation of one of the parent company's vendors. The committee is charged with ascertaining that persons with whom the parent company does business have good character, or more accurately, given the practicalities, that they appear to have good character.

Figuring that diligence is the antithesis of negligence, you intend to advise the regulators that the committee conscientiously checked every item in the personal history disclosure form that the vendor submitted to the committee. In the introductory portion of your draft report to the regulators, you write as follows:

> *The Committee followed its usual practice of confirming prior jobs, college attendance and army service, verifying gaming licenses and professional licenses, and sending inquiries to personal references and local police.*

You list all the information confirmed by the committee—prior jobs, college attendance, army service, gaming licenses and professional licenses—because you feel this show of diligence will earn points with the regulators. To make the list seem longer and the diligence greater, you even create two categories of validation—"confirming" and "verifying"—where one would suffice.

Presenting the detail isn't a foolish strategy. Diligence is commendable, and it does tend to disprove negligence, though not in direct proportion. But the regulators' principal concern is why the company missed the mob affiliation. They want you to get to that issue.

They understand that the personal items were checked and showed nothing amiss, but they are thinking, "Fine, fine. You dutifully went through the list, but you let the most important item slip by. The guy was tight with a mob lieutenant. Tell us about that."

You are itching to tell the regulators about your client's assiduousness, but you are better served to pull back, lest you cause the regulators to think you are raising a smoke screen of diligence to hide the absence of a meaningful response on the key issue—why the company overlooked the vendor's relationship with the mobster.

You can acknowledge the diligence without appearing to rely on it by gathering the items under one term: "information in the disclosure form." The revised sentence regarding confirmation would read as follows:

> *The Committee followed its usual practice of confirming information in the disclosure form and sending inquiries to personal references and local police.*

You lose little by bypassing the detail because none of the checks performed by the committee would have revealed that the vendor had a relationship with a mob lieutenant—not prior jobs, college attendance, army service, gaming licenses or professional licenses. Because none of the confirmations should have revealed the mob connection, none of them will excuse missing it.

You may later wish to bring in the specifics of the committee's efforts in mitigation of the offense, but in your opening section, the burning question in the reader's mind is, "Why did you miss this fact?" The details will slow the reader down and may suggest that you are trying to use diligence to mask negligence. By shortening the response, you fall in line with the regulators' thinking, namely, that diligence is fine but isn't an excuse when something important is overlooked.

Additional Examples

Later in the presentation, you plan to tell the regulators that a person named by the vendor as a reference responded favorably on his behalf. You write:

> *The reference who responded, Steven A. __________, of ___________, New Jersey, wrote that Mr. X [the vendor] was "a reputable, responsible citizen."*

Unless the person providing the reference is particularly notable, such as a clergyman, law enforcement official or CEO of a substantial company, omit the person's name and personal data, in this case the place of residence. The extra facts are irrelevant and may create the appearance that you are invoking the false weight of irrelevant detail. For this particular reference, just say:

> *The reference who responded wrote that Mr. X was "a reputable, responsible citizen."*

Similarly, when you point out that the vendor registered his company with the United States Department of Justice as a seller of coin-operated gaming machines, which is yet another reason why he did not appear to be a mob affiliate, you do not have to say he did so "in a letter to the United States Department of Justice, Organized Crime and Racketeering Section, Criminal Division, Attention: Mr. So-and-So."

This official-sounding language may be impressive in another context, but here, anything beyond "United States Department of Justice" is unnecessary and is subject to the same concerns as above. At a minimum, it would slow the reader down, and at worst, it could create the suspicion that you were using detail to obfuscate.

In the end, the strategy is the same whether you have a good explanation for the company's missing the mob connection or not. If you have a good explanation, you don't want to divert attention from it. If you lack a good explanation, you don't want to compromise the necessary *mea culpa* by suggesting, in essence, "It wasn't really our fault," in other words, that your client had no *culpa*. If you detail how careful the committee was, make sure the reader knows that the diligence goes to mitigation, not to exculpation.

Puzzler

How would you fix the following sentence?

The State Penal Code prohibits, with the intent to further gambling, knowingly owning, manufacturing, transferring, or possession of any gambling device.

Not only is the phrase "With the intent to further gambling" interruptive, but it suggests that the intent of the Penal Code is to further gambling. Move it to the end of the sentence. Change "possession of" to "possessing" to achieve parallel construction.

I drop the comma before the "and" or the "or" at the end of a series unless clarity requires it.

The revised version:

The State Penal Code prohibits knowingly owning, manufacturing, transferring or possessing any gambling device with the intent to further gambling.

Maximize Impact by Making One Point at a Time

In writing, as in art and music, less is sometimes more

Persuasive writing achieves maximum impact by concentrating on one point at a time. That's how people are persuaded—one point at a time. Sometimes writers lose sight of this and try to make two points at a time, perhaps out of fear of leaving a second issue unaddressed, even for a moment.

Consider the circumstance of a liability insurer having refused to accept the defense of an action against its insured (the "underlying action"), forcing the insured to retain its own defense counsel. When the underlying action ends, the insured retains you to sue the insurance company to recover the cost of the defense.

A liability insurer's duty to defend is determined by comparing the face of the complaint to the policy terms. If the complaint alleges a claim covered by the policy, then the insurer has a duty to defend.

You move for partial summary judgment to establish the duty to defend. The insurer argues in response not only that the complaint and the policy terms don't match, but also that the fees charged by the insured's defense counsel were excessive. The latter argument is irrelevant, and you believe it to be untrue.

In your draft reply brief, you try to squeeze into one sentence that the amount of the defense costs is irrelevant on a motion to establish the duty to defend and that the fees weren't excessive because the underlying action was complex and involved millions of dollars:

> *The issue whether the counsel fees incurred by XYZ Corp. to defend this complex litigation demanding millions of dollars of damages are reasonable is not presently before the court.*

The portion of the sentence referring to the amount of the defense costs ("this complex litigation demanding millions of dollars in damages") responds to the contention that defense costs were excessive. If the underlying action was complex and worth millions of dollars, then defense costs had to be substantial.

As a matter of style, the phrase is interruptive; it forces the reader to wait a long time between subject ("issue") and verb ("is not"). More significantly, you are playing into the insurer's strategy by trying to kill two birds with one stone.

The insurer is challenging the amount of the defense costs for two reasons: to gain sympathy—always helpful in the good guy/bad guy game of litigation—and to pick a fight on a fact issue that can't be resolved by summary judgment. The duty to defend can be determined merely by comparing complaint and policy terms and is therefore a good candidate for summary judgment, but a dispute over the reasonableness of lawyers' fees would probably involve material issues of fact and would therefore be inappropriate for summary judgment.

The insurer doesn't need to win the irrelevant argument, that is, to prove that the defense costs were excessive. The insurer merely needs to make the argument appear relevant. Because it involves a fact issue, it is poison for summary judgment. If you blend a response to the merits of the insurer's irrelevant argument into your point that the argument is irrelevant, you make the irrelevant argument appear relevant.

To be sure, you are reluctant to allow the contention of excessive fees to go unanswered, lest the court think you concede the point. Once the duty to defend is established, you will have to prove the reasonableness of the defense costs.

This instinct is good, but don't let it divert you from your point, which is that the amount of the defense costs is irrelevant to the duty to defend. After you make that point, you can add, separately, that you disagree with the insurer's contention that the fees were excessive but refuse to argue the point prematurely. This gives you a chance to reiterate that the amount of the defense costs is irrelevant on a motion to determine the duty to defend.

Some writers might add text or drop a footnote addressing the merits of the defense costs, arguing, for example, that the fees were substantial because the litigation was complex, requiring dozens of depositions and significant motion practice.

Whether to address the merits of the defense cost issue is a judgment call, determined in part by your client's wish to leave no argument unanswered and in part by your sense of whether the insurer has built sympathy with the excessive fees argument. Courts aren't supposed to be moved by irrelevant white-hat/black-hat arguments, but sometimes they can't help themselves.

If the client wants you to respond—and clients usually do—you may have to address the issue. If you are concerned about your client's image with the court, you will want to neutralize the venom.

At this juncture, the court probably doesn't care whether the defense costs were reasonable. The issue is not ripe because neither side has presented proofs on it. If you feel you have to address the issue, the court won't hold it against you. The court once had clients of its own.

Puzzler

How would you tighten and sharpen the following sentence?

Appellate litigants should be aware of their recourse to a motion to the appellate court for a limited remand to the trial court while the appeal is pending where consideration of a particular issue by the trial court will enable full resolution of the controversy by the appellate court.

The posture of the case is implicit in the words "Appellate" and "remand," permitting you to delete "to the appellate court" and "to the trial court." The phrase "should be aware of their recourse to" can be shortened to "can move for [a limited remand]" or "can seek [a limited remand]."

I prefer "can move for" to the shorter "can seek" because it conveys more information. Litigants who do not normally practice in the appellate court might hesitate to use motion practice there.

Shorten "by the trial court" to "below" and improve the passive "will enable full resolution of the controversy by the appellate court" to the more active "will help the appellate court resolve the controversy fully." Place "fully" in the position of emphasis at the end of the sentence because it is the essence of your point.

Delete "while the appeal is pending" as implicit and delete "particular [issue]" as unnecessary. For extra credit, change "where consideration of an issue below will help" to "on the ground that consideration of an issue below will help" because one does not have to prove what will happen on remand to move for, or be granted, the remand.

The revised version:

> *Appellate litigants can move for a limited remand on the ground that consideration of an issue below will help the appellate court resolve the controversy fully.*

Tighten Your Work by Omission and Compression

Eliminate thoughts you don't need and streamline the ones you do

To tighten and sharpen prose, omit what is implicit, duplicative, or irrelevant and compress the rest. Such trimming is more a craft than an art, and it can be learned.

Consider the following 54-word excerpt from a brief:

> *The court denied the plaintiff's motion for sanctions for spoliation in the form of a negative inference. The court distinguished the present facts from those in Smith v. Jones, noting that the e-mail was destroyed by a person who was not a party to the case and who was not instructed to delete the e-mail.*

Because both sentences begin with "The court," you might look to combine them. But this won't work yet. The sentences are too heavy.

The first sentence articulates five concepts: denial, motion, sanction, spoliation and negative inference:

> *The court* ***denied*** *the plaintiff's* ***motion*** *for* ***sanctions*** *for* ***spoliation*** *in the form of a* ***negative inference****.*

You don't need to articulate all five concepts. You can eliminate "motion" and "spoliation" because motion is implicit in the denial, and spoliation is implicit in the destruction of an e-mail. You can also eliminate "sanction" because it is the set within which "negative inference" is a subset. Just say the court "declined to grant a negative inference." Everything else is understood. Though "declined to grant" is longer than "denied," it is tighter than "denied plaintiff's motion for" because it presents only one concept (denial) rather than two (denial and motion).

"The court distinguished the present facts from those in *Smith v. Jones*" can be shortened to "The court distinguished *Smith v. Jones*." Facts are almost always what is distinguished. True, you are reversing which case was compared to which, but they are two sides of the same equation.

The noncommittal "noting" is a frequent dodge. It allows the writer to hint at a position rather than taking one. Did the court distinguish *Smith v. Jones* on the basis of the cited facts or not?

Generally, you should draw the causal connection where the reader expects it. Here, you should acknowledge the link between the court's observation and the court's conclusion with a strong connector such as "because" or "on the ground that"; otherwise, you manifest weakness. If you don't affirm the obvious tie, a reader may wonder why you are waffling.

If you are genuinely unsure why a court distinguished a case, you can use "apparently because." If the causal connection is likely but not certain, you can be assertive with "evidently because."

Thus far, we have reduced 54 words to 37 and made the passage more direct:

> *The court declined to grant a negative inference. It distinguished Smith v. Jones because the e-mail was destroyed by a person who was not a party to the case and who was not instructed to delete the e-mail.*

I would begin the second sentence with "It" because repetition of "The court" sounds grade-schoolish.

You still have plenty of stone to chip away. In the phrase "a person who is not a party to the case," person and party are essentially the same, and "to the case" is implicit. Because "party" duplicates both "person" and "to the case," you can drop both in favor of "nonparty" ("the e-mail was destroyed by a nonparty").

You can also substitute "told" for "instructed," which is longer and has unnecessary academic connotations, and you can use a pronoun—one of the great compressors—in place of "the e-mail." We are now down to 27 words, half the original amount:

> *The court declined to grant a negative inference. It distinguished Smith v. Jones because the e-mail was destroyed by a nonparty who was not told to delete it.*

At this point, you have made significant progress. The only segment left to prune is the concluding dependent clause ("who was not told to delete it"). Because the thought is important, you cannot discard it. Can you compress it?

An adverb describing how the e-mail was destroyed could suggest lack of control by the defendant. I considered "independently," "gratuitously" and "inadvertently," but none fit. Then I considered and chose "innocently" because the nonparty's innocence means the defendant did not tell the nonparty what to do.

This change reduced the passage to 21 words:

> *The court declined to grant a negative inference. It distinguished Smith v. Jones because the e-mail was innocently destroyed by a nonparty.*

This is pretty good. The second sentence goes straight to the "because" (if you can't handle the "because," you can't handle the truth). It encapsulates the core fact in five words ("innocently destroyed by a nonparty"), and it ends with a fact you wish to emphasize (nonparty). To reach this point, you merely had to trim. The pieces were already in place.

Whether to create one sentence is a judgment call. You could change "The court declined" to "Declining," converting the first sentence from an independent clause to a dependent clause:

> *Declining to grant a negative inference, the court distinguished Smith v. Jones because the e-mail was innocently destroyed by a nonparty.*

This saves a word, but I prefer the two-sentence version because the stand-alone first sentence emphasizes the court's ruling.

In the alternative, you could subordinate the second sentence to the first:

The court declined to grant a negative inference, distinguishing Smith v. Jones because the e-mail was innocently destroyed by a nonparty.

Of the two subordination options, I prefer the latter. It emphasizes the court's ruling, albeit with a less staccato pace than the two-sentence version.

Trimming such as the foregoing achieves brevity. Paradoxically, it may also reveal opportunities to add words to good effect. Here, for example, I would add a description of the destroyed evidence in *Smith v. Jones* to contrast the cases and to clarify which case involved the e-mail that was innocently destroyed:

The court distinguished Smith v. Jones because the e-mail there was intentionally destroyed by an employee, whereas the e-mail here was innocently destroyed by a nonparty.

Trimming and augmentation work in synergy. You trim excess words to achieve clarity and emphasis, and you add compelling words to the same end. Sometimes you add and then trim, and sometimes you trim and then add. All roads lead to Rome.

Puzzler

How would you tighten and sharpen the following sentence?

This case addresses the issue of whether the notes would be admissible as they were prepared in anticipation of litigation.

Drop "the issue" as implicit. Change "as" to "because" because as is substandard in a causative role, and change "admissible" to "inadmissible" so the potential status of the notes (inadmissible) and the reason for the status (prepared in anticipation of litigation) are consistent.

The revised version:

This case addresses whether the notes would be inadmissible because they were prepared in anticipation of litigation.

Alternate version:

This case addresses whether notes prepared in anticipation of litigation are inadmissible.

Precision Brings Your Idea to a "Point"

Save the reader the trouble of sorting through multiple meanings

Except in the rare instance where you wish to avoid an issue rather than confront it, be precise. Precision narrows your focus; it helps you home in, which is necessary if you wish to arrive at, and thus make, a "point."

Imprecision, in contrast, generates ambiguity, which burdens and may confuse the reader. If the burden or the confusion becomes too great, the reader may lose confidence in the story and in you.

Suppose you represent a company that bought a data processing business, including software. The company contends that it bought not only the "applications," such as spreadsheet programs, but the source code as well (proprietary code written in letters, numbers and symbols). With source code, one can modify an application. The seller contends that the contract price was far too low for source code to have been included in the sale and that the buyer didn't need the source code anyway because the seller would continue to service the system.

You rely on a clause in the contract stating that the transferred assets included "computer programs," a term that may be broad enough to encompass source code as well as applications. Which sentence is better for your client ABC Co., Version A or Version B?

Version A:

The contract for the sale of XYZ Corp's. data processing system to ABC Co. covered "computer programs."

Version B:

Under the contract for the sale of XYZ Corp's. data processing system to ABC Co., the assets sold included "computer programs."

Version B is better because it more strongly suggests that source code was sold. The reference to "assets sold" reinforces the idea of a transfer, and the word "included" brings computer programs within the set "assets sold."

In Version A, "covered 'computer programs'" could mean that computer programs were sold or merely that computer programs were discussed. The reader may figure you mean the former, but that's the problem—"may" and "figure." Figuring requires work and does not ensure that the reader will draw the conclusion you intend.

In wordsmithing, I tend to select the general before the specific. I think "the contract covered" before I think "the assets sold included." In other words, I think of the set before the subset. To improve precision, I examine a concept (a set) until I find a subset helpful to my argument, and then I look for an even better subset.

Here, the intent is to reinforce the likely inclination of the reader to agree that source code was sold because "computer programs" were sold. By asserting that "assets sold included 'computer programs,'" the writer dares the reader to deny that source code is a "computer program" and lays the groundwork for invoking the doctrine that contracts should be given their plain meaning.

A Second Example

Contracts are about risk. If the parties correctly evaluate the risks, they will probably make money. If they are wrong, they may lose money. The strength of our economic system is in that risk. Through it, the parties extend themselves and grow. As they grow, so grows the economy.

Generally, the law does not insulate contracting parties from risk. But the "frustration of purpose" doctrine may excuse performance where contracting parties did not anticipate, and thus did not provide for the consequences of, an extraordinarily destructive event. The doctrine provides that in fairness, neither side should bear the consequences where neither side knew or should have known of the risk.

Which of the following versions of a statement regarding the frustration of purpose doctrine is better for the party that wishes to invoke the doctrine?

Version A:

Under the frustration of purpose doctrine, a condition is implied into the contract to account for something the parties overlooked.

Version B:

Under the frustration of purpose doctrine, a condition is implied into the contract to account for a risk the parties did not allocate.

Both statements are true. "Something the parties overlooked" and "a risk the parties did not allocate" both address foreseeability, which is an element of the frustration of purpose doctrine. But "something overlooked" is broader than "a risk the parties did not allocate" because risk is only one item (one subset) that can be overlooked. "A risk the parties did not allocate" is more precise.

"Overlooked" has bad connotations. It suggests that something visible was missed. Courts won't excuse contract performance just because a party overlooked something. Overlooking is a moral failing for which a person deserves to suffer the consequences.

On the other hand, if both parties failed to account for a significant risk, then arguably the court should not burden one party with the entire loss. If a risk was not foreseeable, neither party can be faulted for failing to account for it.

In Sum

Writers sometimes rationalize that attention to precision is unnecessary because the reader will get the point from the broad strokes. Sometimes, they are right, especially if they have done a good job theming and organizing their piece.

Nevertheless, because your job is to maximize your chances of victory, you should put your writing through at least one precision revision. Subject every word to the question, "Is this the most precise word possible?"

In a sense, recommending that you begin with one precision revision is like recommending that a healthy person begin an exercise program with one pushup. Nevertheless, you have to start somewhere. If you see progress, maybe you will make precision a habit.

Puzzler

How would you tighten and sharpen the following sentence?

The rule accepted by the overwhelming majority of courts is that appeal does not deprive the trial court of jurisdiction as to matters collateral to the issues on appeal.

Favor the active and the affirmative over the reactive and the passive. Replace "The rule accepted by the overwhelming majority of courts is" with "The overwhelming majority of courts hold." The active phrase "courts hold" is more forceful than "The rule . . . is."

To emphasize the continuing power of trial courts over matters collateral to an appeal, state affirmatively that trial courts "retain" jurisdiction rather than that the appeal "does not deprive" them of it. For the same reason—to establish power and control—say that the courts retain jurisdiction "over" rather than "as to" such matters.

"Issues" can be deleted because their presence is implicit.

The revised version:

The overwhelming majority of courts hold that trial courts retain jurisdiction over matters collateral to an appeal.

Skip the Unnecessary Tack-On Explanation

Stating the obvious slows the pace

Developing a thought is good, but lawyers sometimes overdo it by tacking an explanation to the end of a sentence that has already made its point. Consider the following statement regarding the need to update document retention programs:

> *A company's document retention program should be reviewed regularly and should be updated to reflect changes in the law and changes in the company's business that may require adding or deleting document retention requirements.*

The point of the sentence is that document retention programs should be regularly reviewed and revised ("updated") in light of changes in the law and changes in the company's business. The concluding clause—"that may require adding or deleting document retention requirements"—is unnecessary because revision of a document retention program implicitly involves adding or deleting document retention requirements. That is what "updated" means.

Writers sometimes extend a sentence unnecessarily because they sense they are making a point, and they figure, incorrectly, that the longer they keep the sentence going, the more of a point they are making.

Additional Examples

The author of the following sentence did not have to state that on remand, a hearing must be held by the trial court:

> *For the foregoing reasons, the Appellate Division should deny the motion for reconsideration and not further delay the remand hearing which must be held by the trial court.*

Of course the remand hearing must be held by the trial court. That's where jurisdiction resides on remand. The writer may have been thinking something like, "Please hurry up and deny this motion for reconsideration so the trial court can get down to business." But the writer couldn't say it, and fortunately, the tack-on clause did not convey it.

(A grammatical note: Putting aside the redundancy issue, the concluding clause should have read "that must be held by the trial court" rather than "which must be held by the trial court.")

If the reader is likely to draw a logical inference, you can leave a thought implied. In the following sentence (as in the above examples), the writer could have left out the concluding phrase because the thought is implicit.

> *The term "reasonable effort" is not defined in the contract and must therefore be interpreted.*

If a contract doesn't define an important term, then the term has to be given definition by reference to custom in the industry, terms in the contract, the conduct of the parties, and other indicia of the parties' intent. In other words, the term has to be interpreted. Because lawyers know that, you don't have to say it. Drop the phrase "and must therefore be interpreted" and move on to the method of interpretation as follows:

The term "reasonable efforts" is not defined in the contract. Its meaning can be found in the custom in the industry and in the conduct of the parties.

Where motive is obvious, you need not state it. Consider the following:

Parties may withhold privileged or confidential information if they identify it, but they are prohibited from destroying, altering or hiding information in an attempt to conceal potentially damaging evidence.

Because readers know that parties who destroy, alter or hide information are probably attempting to conceal potentially damaging evidence, the above sentence should end with "hiding information." The tack-on phrase "in an attempt to conceal potentially damaging evidence" is unnecessary.

The tack-on phrase should be dropped for the additional reason that it limits the idea. Destroying or altering information is prohibited whether the purpose is to conceal or not ("hiding" presumes intent to conceal). Even inadvertent destruction or alteration is likely to be prohibited.

You can sense what the writer had in mind. Attempting to destroy, alter, or otherwise conceal potentially damaging evidence manifests an ill motive, which gives the opposing party a "black hat." That is, the party appears to have acted in a morally reprehensible manner. The writer sought to make sure the reader knew the opposing party wore a black hat. "Destroying, altering or hiding" was enough to convey that.

In Sum

The instinct to explain is good. You are better off over-explaining than leaving the reader uncertain. But stating the obvious may add length without adding meaning. Tack-on explanations slow the pace, and they may offend readers because articulation of the obvious suggests that the reader isn't sharp enough to draw an obvious conclusion without assistance.

Puzzler

How would you tighten and sharpen the following sentence?

There are four statements made by defendant to the press which are the basis for this defamation action.

"There are" is almost always unnecessary. Deleting it allows you to drop "which" as well.

"Which" is not only unnecessary but confusing. Initially, it seems to refer to "the press" (the press which) rather than to the four statements. The reader expects to see "the press which is . . . " rather than "the press which are," perhaps with a comma before which ("the press, which is . . . ").

But the reader is immediately redirected by the verb "are" and is momentarily confused by the apparent nonagreement of singular subject (press) and plural verb (are). Eventually, the reader will realize that "are" goes with "statements" and may realize that "which"—if such a word had to be there at all—should have been "that."

"Made" is unnecessary because it is understood, and so is "by defendant" because the defendant always makes the statements that result in a defamation action. This solves the problem of whether to say "by defendant to the press" or "to the press by defendant."

Finally, "are the basis for" can be shortened and converted to active voice as "underlie" or "led to."

The revised version:

Four statements to the press underlie [led to] this defamation action.

Alternate version:

This defamation action is based on four statements to the press.

Do Not Make a Thought Long Just Because It Is Good

Unnecessary elaboration can produce a net loss rather than a net gain

Good ideas can be hard to come by, so when we have a decent point, we sometimes drone on, repeating ourselves in the mistaken view that more is better, that if we keep railing against the other side's argument, our position will appear stronger, and the reason for our righteous indignation will be confirmed. Sometimes we elaborate because we are afraid we have nothing else to say.

Suppose your client, the defendant XYZ Corp., prevailed in a jury trial against claims for fraud and breach of contract. Before the court sent the case to the jury, you asked the judge to require separate verdicts on each count, but plaintiff ABC Co. demanded—and the court agreed—that the jury should render a single general verdict, either for or against recovery. To plaintiff's chagrin, the jury found "no cause."

After the verdict, plaintiff interviewed jurors and concluded that they were confused by the court's instructions, thinking they couldn't find fraud unless they also found breach of contract. Apparently, several jurors thought they had to find for plaintiff on both causes of action to render a general verdict in plaintiff's favor.

Your associate drafts a brief in opposition to the motion for a new trial and makes two points—that the jury instructions were not confusing (which is not discussed here) and, by way of the following example, that plaintiff got what it deserved by insisting on a single general verdict:

> *Plaintiff ABC Co. sought an undifferentiated general verdict despite defendant XYZ Corp.'s objection. XYZ Corp. requested that the jury be asked to render a verdict on each count, but ABC Co. convinced the court that a single general verdict would be more appropriate. ABC Co. must now be compelled to accept the consequences of having prevailed on that issue. Dissatisfied with the result, plaintiff now seeks to discredit the very process it proposed.*

This is a good thought. Plaintiff demanded a single general verdict, prevailed over objection, and should be stuck with the result. But the writer elaborates unnecessarily.

The writer initially considered using a metaphor, either that the plaintiff "made its bed and must sleep in it" or that plaintiff was "hoist on its own petard." The former seemed too casual, and the latter seemed too esoteric, especially because the writer didn't know what a petard is. So the writer chose length, as if elongating the thought would drive the point home.

Let's see what length added. The first sentence says the plaintiff ABC Co. sought a unitary general verdict rather than separate general verdicts for each count "despite" defendant XYZ Corp.'s objection. "Despite" isn't the right word—

it should have been "over"—but we get the point: that plaintiff has no basis for objecting to the form of verdict it requested other than being unhappy with the result, which isn't an acceptable basis.

The second sentence says exactly the same thing, adding only that the court ruled for the plaintiff. This reiteration is unnecessary as an aid to comprehension because the thought is simple. It describes a straightforward procedural request with which the reader is likely to be familiar.

Reiteration does create emphasis, but that rhetorical gain has to be balanced against other consequences. For example, you have to factor in the potential insult to the reader's intelligence from spelling out what an ordinary reader should be able to grasp. Or, the reader may suspect you are elongating the thought to create an appearance of weight that the substance won't sustain.

You also have to consider the impact on pace. When more words cover the same distance, the story slows. To use a vehicular metaphor, one adds strong words and ideas to gain "traction" and culls duplicative words and ideas to reduce "friction."

The last sentence in the sample paragraph has an additional problem. "Dissatisfied with the result" is *ad hominem*, directed to the person rather than to the point. It merely states the obvious, and it identifies the writer with advocates who make personal attacks because they lack a basis on which to attack the issues.

The sample paragraph has the feel of a writer extruding a story, as casual speakers do, extending it to hold the floor. Casual listeners don't mind the repetition, but judicial readers do.

Judicial readers prefer compression. If elaboration will drive a point home or help the reader understand, fine. But otherwise, compress. Get to the point and save the reader time.

Following that advice, we might rewrite the above paragraph as follows:

Plaintiff ABC Co. sought a general verdict, prevailed over objection, and must accept the consequences.

The idea is now conveyed in 15 words rather than 73. The good news is that brevity has been served. The bad news for the writer is that the illusion of power that may have attended the sheer weight of words is now dissolved. Realizing that one has less to say than anticipated can be unsettling. It is one reason writers don't trim as much as they should.

Puzzler

How would you tighten and sharpen the following sentence?

The destruction of electronic data or the data's inadvertent loss after a litigant is on notice of a potential dispute can subject the litigant to very significant sanctions or even an adverse instruction to a jury that may seriously compromise the likelihood of success in an otherwise meritorious action.

Say "intentional" destruction to contrast it with inadvertent loss and to create parallel adjectives and nouns (intentional destruction and inadvertent loss). Drop "The" at the beginning because it is implicit. Add "even" in front of inadvertent loss to indicate that losing electronic data is serious even if inadvertent. Use "and" rather than "or" between intentional destruction and inadvertent loss because, together with "even," it builds.

The phrase "after receiving notice" would be an improvement because it is shorter than "after a litigant is on notice," but you don't need "receiving." "After notice" implies receipt. Compress "instruction to a jury" to "jury instruction." This not only tightens the phrasing, but it eliminates the gratuitously ambiguous combination, "a jury that may seriously compromise."

Don't use "or" between "very significant sanctions" and "adverse jury instruction" because an adverse jury instruction is included in the set called "significant sanctions," not coordinate to it. Use "including" instead of "or" and set it off with dashes rather than commas to highlight the seriousness of the sanction.

Delete "the likelihood of success in" as implicit. The word "compromise" conveys the concept. Also, you don't need both "significant" and "seriously." Minimize your editorials.

In what appears to be a close call but isn't, I would use "that" rather than "which" after the second dash. The dashes and the material between them create a pause, like a comma, suggesting that "which" might work, but the operative phrase is "sanctions . . . that may seriously compromise." Because not all sanctions seriously compromise, the clause is restrictive and takes "that" rather than "which."

Keep the phrase "otherwise meritorious." It highlights the harshness of the sanctions.

The revised version:

> *Intentional destruction and even inadvertent loss of electronic data after notice of a potential dispute can subject a litigant to sanctions—including an adverse jury instruction—that may seriously compromise an otherwise meritorious action.*

Unpack Your Generalizations for Greater Effect

Where possible, create images for the reader to visualize

As writers, we tend to forget that the reader isn't as familiar with the details of our case as we are. We are so intimate with the facts and the relationships among them that our recollection of fact patterns is easily triggered, even by superficial references.

Not so for the reader, who hasn't been working the case. Images of the litigants and their conduct don't take shape as readily in the reader's mind. Conceptual phrases that can remind the writer of entire gestalts may do nothing for the reader.

Suppose you represent a corporation in a proxy fight with dissident shareholders over the composition of the board of directors. Management and challengers both seek written authorization (proxies) to vote shares at the shareholders' meeting. The two sides compete for the right to stand in the place of (as proxies for) the shareholders.

Assume the dissidents have made false statements about the qualifications of the current directors in a draft "proxy statement" (position paper) filed with the Securities and Exchange Commission (SEC). You bring an action to compel the dissidents to correct their draft proxy statement, contending that the dissidents have to do more than just delete the offending material. They have to include a *mea culpa*, an acknowledgement that assertions in the draft proxy statement were false.

Your rationale is that draft proxy materials filed with the SEC are public documents, available on the Internet through EDGAR and scrutinized by shareholders, especially the large institutions. Because a bad first impression is difficult to overcome, the dissidents should not only remove but acknowledge earlier falsehoods.

You write the following in a brief supporting your request for an order compelling the dissidents to correct their proxy materials and include a *mea culpa*:

Proxy solicitation begins well before the definitive proxy statement is issued.

You argue that proxy solicitation begins not with the definitive proxy statement—the version mailed to shareholders—but much earlier, with the first draft of the proxy statement. You figure that you make your point about the need for *mea culpas* by establishing that proxy solicitation begins with the initial draft. If the court accepts that proposition, you believe, then the court will realize that corrective disclosure must include an acknowledgement of falsity.

Unfortunately, one conclusion does not compel the other. That proxy solicitation begins with the draft proxy statement does not automatically require *mea culpas*. You have to make the court want to order a *mea culpa*. To do that, you need to trigger images in the court's mind.

The phrase "proxy solicitation" is difficult to visualize. Give it shape as follows:

> ***The stream of information disseminated to shareholders to solicit their proxies*** *begins well before the definitive proxy statement is issued.*

The added detail ("the stream of information disseminated to shareholders to solicit their proxies") is, in a sense, just another way of saying "proxy solicitation," but it creates an image of dissidents soliciting shareholder votes. The metaphorical word "stream" connotes both volume and flow, and flow connotes a source as well as a destination. The source is the draft proxy statement.

The phrase "disseminated to shareholders" is also helpful. It indicates that draft proxy materials are intentionally being made available to shareholders by way of the Internet to convince them how to vote. Together, "stream of information" and "disseminated to shareholders" paint a picture of dissidents intentionally placing false information in publicly available draft proxy materials to deceive shareholders. This mini-story is more likely to move the court than is the conceptual phrase "proxy solicitation."

Note: If the foregoing were a Puzzler, I would not tell you to delete "the stream of information disseminated to shareholders" even though it is implicit in the term "proxy solicitation." Useful words should be stripped only when the purpose they serve isn't worth the time needed to read them.

A Second Example

The tactic of fleshing out a generalization applies to another sentence from the same brief:

> *Merely removing the offending language from a proxy statement does not correct the problem.*

"Correct the problem" is the underperforming generalization. It doesn't say what the problem is.

The problem is the potentially indelible misimpression created by the false statements in the draft proxy statement. Such misimpressions don't disappear magically merely because they are false. They have to be neutralized. To make that point, begin as follows:

> *Merely removing the offending language from a draft proxy statement does not* ***neutralize false impressions created by the misstatements.***

By going deeper than the phrase "correct the problem," you remind the reader that false statements, even in draft documents, create false impressions that don't disappear automatically. They have to be "neutralized," meaning that the person who has formed the false impression may not change it until the person receives new information, and the new information may not override the old unless the reader is told that the earlier information was false. All this is implicit in the word "neutralize," a powerful verb in this context because the poison of the early falsehoods must be neutralized by later truths.

A Third Example

Suppose you represent an investor suing a person who claimed to have $50 million in certificates of deposit to serve as security for your client's investment in a construction project. The project falls through; the certificates of deposit turn out not to exist; and your client's investment is lost. A sentence in your motion brief reads as follows:

> *Mr. Big was presented as a man of means whose certificates of deposit totaling $50 million would serve as collateral for the proposed project.*

You don't say what you mean by the certificates of deposit serving as collateral "for" the proposed project, namely, that the certificates would comfort investors by ensuring that the project would not fail. You can improve the sentence by putting a human face on the purpose of the collateral:

> *Smith was presented as a man of means whose certificates of deposit totaling $50 million would serve as collateral* ***to assure investors they could safely participate*** *in the proposed project.*

The purpose of proffering collateral was to comfort investors, inducing them to invest. Showing the human side—the investors' concerns—fleshes out the story and gains sympathy.

Usually, edits that unpack generalizations are made late in the process, if at all, because the writer has been focusing on theme, factual and legal support, organization and flow. Generalizations can remain unedited through several reviews as you continue to imagine, but fail to articulate, the embedded facts.

Puzzler

How would you improve the following sentence?

> *The reports were factual rather than speculative.*

To emphasize "factual," insert a comma as an interim stop and replace "rather than" with "not."

The revised version:

> *The reports were factual, not speculative.*

Where Else Would a Court Rule But "In Its Opinion"?

In stating the obvious, you may be sidestepping the point

One of the comedy channels on satellite radio features a fellow who mocks people for asking questions that he considers stupid because the answer is so obvious, for example, a person who sees you jacking up your car to remove a deflated tire and asks, "Got a flat?" The question is well-intentioned, even neighborly, but it irritates.

Perhaps I am too quick to draw analogies (a habit developed through years of comparing and contrasting sets of facts), but I see a similarity between that kind of unnecessary question and the unnecessary warm-up phrase, "In its opinion, the court held (ruled or reasoned) . . ." The phrase "In its opinion" is unnecessary because the only place a court would hold (rule or reason) is, almost by definition, in its opinion.

A court might rule from the bench, as opposed to "in its opinion," but the context would make that clear without the phrase "in its opinion." For reported opinions, where no bench is involved, no such confusion is possible.

A closely related transition, just as unnecessary, is an expression frequently used to introduce a court's rationale: "In reaching its decision, the court reasoned . . ." The phrase states the obvious.

Why else would a court engage in reasoning other than to reach a decision? And when else would the court do this reasoning—after reaching its decision? We hope not. Implicitly, a court goes through a reasoning process in reaching a decision. Therefore, the phrase "in reaching its decision" is superfluous.

That phrase appeared in a memo addressing whether a municipality's decision to transfer a police officer from detective work to patrol duty was arbitrable:

> *The New Jersey Public Employment Relations Commission (PERC) held that the decision to transfer or reassign a police officer is not arbitrable.* ***In reaching this decision,*** *the Commission noted that no statute or regulation preempts negotiations. The Commission focused on whether the arbitration would place limitations on the policy-making powers of the employer. [Emphasis added.]*

In the above example, "In reaching this decision" purports to be helpful because it repeats the word "decision" from the prior sentence and thus links the sentences, superficially creating a sense of flow. The connecting phrase lulls the reader into thinking that the logical chain is intact.

But the second sentence does not flow logically from the first. The nonarbitrability of a decision to transfer a police officer has no apparent connection to the phrase "no statute or regulation preempts negotiations." In other words, you can't tell from the memo what the preemption of negotiations by statute or regulation has to do with nonarbitrability. A better segue after "arbitrable" would be something like, "PERC's rationale for this holding was that . . . "

Not only is the phrase "In reaching this decision" unnecessary, but it may signal deeper trouble. The phrase often precedes a tedious recitation of the court's reasoning process, which means at best that the reader will have to wait for the point and at worst that the reader will get lost in a *non sequitur*, as in the example here.

This writer of this memo knew that a decision to transfer a police officer within the department is considered nonarbitrable because arbitration of such decisions would interfere with the governmental prerogative. But the writer didn't say that clearly or directly. Using the phrase "In reaching this decision" as an introduction, the writer provided, out of context and without warning, a disembodied slice of the series of questions that PERC must answer in determining if a matter is arbitrable:

- Does a statute or regulation determine if an item is eligible for negotiation between union and municipality and thus eligible for the arbitration of grievances?
- If not, does the item intimately and directly affect the work and welfare of the employees and not significantly interfere with the exercise of express management prerogatives?
- If so, the item is mandatorily negotiable, and grievances regarding the negotiated item are arbitrable.

In the example above, the memo writer mentioned the first item in this reasoning process—preemption by statute or regulation—but provided no context for it, leaving the reader at sea. The memo writer said only that PERC "noted" the absence of preemption, which is true, but as far as the reader can tell, the idea connects to nothing.

Weak transitions like "in reaching its decision" or "in its opinion" often precede a recitation of what a court noted rather than what the court held and why. Sometimes, the weak transition precedes a *non sequitur*—an interval of illogic. In short, "In reaching its decision" is more than just four unnecessary words. It's a signal that the writer isn't getting to the point and may not understand the point.

Lawyers often use "In its opinion" and "In reaching its decision" to avoid the challenge of drafting an effective transition. If you are tempted to begin a sentence this way, ask yourself what task you are avoiding. It may be the task of formulating a helpful transition.

A Related Offense

The phrase "In its brief, plaintiff argues . . . " is a similar space holder. The brief is the only place plaintiff would argue. Even if the courts in your state permit argument in affidavits, the context would make clear which document embodied plaintiff's argument—the brief or the affidavit. Thus, the phrase "In its brief" has nothing but mild rhythmic value. Don't use it.

Puzzler

How would you shorten the following point heading?

FACT ISSUES REGARDING THE AMOUNT OF DAMAGES ALLEGEDLY OWED TO ABC CORP BY THE DEFENDANTS DO NOT PRECLUDE THE GRANT OF SUMMARY JUDGMENT AS TO THE LIABILITY OF THE DEFENDANTS ON THE CLAIM FOR TORTIOUS INTERFERENCE

You have one point—that fact issues regarding damages do not prevent the court from resolving liability issues as a matter of law. Let's see why you can say it pretty much that way.

The following phrases can be dropped as implicit:

- "The amount of" (The amount of damages doesn't matter; we assume fact issues on damages.)
- "Owed to ABC CORP" (To whom besides plaintiff ABC CORP would damages be owed?)
  Note: If you use "owed," you need "allegedly" to defuse the phrase "damages owed" because smoke (damages owed) suggests fire (liability). If you drop "owed," you don't need "alleged."
- "By the defendants" (By whom else would damages be owed?)
- "The grant of" (Does summary judgment ever occur without its being granted?)
- "Of the defendants" (Who else would be liable?)
- "On the claim for tortious interference" (The court knows what claim is the subject of the motion for summary judgment. As counsel for the defendants, don't reiterate the nasty phrase "tortious interference" if you can help it.)

The new version:

FACT ISSUES REGARDING DAMAGES DO NOT PRECLUDE SUMMARY JUDGMENT ON LIABILITY

Trust Your Reader to Fill in Some Blanks

Implicit steps of a procedural history can usually be omitted

Briefs often recite procedural histories from soup to nuts, setting forth precise dates when the complaint and answer were filed, when motions and cross-motions were made and argued, and so forth. Procedural histories can go into excruciatingly boring detail.

Much of what is typically included in a Procedural History can be referenced in passing or omitted altogether because it is implicit. Either the reader can deduce the information without your articulating it, or the reader doesn't need the information.

Consider, for example, this entirely accurate but very long recitation from the Procedural History of an appellate brief:

> *ABC Corp. filed a motion for summary judgment on December 5, 2005. XYZ Co. opposed ABC Corp's motion for summary judgment and filed a cross-motion for summary judgment on December 19, 2005. ABC Corp opposed XYZ Co.'s cross-motion, and after the motions were fully briefed, the trial court heard oral argument on January 20, 2006. The trial court issued its written decision immediately after oral argument, granting ABC Corp.'s motion for summary judgment and denying XYZ Co.'s cross-motion for summary judgment.*

Let's lay out the elements of this recitation:

- ABC Corp. moves for summary judgment on December 5.
- XYZ Co. opposes and cross-moves on December 19.
- ABC Corp. opposes the cross-motion.
- The matter is fully briefed.
- Oral argument is held on January 20.
- The court grants ABC Corp.'s motion in a written opinion on the same day.
- The court denies XYZ Co.'s cross-motion.

How many of these elements should the Procedural History articulate?

In the adversary system, opposition of the cross-motion is assumed, as is full briefing. Both elements can be omitted. Also, the court won't care that the motion was filed on December 5 and that the cross-motion was filed two weeks later unless a party is making an issue of the filing dates, which does not appear to be the case here. Omit the filing dates as well.

At all times, think in terms of compacting.

But mind the forms, which in this case may call for an exception to the rule-of-thumb that a writer should trim what is implicit. When both sides move for summary judgment, one side will win and the other will lose, or, more often, both will lose (putting aside the possibility that either party could seek partial summary judgment).

If one side wins summary judgment on the entire case, then by definition the other side loses. Why, then, should the Procedural History say that the court granted one motion and denied the other? Isn't it enough to say that the court granted one side's motion for summary judgment? Theoretically, it should be, but courts and brief writers invariably report that "the trial court granted the plaintiff's motion for summary judgment and denied the defendant's motion for summary judgment."

One member of my informal polling group says that writers don't trust readers to see the implication. Another says that stating the obvious shows respect for the formality of a motion—the mere fact that a motion is made merits comment on its disposition. Another says that clarity and neatness require that the writer specify what happened to all motions, eliminating the possibility, among others, that one party or both moved for partial summary judgment.

I also received a good suggestion for revision: "The court granted ABC Corp.'s motion and entered final judgment against XYZ Co." This conveys the sense of XYZ Co. losing without stating the obvious—that XYZ Co.'s motion was denied.

A shortened version of the procedural history might read as follows:

> *ABC Corp and XYZ Co. cross-moved for summary judgment. On January 20, 2006, the trial court granted ABC Corp.'s motion and entered final judgment against XYZ Co. in a written opinion handed down immediately after oral argument.*

Be Careful How You Criticize the Trial Court

As an appellant, you like the suggestion that the trial court denied the loser its "day in court" by apparently having made up its mind before oral argument (the court issued a written opinion immediately after oral argument).

I would not deliver this criticism overtly, if at all. Appellate courts do not like criticism of trial courts' motives or methods. Such lack of respect for the trial judge demeans the whole judiciary. It also reflects poorly on your case because your election to criticize the trial judge suggests you don't have confidence in the merits of your case, and it suggests that the law so clearly disfavored your client that the court granted oral argument only as a courtesy, albeit an empty one.

If I were the appellant, I would not mention the timing of the trial court's decision because I can't control how the appellate court will read it. The court might view the trial court as cavalier, but the court might also think my case is so weak that the trial court didn't need oral argument to help resolve it.

Taking that concern into consideration, a streamlined procedural recitation might read as follows:

> *ABC Corp. and XYZ Co. cross-moved for summary judgment. On January 20, 2006, the trial court issued a written opinion granting ABC Corp's motion and entering final judgment against XYZ Co.*

Events move fast these days. Courts aren't interested in savoring procedural details that don't bear on the result. If you cut through the details, you will give the court the impression that you know how to get to the point. The court may then continue reading with a feeling of optimism ("Let's see what we have here") rather than a feeling of resignation ("Here we go again.").

Puzzler

Which version of the following sentence is better?

Version A:

On February 4, at an informal meeting, members of the Commission staff presented their views.

Version B:

At an informal meeting on February 4, members of the Commission staff presented their views.

Version A homes in from the widest view to the narrowest—from the date, which covers the entire day, to the meeting on the day, to the persons who attended the meeting, and finally to what was said at the meeting. It is like a camera zooming in.

The progression has a rationale, but the prose is choppy. The step-wise focus requires two commas. At each comma, the reader pauses. Because of the pauses, the information takes too long to come out.

Version B begins with geography rather than date. The reader envisions a room, a conference table, and people around it. If the reader sees "On February 4" first, the reader doesn't envision anything except a calendar.

If the sequence of dates is important, Version A can be useful if revised (*e.g.*, "On February 4, members of the Commission staff presented their views at an informal meeting.").

Version B is better.

7

Emphasis

Driving the Point Home

Emphasis

Driving the Point Home

If readers were computers, you could make a point once; the computer would remember it; and if it were a dominant point, you would win. But readers are human. They have attitudes, preconceptions, and gaps in their data bases. They can be ambivalent and confused, and they forget. Points have to be embedded—bound to the reader's brain by reiterated facts, revisited arguments, and structural devices such as positioning a key fact at the end of a sentence.

Don't confuse emphasis with intensification. Words like "clearly" and "obviously" add no value, nor does vilification of opposing counsel (who "falsely" claim) or the trial court (who "incredibly" ruled). If you must put such words into your drafts to vent, delete them as you would destroy angry letters before sending them to friends and family.

Eschew Exaggerations, Disparagements and Other Intensifiers

Let the facts speak for themselves

An advocate's instinct is to disparage the other side. Motivated by indignation at the perceived insult to our intelligence and to the cause of truth, we say the other side's position is "obviously" or "clearly" wrong; their reading of a statute is "preposterous," and they cite no law "whatsoever." We almost cannot help ourselves.

Such characterizations of the other side's arguments are not effective writing. They are more likely to trigger disbelief than agreement because they are the known refuge of persons whose positions are weak. They are a way of pounding the table when you cannot pound the law or the facts. If you pound the table with "clearly," "obviously" and "whatsoever," the reader may figure you have nothing substantive to say.

Just as bad, if not worse, are statements disparaging the opposing advocate. In the following examples, the italicized words should be eliminated:

1. Plaintiff's *disingenuous* reading of the rule is inconsistent with the public policy that supports the rule.
2. Defendant *blithely* ignores the fact that he was present when the statements of which he claims ignorance were made.
3. *In an outrageous show of chutzpah,* the plaintiff blames his injury on the defendant rather than on his own inattention.

Words should speak for themselves—you should not have to speak for them. Consider the following intensifier in a brief submitted by a condemnee appealing for the third time from a trial court's refusal to value the condemned property fairly:

> *An appalling ten years after the taking, condemnee comes before the Appellate Division for the third time.*

The word "appalling" is unnecessary because the egregiousness of the condemnee's having to wait ten years for a shot at justice is evident merely in the recital, without need of editorial gloss. The passage of time speaks for itself, and the point is made just as well without the word "appalling":

> *Ten years after the taking, condemnee comes before the Appellate Division for the third time.*

Some writers vigorously defend the use of "strong language," deeming it a matter of taste and contending that those who shy from the practice are wimps. This view has some merit, but not much. Aggressive writing may intimidate a few adversaries, and more importantly, it may give some clients the sense that you are vigorously advocating their cause; but experienced lawyers are not easily intimidated, and they frequently turn strong language back on the writer, portraying the writer, and, by dint of association, the writer's client, as offensive rather than thoughtful or thorough.

Judges are largely unmoved by intensifiers. If the words are *ad hominem* attacks on the other side (*e.g.,* contending that an argument is "disingenuous"), the court may deem it unseemly. If they are used to pump up your own argument (*e.g.,* contending that your point is "clear" or that a delay was "appalling"), the court may be insulted because you deem it necessary to point out the obvious (*e.g.,* that a ten-year odyssey in court is appalling). If the facts don't speak for themselves, they probably aren't good enough facts.

Though you may wish to express indignation if the other side is caustic, don't sink to their level. In the end, the best way to persuade the client that you are a dedicated and effective advocate is to prevail in court, and the best way to prevail in court is to make your point and back it up with authority.

Persons who use intensifiers are often trying to make up for a failure to highlight good facts. Consider the following first sentence in the preliminary statement to the aforesaid condemnee's brief, where the condemnee argued that the trial court had undervalued the condemned property. Which version would you use, A or B?

Version A:

> *Condemnee seeks a redetermination of fair market value based on the value that a hypothetical willing buyer would have paid for the property at the time of the taking.*

Version B:

> *Condemnee seeks a determination that a person buying into the Jersey City waterfront real estate boom in April 1986 would have seen the potential of this choice parcel and would have paid a premium for it.*

The best fact for the condemnee is that its condemned property was situated in the midst of a waterfront real estate boom, which means that a willing buyer would have paid a premium for the property. Using version B, the writer integrated the most important fact ("waterfront real estate boom") into the first sentence of the preliminary statement. With version A, the writer would have presented nothing more than a statement of the law. Thus, version B is persuasive, and version A is not. The facts in version B supply the "intensity" for which intensifiers are a poor substitute.

Just as someone always votes for the other side in an election, some writers would use version A anyway, reasoning that (a) they don't want to appear to be too much the advocate too soon or (b) it is important to invoke the key terms in the relevant principle of law, such as "fair market value," "hypothetical willing buyer" and "time of the taking." These rationales are unimpeachable as general statements, but taken in context, they are outweighed by the more important principle that persuasion begins with good facts.

Puzzler

How would you tighten and sharpen the following sentence?

ABC Co. is in the business of collecting information about the condition of new and used cars and providing said information to various clients in the automotive industry.

"In the business" can be deleted because it is assumed. The collection of information can be assumed if the information is provided, so "collecting" can be dropped, and the concept of providing can be moved to the front of the sentence, which eliminates duplication of the word "information" and removes the awkward word "said." "Various" is almost always unnecessary.

The revised version:

ABC Co. provides information about the condition of new and used cars to clients in the automotive industry.

Don't Take Refuge in "Common Sense"

Like the phrase "it is important to note," it may indicate fuzzy thinking

One of the themes of this column is that flaws in our writing can serve as "red flags" to help us spot when our thinking is unclear or unfinished.

Typical red flags are the words "clearly" and "obviously," which may signal that our thinking is anything but clear and obvious. A red flag we often overlook is the expression, "It's a matter of common sense," which we think encapsulates the wisdom of our position but, more often than not, is just a dodge.

"It's common sense!" we exclaim in frustration. We wonder how anyone cannot see the point, and we resent having to explain it. So we don't.

Ironically, the frustration and resentment may reflect our inability to explain why our position is a matter of common sense. We are as frustrated with our own lack of analysis as we are with the adversary's. When you feel a desire to say that something "is a matter of common sense," think twice. You may be avoiding the hard job of making a point.

That the phrase "common sense" may not be up to the task we assign it isn't surprising. If you are asked to write a memo, chances are the answer to the question is not crystal clear. That is why someone needs a memo.

Similarly, if you have to write a brief, you are probably in a dogfight on a contested issue. Therefore, common sense is not likely, by itself, to supply an answer. The phrase "common sense" means "sound and prudent judgment based on a simple perception of the situation or facts."[1] It implies a resolution "from the gut," which is the antithesis of the thorough analysis you need to perform.

Someone not convinced of your thesis could even view the expression "It's a matter of common sense" as fighting words. If you contend that anyone with common sense must agree with you, where does that leave the unpersuaded reader? Are you implying the reader has no sense? Be careful, or you may unwittingly insult your audience as you voice a frustration that derives from your own inability to make a point.

It Is Important To Note

Another expression that may conceal more than it promotes is, "It is important to note," which, at best, is unnecessary:

It is important to note that the information in these records is unavailable from other sources.

The unavailability of the information speaks for itself. If the fact were not important, you would not use it. Declaring it important adds nothing.

---

1 *Merriam-Webster's Collegiate Dictionary* (2004).

Consider what you mean when you write, "It is important to note." Are you asking the reader to pay attention? If your writing is effective, the reader is already paying attention.

Are you suggesting the point you are about to make is more important than the point you just made? Don't rank order your points like that—the reader may discard what you demote. Perhaps you are really saying, "I sense that what I am about to say helps my case (thus its importance), but I am not sure how."

Your urge to write "It is important to note" may signal that you don't know how the thought you are about to impart relates to the thought you just imparted or that you don't know how the "important" thought fits into your argument. For example, you may say "it is important to note" a fact that appears to weaken the other side's position, but you don't identify the element of the cause of action to which it relates.

Facts aren't just important; they are important to something. If you leave it for the reader to deduce, you lose control of the persuasive process. Moreover, if you say that something is important but don't say why, you break an implied promise to the reader to back up your assertions. Failing at this or any rhetorical task costs you credibility as an advocate.

Puzzler

How would you tighten and sharpen the following sentence?

Insurer X takes the position that it has "fully responded" to ABC Co.'s request that Insurer X identify the specific facts which support its continued reliance on each policy provision that Insurer X has identified as providing a basis for its coverage decisions to deny insurance coverage and/or to "reserve its rights" to deny coverage for ABC Co.

The sentence is thick with words. "Takes the position that" can be shortened to "contends." "ABC Co.'s request that Insurer X identify the specific facts" can be shortened to "the demand for facts." (Who besides ABC Co. would make the demand?) "Which support its continued reliance on each policy provision Insurer X has identified" can become "supporting its invocation of specific policy provisions" or "supporting each of its policy defenses." (You may have to use new words to cut out old ones.)

"As providing a basis for its coverage decisions to deny insurance coverage and/or to 'reserve its rights' to deny coverage for ABC Co." either falls away altogether, as in the alternate rewrite below, or it becomes "to deny coverage or reserve rights." In the insurance business, the expression "reserve rights" implicitly means "reserve the right to deny coverage."

The revised version:

Insurer X contends it "fully responded" to the demand for facts supporting its invocation of specific policy provisions to deny coverage or reserve rights.

Alternate version:

Insurer X contends it "fully responded" to the demand for facts supporting each of its policy defenses.

Bonus: The sentence also smacks of "free airtime"—a naked restatement of the other side's position. To avoid giving free airtime, I would look to encapsulate the insurer's discovery shortcomings in introductory language:

Having supplied only skeletal facts or nothing at all in response to Interrogatories regarding its second, fourth, fifth and seventh policy defenses, Insurer X contends it "fully responded" to the demand for facts supporting each of those defenses

"Indeed," "Simply" and "Certain" Are Unnecessary Additives

They are likely to achieve the opposite of what you intend

Some lawyers challenge themselves to get through a brief without using the word "indeed." Others permit themselves one per brief, like one dessert per day or one cigarette. The word is tempting, but it can generally be deleted or replaced without loss of emphasis, as in the following example:

Plaintiff offers no justification for filing his motion late. Indeed, the moving papers even fail to mention that the filing was late.

You can drop "indeed" because "even" does the intensifying. In the following paragraph, would you use "indeed" or "to the contrary"?

Investigation turned up no evidence of illegal dumping. [Indeed] [To the contrary], documents accounted for the disposition of every load.

"Indeed" merely tells the reader that something is about to be intensified. It could mean the investigation was particularly thorough, the waste was not even toxic, or the dumping was properly documented, which turned out to be the case.

"To the contrary" is more helpful because it suggests the investigation not only failed to find evidence of illegal dumping, but it turned up evidence inconsistent with illegal dumping. The greater specificity of the phrase "to the contrary" connects the second sentence more closely to the first and thus retains a stronger grip on the reader's attention.

Try one more example:

XYZ Corp. acknowledges that the silicon chip industry is highly competitive. Indeed, all XYZ Corp. employees must sign a secrecy agreement.

"Indeed" does help, but you can link the sentences better and begin the crescendo sooner, thus magnifying the impact, by changing "acknowledges" to "does more than just acknowledge." With an adjustment to the second sentence as well, the thought reads as follows:

XYZ Corp. does more than just acknowledge that the silicon chip industry is highly competitive: It requires all its employees to sign a secrecy agreement.

In short, "indeed" is a nonspecific intensifier that can usually be dropped or replaced to good effect. Limit its use.

Simply This and Simply That

Another word I avoid is "simply," which is often found in a "no-no statement," that is, an unsupported negation of the other side's position:

- The defendant is simply incorrect.
- The plaintiff's position simply has no basis in fact.
- Plaintiff's accusation that ABC Co. violated the Court's Order requiring ABC Co. to produce documents is simply wrong.

"Simply" is an unnecessary intensifier. The contentiousness of the adversary system hasn't escalated to such a degree that one must exaggerate to make a point, as one must ante to participate in a poker game. You don't have to say the other side is "simply wrong" to persuade the court they are wrong.

Just set forth the facts and the reasoning in support of your position. Then, if you wish, finish your presentation—and satisfy your perceived obligation as a forceful advocate—by saying:

> *Thus, plaintiff's accusation that ABC Co. failed to comply with the Court's Order is wrong.*

That is enough. The other side's being wrong is just as bad as their being "simply wrong." Look at it this way: If you haven't presented enough facts and deductions to persuade the court that the other side is wrong, then you aren't going to tip the scales with "simply wrong."

Not only is "simply" unnecessary, but it may undermine the credibility of your thesis because it often marks a lack of analysis, just as bad grammar often marks a bad student. Ironically, though the word is intended to enhance clarity, it may highlight the absence of facts and reasoning needed to support the writer's position.

Finally, the word may even be taken as an insult, as if the writer were suggesting that anyone with half a brain would see—because it so "simple"—that the writer's position is correct.

"Certain" Often Waffles

Another word best omitted is "certain." It is usually unnecessary and sometimes counterproductive. Consider the following:

> *The environmental regulators notified ABC Co. of certain concerns that arose in the State's investigation of the dump site.*

Why qualify "concerns" with "certain"? Did the regulators also have concerns of which they did not notify ABC Co.? That sounds ominous, and you don't want to suggest it. Try the sentence without the word "certain":

> *The environmental regulators notified ABC Co. of concerns that arose in the State's investigation of the dump site.*

It works fine this way.

Writers waffle with "certain." In the above sentence, it was an attempt to minimize the seriousness of the concerns. The author was saying, "Yes, there were concerns. But it was only certain concerns. It wasn't numerous concerns. It wasn't an array of concerns. It was only certain concerns. Therefore, the concerns didn't amount to much."

That is, of course, hogwash. "Certain" broadcasts that you are waffling, and the reader will pick up the signal.

The word "certain" reminds me of Jim Carrey's movie "Liar Liar," in which Carrey is under a spell that requires him to tell only the truth for 24 hours. Carrey is a lawyer and assumes that as part of his job, he has to lie. When he is forced to tell the truth, he discovers that he is freed by it. Writing is the same way. When you stop waffling and tell the truth, you are freed by it.

Puzzler

Which of the following versions is better?

Version One:

Under statutes pre-existing the current Criminal Code, offenses termed "misdemeanors" are now deemed crimes of the fourth degree.

Version Two:

Offenses termed "misdemeanors" under statutes pre-existing the current Criminal Code are now deemed crimes of the fourth degree.

In Version Two, the prepositional phrase beginning with "under" is interruptive because it separates the subject (offenses) and verb (are deemed), but the sentence is better than Version One, which is inaccurate. Misdemeanors aren't deemed crimes of the fourth degree "under" pre-existing statutes. Only a section of the current Criminal Code could deem acts that were called "misdemeanors" under the old statutes to be crimes of the fourth degree.

Show Every Step of Your Reasoning on Key Points

Elaborating the obvious isn't necessarily beating a dead horse

Brief writers are sometimes reluctant to elaborate obvious points because they are fearful of being viewed as simplistic if not transparent. Ironically, the more evident a point is, the more inclined a writer may be to deem it too clear for extended comment.

Suppose you represent a bidder on a public contract to drain and fill a small municipal lake and build athletic fields over it. The contractor won't be paid directly by the town. It will receive its revenue from the "tipping fees" charged to haulers who dump fill into the dry lake bed. The request for proposals (RFP) asked the contractors to state what percentage of the tipping fees they would share with the town. The bidder proposing to share the greatest percentage would win the contract.

Your client offered to share the second highest percentage of tipping fees with the town. The contractor that offered to share the highest percentage won the contract, but the winner's proposal deviated from the contract specifications.

The RFP called for fill suitable for residential use. The winning proposal said the project was not viable using residential-grade fill because not enough fill would be available within the desired time frame, and the tipping fees would be too low for the contractor to turn a profit. Because residential-grade fill can be dumped almost anywhere, competition among disposal sites keeps the tipping fees for that grade of fill very low.

The winning contractor proposed to accept not only residential-grade fill but also non-hazardous industrial-grade fill, which is more plentiful and would serve the project as well. If both grades of fill were used, the project could be completed sooner, and the contractor could charge higher tipping fees, generating more money to share with the town. The town accepted the contractor's proposal.

As counsel for the bidder who came in second, you seek an order enjoining the town and the contractor from proceeding with the project on these terms. You argue that the change in fill should invalidate the winning proposal because the change gives the winning contractor an advantage over the other bidders and thus constitutes a material deviation from the specifications. If you are correct about the deviation, you should win the case because bids that contain material deviations are void.

Instinct tells you that the proposed change in the type of fill is a material deviation, but you are unsure how extensively to develop that thought. It seems self-evident. Any reader can see the importance of fill to the contract. The lake bed could not be covered without the fill, and the athletic fields could not be built.

You fear the court may think you have nothing better to say if you tediously explain why fill is an important element of the contract and why a proposed change in fill is a material deviation from the specifications.

In this case, the fear is misguided. The closer you come to the core of your argument, the more you should elaborate.

Lay It on Thick

Because your argument depends on fill being a material element of the contract, explain the importance of fill from several perspectives. For example, after noting the physical role of fill in the project (backfilling the lake; supporting the athletic fields), call attention to its financial role with something like, "Fill is the sole source of funding for the project. Without tipping fees, nothing gets built."

Then reinforce the idea by referencing the outflow of cash as well as the inflow: "Every other aspect of the project requires an outflow of cash, but the tipping fees bring in revenue." Do you need to juxtapose the inflow and outflow of revenue? No, but repetition regarding the crucial function of the tipping fees solidifies the point.

Good arguments are built on obvious facts, such as fill being the primary physical element of the contract and the only source of funding, and industrial-grade fill being more plentiful and bringing in more money through higher tipping fees.

The first set of facts shows the importance of fill to the contract, which goes to materiality, and the second set of facts differentiates one kind of fill from another, which goes to the advantage obtained by the winning bidder.

Don't be shy about spelling out that advantage. In addition to stating that industrial-grade fill will bring in more money because haulers will pay higher fees to dispose of it, explain why haulers will pay more to dump lower grade fill. The exposition may seem so basic that you are embarrassed to discuss it, but don't be. The court will welcome your discussion because it may help the court write its opinion.

After you establish that the tipping fees are determined by the nature of the fill, you are ready to argue that the amount of the fees bears on what percentage the contractor is willing to share with the town. The more cash the contractor receives, the more it can afford to share with the town.

In this way, the nature of the fill affects the contractor's competitive status vis-a-vis other bidders. If the contractor can accept a more lucrative kind of fill than what the RFP requires, the contractor can offer the town more money and still make a profit. This gives the contractor a competitive edge.

Again, the point is so obvious that you fear the court may think you are patronizing it or beating a dead horse. You aren't.

If you have an important point, explore it. Every story has two sides, and you don't really know the strength of your case until you fully work it out. Assuming your analysis is correct and your exposition clear, then as each element of the analysis locks into place, you further persuade the court that your reasoning is sound. The more time you spend on a winning point, the more the court sees you as a winner.

Although you discuss at length what could be set forth in a few sentences, the rigorous treatment is worth the effort if the subject matter goes to the core of your argument. In reasoning out the obvious, you drive your point home.

Puzzler

How would you tighten and sharpen the following sentence?

A "germane" claim is one which is related to the validity of the mortgage, the right to foreclose, or to the amount of the debt.

Drop the phrase "one which is" as unnecessary. The quotation marks around "germane" alert the reader that a definition is coming. To achieve parallel construction, change "right to foreclose" to "right of foreclosure" and eliminate the last "to." Use the active "relate" rather than the passive "is related."

Keep the prepositional phrases—even though they add words—so the elements that make the claim germane (*e.g.*, validity, amount) quickly answer the question, "Relates to what?"

The revised version:

A "germane" claim relates to the validity of the mortgage, the right of foreclosure, or the amount of the debt.

Don't Take Pot Shots at Court or Counsel

Gratuitous zingers are offensive and unpersuasive

The name of the game is not to fight but to sell,
and for this purpose alone should words be selected.
—Girvan Peck, *Writing Persuasive Briefs* (1984) at 146

When litigators become inspired with the perceived righteousness of their cause, they sometimes view the other side as evil and demonize them. If the lawsuit does not go well, and especially if the court gives counsel's arguments short shrift, counsel may demonize the court as well.

Below is an example of a lawyer allowing animosity toward the trial court to color an appellate brief:

After plaintiff's expert testified, defendant's expert disagreed with much of the testimony, but the trial court chose to disregard defendant's expert without justification.

Counsel truly believed the trial court had ignored the testimony of the defendant's expert without analysis. Suspecting bias, laziness, or just plain orneriness on the part of the trial court, counsel could not resist the urge to suggest—though counsel would not overtly say—that the trial court had breached its judicial duty. Instead, counsel left the accusation ambiguous:

". . . the trial court chose to disregard defendant's expert without justification."

This could mean either that the court knowingly disregarded the expert's testimony without analysis—a serious omission—or that the court, well-intentioned but misguided, merely misunderstood or undervalued the expert's testimony. Being angry, counsel probably hoped the reader would take the harsher meaning.

That was a mistake. "Chose to disregard . . . without justification" may irritate appellate judges, who have spent their lengthy judicial careers trying to do the right thing. They may resent any suggestion—because it reflects poorly on all judges—that a colleague acted unethically.

The writer should have said that the trial court disregarded the expert's testimony "without explanation," not that the court "chose" to disregard it "without justification." The toned-down approach is more persuasive because it is more accurate and carries no baggage. Counsel doesn't know the trial court's reasoning or intent. The court may have carefully considered the testimony but found it incredible.

A Second Example

The following gratuitous shot was taken in a plaintiff's reply brief:

Defendant claims falsely that the court's decision not to hold a hearing and deprive plaintiff of due process was somehow within the court's discretion.

Suggesting that the court intentionally deprived the plaintiff of due process attributes a motive that counsel can't prove. Similarly, stating that defendant "falsely" claimed something strongly implies an intention to dissemble, which is hard to prove. The better word is "incorrectly," even if counsel is sure the adversary is lying. If the facts are well marshaled, the court will sense that the adversary is lying. Courts find mud slinging unseemly.

Re-written, the sentence might read:

> *Defendant claims incorrectly that the court's failure to hold a hearing, thus denying plaintiff due process, was within the court's discretion.*

Unfortunately, when we become indignant on behalf of the client, we may take things personally and may suspect, usually wrongly, that the court is out to get us, the client, or both. We may be so irate at what we deem the laziness, stupidity, or prejudice of the trial judge that we feel the only way to convey how far the court has strayed is to show disrespect.

If you are about to vent such sentiments in an appellate brief, don't. At best, you will accomplish nothing, and at worst, you could find yourself at the wrong end of a disciplinary action.

I don't suggest that you stifle your indignation. Being worked up fosters optimism and sustains energy. It stimulates the juices and helps the words flow. Sometimes it even leads to good ideas. All that is productive.

But enthusiasm is neither evidence nor logic. A verbal manifestation of your anger cannot replace good facts and good law.

A Third Example

Suppose you are appealing an award of counsel fees where the trial court shaved plaintiff's arguably bloated fee application only minimally. You write:

> *The trial court granted a minimal reduction of the more than $268,000 in claimed fees,* ***ignoring*** *plaintiff's failure to survive summary judgment on claims of malicious interference with contractual relations, malicious interference with prospective economic advantage, and intentional infliction of emotional distress. [Emphasis added.]*

The accusatory "ignoring" assumes an approach by the court that you can't prove. You don't know that the trial court ignored anything, and the appellate court knows you don't know.

The better technique is to say "making no adjustment for plaintiff's failure, etc." This is strictly factual, without editorial content. The appellate court will be well aware that in your view, the trial court's failure to make an adjustment was erroneous. You have to show why it was erroneous.

The right to have arguments taken seriously seems almost an entitlement. When a court fails to respond to a point, we feel as if the court has broken an agreement that all judges make with all lawyers—to give serious consideration to everything we assert.

Sooner or later, we realize that such an agreement does not exist. On the one hand, judges don't have infinite time to review and respond to briefs, and on the other hand, they know they can achieve substantial justice, or at least come close, without fully evaluating every point.

Like the illusion that we will live forever, the illusion that courts will read and analyze everything we write is dispelled slowly. Even senior attorneys are vulnerable to it (some of them don't plan to die or retire, either). Whatever our resentments and suspicions, we must not let them color what we file in court.

Puzzler

Which is correct, Version A or Version B?

Version A:

They began to home in on a better solution to the problem.

Version B:

They began to hone in on a better solution to the problem.

Once you know the preferred word, you will remember it, but initial confusion is understandable, given the similarity of the words "home" and "hone" in sound and function. We home in on a solution (proceed toward it, like finding our way home) but hone the solution once we find it (make it more effective, like sharpening [honing] a knife). We home in on the right answer (find our way toward it, like a homing pigeon) and then hone it (give it a sharper edge). Version A is correct.

You Don't Need Intensifiers to Mark the Absence of Evidence

Emphatics such as "whatsoever" and "in any way" tend not to persuade

Brief writers are drawn to "whatsoever" like fruit flies to an open melon. They seem to think that "Plaintiff presented no proof whatsoever" is better than the shorter, crisper, "Plaintiff presented no proof," as if "no proof" meant "almost no proof," and "no proof whatsoever" meant "no proof at all."

Intensifiers such as whatsoever are used by experienced attorneys as well as novices to express partisan zest—to say, in effect, "Not only did these guys fall short, but they fell really short."

A member of my informal polling group feels that whatsoever adds emphasis and has "a certain flow to it." He believes it is acceptable if backed by reasons. (I would say it is "forgivable" if backed by reasons.)

Another writer uses whatsoever to "flag the point like a billboard in Times Square." She likes to "hit the court over the head with it." A third writer uses the word because she feels that "no" is very short, and she is afraid the court may skip over it.

The intention of these writers is good—they wish to drive their points home—but using intensifiers such as whatsoever is counter-productive. Often, the amplified sound merely covers a shortfall of sense.

Intensifiers are not inherently persuasive; they represent neither fact nor logic. They are frequently used by advocates with weak cases or weak points, which means that you and your case may be identified with weakness; and they are intrusive, purporting to declare a conclusion that readers may prefer to reach on their own. In balance, they subtract more than they add.

Writers looking to call attention to an absence of evidence also use "devoid," "in any way," and "ever" or "never." They say the record is "devoid of evidence" (or contains "not a single shred of evidence"), just as they would say a party "presented no evidence whatsoever." Instead of intensifying "evidence" (no evidence whatsoever), the writer intensifies "record" (the record is devoid).

A similar function is performed by "in any way," which sometimes appears as "in any way whatsoever." In the brief where I found the following, the issue was whether Jones had apparent authority to act on behalf of Smith:

Jones did not represent that he was acting on behalf of Smith in any way.

The writer seemed to fear that the court wouldn't believe Jones lacked apparent authority to act for Smith if the writer said only that Jones "did not represent that he was acting on behalf of Smith."

The concern was, I suppose, that the court might think Jones made some other representation, less direct, that could be taken as a declaration of apparent authority. Perhaps the writer added "in any way" to preclude the perception that he was splitting hairs.

This was incorrect psychology. A court does not suspect hair splitting from the absence of intensifiers. To the contrary, a court may distrust the advocate who uses them because lawyers who misrepresent, mischaracterize, or omit facts or law often hide behind intensifiers.

If you dress up your prose as those lawyers dress up theirs, you may become aligned with them in the court's mind. Worse, you may incorrectly think you have made a point where you haven't. As a consequence, you may overvalue your argument and your case.

Yet another intensifier is "ever" or "never." Suppose that in an action against an insurance company, the claimant's lawyer alleges that his client received no communications from the insurer in response to his claim:

> *No one from ABC Insurance Company ever communicated with Plaintiff regarding his claim.*

"Ever" is unnecessary. "No one . . . communicated" is definitive enough. A good brief would use details to establish that no one from the insurance company communicated with plaintiff:

> *Plaintiff received no letters, faxes, e-mails, instant messages or telephone calls from the defendant insurer, either acknowledging his claim or inquiring about it.*

Naming each medium in which the insurer failed to communicate obviates the need for "ever." Were the writer to use "ever" instead of the details, the presentation would be much weaker.

Could the writer use both "ever" and the details? I recommend against it. The intensifier would divert attention from the details.

As used here, "ever" is a kind of editorial —more opinion than fact. Not only does it smack of exaggeration, but it may insult the reader by declaring a conclusion that the reader feels fully capable of reaching from the facts. Let the facts speak for themselves.

As suggested above, writers are sometimes concerned that if they don't use an intensifier (*e.g.,* whatsoever, in any way, ever), the reader may suspect that the writer truncated the details to include only good ones, omitting what might be harmful to the writer's case. After all, lawyers in our contentious adversary system tend to be tricky.

The reader won't suspect trickery if the details are complete and well-conceived. For example, if you say the insurance company failed to communicate with plaintiff by letter, fax, e-mail, instant message or telephone, you have covered the field. What is left—pigeon?

As with gratuitous editorials such as "clearly" and "obviously," intensifiers such as "whatsoever" are less offensive, and may be forgiven (though they still add nothing) if they appear after you have presented good facts and strong law. In contrast, if you use them before you earn the right to indulge—in other words, before you present good facts and strong law—you are likely to undermine your credibility and your case.

Puzzler

How would you tighten and sharpen the following sentence?

There are no cases that provide any insight into the meaning of the definition of "instrument."

Delete "there are," losing "that" as well. Drop "any" as an unnecessary intensifier and drop "the definition" as duplicative of, and less precise than, "the meaning."

The revised version:

No cases provide insight into the meaning of "instrument."

Alternate version:

No cases [illuminate; address] the meaning of "instrument."

Dashes Are Powerful Punctuation Marks

They add a third option to commas and parentheses

Dashes aren't taught, and most writers don't use them. Like commas, dashes separate and pause, but more starkly. They are a strong spice, to be used sparingly, but they add excellent flavor in the right spots.

Suppose you represent a person sued for negligent failure to preserve evidence in an action to which your client was not a party. The law requires a nonparty to preserve evidence only under extraordinary circumstances. You want to emphasize to the court that your client does not fall within any of the extraordinary circumstances identified in the case law, so you write:

> *Only in extraordinary circumstances—not present here—will a court impose a duty on a non-litigant to preserve evidence for a litigant.*

The dashes set off and thus highlight the phrase "not present here," stressing that the required extraordinary circumstances are absent. Commas would not have the same oomph:

> *Only in extraordinary circumstances, not present here, will a court impose a duty on a non-litigant to preserve evidence for a litigant.*

Set off only by commas, the phrase "not present here" is less likely to catch the reader's attention. It lacks confidence, as if the writer were not entirely sure it was true.

What about parentheses?

> *Only in extraordinary circumstances (not present here) will a court impose a duty on a non-litigant to preserve evidence for a litigant.*

Parentheses may be even less effective here than dashes or commas. The parenthetical is an aside, as if the writer were sharing a collateral thought. The point is too important for an aside.

A Second Example

Suppose you represent a developer competing for limited sewage capacity. Your client is ready to build, but a developer who is years away from breaking ground contends that the available sewage capacity should not be awarded to your client because the sewer authority agreed in writing years ago to grant the developer first claim on available capacity.

You contend the authority's promise was contingent on the developer being ready to build, and you contend the developer admitted as much (albeit inadvertently) in two sworn statements—the verified complaint and the affidavit that the developer filed in support of an application to enjoin the award of sewage capacity to your client. After quoting from the documents, you sum up:

Thus, in two sworn statements—the verified complaint and a supporting affidavit—plaintiff admitted that its claim to sewage capacity would not ripen until plaintiff was ready to build.

You could write this sentence without reference to the two documents:

Thus, in two sworn statements, plaintiff admitted that its claim to sewage capacity would not ripen until plaintiff was ready to build.

But you wish to re-invoke the dignity and gravity of the legal process and the inherent demand for the truth reflected in the words "verified" and "affidavit." So you name the documents and set them off with dashes (two hyphens or an "em dash").

Parentheses would not work as well:

Thus, in two sworn statements (the verified complaint and a supporting affidavit), plaintiff admitted that its claim to sewage capacity did not ripen until plaintiff was ready to build.

The parenthetical is more a reminder than a highlight. You don't want merely to remind the reader of the documents; you want to feature them. For this purpose, dashes are more assertive and more effective.

Commas would be worse than parentheses:

Thus, in two sworn statements, the verified complaint and the supporting affidavit, plaintiff admitted . . .

If you use commas, a reader could momentarily think the verified complaint is part of a compound subject (complaint and affidavit—until the word "plaintiff" appears) or the second item in a series of three (sworn statements, verified complaint and affidavit). A dash, in contrast, clearly announces that the two sworn statements are about to be identified.

Dashes provide emphasis and help govern pace. Because they are assertive, they project confidence as well. Add them to your writer's toolbox.

Puzzler

How would you tighten and sharpen the following sentence?

The Oppressed Shareholders Act contains no directive regarding the methodology that the parties or the court must employ to calculate fair value.

"Methodology" sounds more important than "method" but is probably too broad for this application. It connotes a body of procedures employed by a discipline.

"Provides no method" is shorter than "contains no directive regarding the method," and it adds the assertive connotation of the Act failing to do something it should have done (provides no) rather than merely omitting something (contains no).

The phrase "for calculating" is shorter than the clause: " . . . that the parties or the court must employ to calculate."

The revised version:

The Oppressed Shareholders Act provides no method for calculating fair value.

Favor Facts Over Law for Initial Reader Contact

If you can, use metaphors to interest the reader and intensify the image

> Any instructor can remember . . . grading papers, grading papers, grading papers . . . at the same deadly level of mediocrity, only to come unexpectedly upon a paper with flashes of humor, an occasional genuinely penetrating remark, a wealth of specific details. You know well what grade he places upon such a paper.
>
> —J.N. Hook, *How to Write Better Examinations* (1941) at 19

Facts engage because they tell a story—everyone likes stories—and they persuade because they suggest, if not conclusively show, how the dispute should be resolved. A mere statement that unspecified facts satisfy an element of a cause of action, *e.g.,* "Seller made false representations," creates no images and provides no context for a moral judgment.

Suppose your client bought all the stock of a company that needs a license in each state where it sells gaming equipment. The seller represented in the purchase agreement that it was unaware of any pending or contemplated regulatory proceedings challenging the company's licenses. The seller failed to reveal that one state regulator had informally advised the company that it would likely be asked to explain a longstanding association with a reputed mobster.

Now it is a year later. Several states have investigated the company's association with the reputed mobster, and one state has scheduled a hearing in which the company must show cause why its license should not be revoked. If that license is forfeited, the others may fall like dominoes.

Your client sues the seller for fraud and breach of contract. The seller makes a motion (whether to change venue, to dismiss the complaint, to compel discovery or to obtain summary judgment), and your associate drafts a responding brief. An introductory paragraph, whether in the preliminary statement or the first point of the argument, begins as follows:

> *Seller made specific representations in the Purchase Agreement to induce the purchase of Seller's business. These representations concerning the condition of the business, however, were false. Plaintiff, though, reasonably relied on the representations, which the Seller knew were false, in entering into the Purchase Agreement. Buyer's reliance has caused it considerable damage.*

Putting aside the relentless pauses, the unnecessary "however," the gratuitous shift from "plaintiff" to "buyer," and the useless references to reliance and damages, the paragraph has no bite because it creates no images. Try to envision someone making a "specific representation."

It is true that if the defendant seeks dismissal or summary judgment, you have to proffer allegations or material issues of fact going to each element of your causes of action, but you don't persuade by citing the elements. You persuade by showing the lie.

To improve the above paragraph, delete the references to reliance and damages, which take the focus off the wrongdoer; eliminate words to improve the pace; and present facts rather than concepts. Instead of running a litany of the elements of a cause of action for fraud (*e.g.,* seller knowingly made false representations on which buyer relied to its detriment), concretize the seller's deception. Make the court want to compensate your client for the seller's bad acts:

> *Knowing that the association with Bad Guy Mobster could seriously impact the value of the company, and well aware that the Gaming Commission's expressed concern suggested that the impact might be imminent, Seller concealed both the association and the regulatory concern.*

The new version is better. It includes facts: the name of the mobster, the warning from Commission staff, and the seller's motive. It begins to tell a story, which a recitation of elements cannot. If you get this far in your editing, you have done a nice piece of work.

Some writers will take the presentation to another level with a metaphor—a rhetorical device that can tell a story in a phrase. A common sight in a courtroom on motion day is the well-heeled practitioner with handkerchief in breast pocket, raising forefinger in the air and brandishing a metaphor, perhaps something as simple as, "Plaintiff is looking to have his cake and eat it, too," or something more creative, like, "Plaintiff's attempt to fulfill this requirements contract was like the little engine that could: 'I think I can. I think I can. I think I can. I think I can.' The trouble was, this little engine couldn't."

Metaphors condense and encapsulate. In the context of the gaming company sale, a metaphor might develop as follows:

> *Seller knew that a regulatory storm was coming even as it warranted that the seas were smooth as glass. The company's association with Bad Guy Mobster and the warning from Commission staff were the "red sky in the morning" of which Seller should have given clear notice. Seller knew the gathering storm would be severe and license-threatening, but Seller kept silent. Worse, Seller swore that nothing was amiss.*

The maritime metaphor creates an image of angry regulators hurling hurricane-force rulings that leave the company's licensing status in shambles. The metaphor engages the reader because it is colorful, and it imprints the image of serious harm without your having to say, "Buyer was damaged."

The "red sky in the morning" is not only metaphor but allusion. It alludes to the anonymous saying, "Red sky at night, sailor's delight. Red sky in the morning, sailors take warning."

The allusion delivers a pointed message. Just as a sailor would be foolish to ignore a red sky in the morning, so would a purchaser of a licensed business be foolish to ignore a license-threatening circumstance of which the purchaser was aware. The metaphor conveys the materiality of the deception.

A further allusion may appeal to a smaller audience: The likely source of the red sky metaphor is a passage from the Gospel According to St. Matthew:

The Pharisees also with the Saducees came, and tempting desired him that he would shew them a sign from heaven.

He answered and said unto them, When it is evening, ye say, It will be fair weather: for the sky is red.

And in the morning, It will be foul weather today: for the sky is red and lowring. O ye hypocrites, ye can discern the face of the sky; but can ye not discern the signs of the times? [Matthew 16:1-3; King James version].

The biblical allusion may be lost on the court, but if the court knows the Bible, you may gain points for your erudition even as you invoke connotations of Heavenly wrath descending upon those who would conceal the truth.

One final note: Your revised paragraph concludes with the statement that the seller swore nothing was amiss. Did the seller actually swear? No, but the word is close enough for our purposes. The seller made an explicit promise by warranting that it was unaware of any pending or contemplated regulatory proceedings. The seller won't dare respond that it didn't "swear," that it merely promised.

Puzzler

What is the problem with the following sentence?

When you review the documents provided by our client, I would appreciate your looking for evidence of insurance coverage.

Read literally, the sentence suggests that the writer's appreciation will occur during the document review ("When you review . . . I would appreciate . . . "). This is not what the writer means. Improve the sentence in either of the following ways:

Version A:

When you review the documents provided by our client, please look for evidence of insurance coverage.

Version B:

I would appreciate your looking for evidence of insurance coverage when you review the documents provided by our client.

Tell a More Powerful Story in the Active Voice

Use active verbs to convey a sense of fault or failure

A classic piece of writing advice is to use the active rather than the passive voice. Few lawyers know what "voice" means, but most know the difference between active and passive.

"John filed an action" is active.
"An action was filed by John" is passive.

The active voice is direct and assertive. It gets more quickly to the verb, and it conveys a sense of control, of doing rather than being done to. It also suggests you have confidence in your point.

Suppose you represent XYZ Corp. in a proxy contest with Takeover Co., which has nominated a slate of directors and is looking to take control of the XYZ Corp. board. You ask the court to enjoin Takeover Co. from disseminating proxy materials that contain misleading statements about the company's directors. Takeover Co. previously made the same statements in press releases.

Assuming the structure of your sentence isn't dictated by transitional needs, would you use Version A or Version B?

Version A:

The misleading statements were previously disseminated by Takeover Co. in press releases.

Version B:

Takeover Co. previously disseminated the misleading statements in press releases.

You would use version B, in which Takeover Co. is the actor. The active voice ("Takeover Co. . . . disseminated") makes the wrongdoing more immediate. In the passive construction, Version A, you don't have as clear a target. The bad actor, Takeover Co., is buried in the middle of the sentence.

The active voice encourages the reader to visualize the persons who control Takeover Co. as drafting and then distributing misleading statements. In contrast, the mental image one can develop of "misleading statements" is nebulous. In passive voice, the story has less grip partly because it has less shape.

A Second Example

You appeal a trial court's refusal to enjoin a former employee of your client from contacting the client's customers. Would you use Version A or Version B?

Version A:

The trial court declined to bar Smith from calling the Company's long-term customers on behalf of his new employer.

Version B:

Smith was not barred by the trial court from calling the Company's long-term customers on behalf of his new employer.

Use Version A. Focus on the court, not on Smith. If the court not only made a mistake but, in your view, did so with attitude, you may wish to cultivate that connotation by stating that the court "refused" to grant the requested relief. But be careful. If the trial court is well respected at the appellate level, "declined" may be the more prudent word.

A Third Example

You represent a company whose retired CFO gave notice of her intent to exercise stock options four days after the options expired. When the company refused to honor the request, the CFO sued. Would you use Version A or Version B in a Statement of Facts?

Version A:

The expiration date passed before Ms. Jones exercised her options.

Version B:

Ms. Jones failed to exercise her options before they expired.

You would use Version B because it highlights Ms. Jones' failure to exercise her options in time. Because she failed, she deserves to lose. It was her fault. She did it to herself.

If you say only that the expiration date passed, you leave a loophole. Maybe the options didn't actually expire. Maybe Ms. Jones has an excuse, and maybe the law will afford her a remedy. After all, she missed by less than a week. She has equity in that fact and in the public policy that the law abhors a forfeiture. Pre-empt those equities by placing responsibility on Ms. Jones for having missed her deadline.

A Final Example

You represent a housing authority that lost a jury verdict to a plaintiff who tripped and fell in a dimly lit parking lot. Plaintiff's lawyer argued strenuously in his closing that a broken light bulb above a door some 70 feet from the accident site established the authority's negligent failure to illuminate the parking lot. Plaintiff did not call a lighting expert at trial. On appeal, would you use Version A or Version B?

Version A:

There was no testimony, lay or expert, that the broken bulb was intended to illuminate the parking lot.

Version B:

Plaintiff offered no testimony, lay or expert, that the broken bulb was intended to illuminate the parking lot.

Version B is better because it places the blame for the absence of testimony directly on plaintiff. Version A's amorphous "There was no testimony" ascribes no responsibility, leaving open the possibility that the absence of testimony wasn't plaintiff's fault.

Above all, you wish to ascribe fault. Do so assertively, using the active voice.

Puzzler

How would you tighten and sharpen the following sentence?

There is no ethics rule that is specifically applicable to the issue of whether a judge should recuse himself where counsel for one of the parties is a former law partner of the judge.

To determine what to prune, select the elements you wish to save:

- lack of specific ethics rule
- a verb associated with the missing ethics rule (*e.g.*, "is")
- the judge
- recusal
- counsel
- former law partner

You can't remove any of these elements without losing meaning, but everything else is fair game. Eliminate "There is...that" as excess. Eliminate "for one of the parties" as implicit and reduce "the issue of whether a judge should recuse himself" to "recusal." Change the passive "is applicable" to the active "addresses" or "requires."

The revised version (if you seek recusal):

No specific ethics rule addresses recusal where counsel is a former law partner of the judge. [Presumably, you will invoke a catchall ethics rule. You will have to invoke something.]

Alternate version (if you oppose recusal):

No ethics rule requires recusal where counsel is a former law partner of the judge.

End Sentences with Your Most Important Thought

The last word delivers the greatest impact

Every sentence tells a story. It has an actor and action (a noun and a verb), and it makes a point. It has a beginning, a middle, and an end. The last word in a sentence commands attention because it is the end of a story, albeit a short one.

By reserving your most important fact for the end of the sentence, you create anticipation—dramatic tension. The reader stays interested. Think of the important fact as the climax. If you place it in the middle of the sentence, you resolve the tension prematurely. Then the rest of the sentence is merely denouement. The reader may skip forward, looking for action.

Suppose you wish to call attention to the maximum number of days by which a record date can precede a shareholders' meeting under the State's Business Corporation Law (BCL). Only persons registered as shareholders as of the record date are entitled to vote at the shareholders' meeting. You write:

> *Section 605 of the BCL provides that the record date must be not more than 60 days before the date of any shareholders' meeting.*

The key fact of 60 days is buried in the middle of the sentence, where it is least likely to be noticed. The message is further clouded by the absence of a reference point prior to the first mention of 60 days. The reader has to make a mental note of the number of days, read further to answer the question "60 days before what?" and then go back and plug in "60 days."

You can improve the sentence as follows:

> *Section 605 of the BCL provides that a record date may precede a shareholders' meeting by no more than 60 days.*

In its position of prominence at the end of the sentence, the key fact makes a greater impact and is more likely to be remembered. The relevant period (60 days) now follows rather than precedes the reference point (the shareholders' meeting), creating a logical sequence: First one learns the reference point, then the distance to it.

A Second Example

Suppose you represent a manufacturer whose supplier precipitously and unjustifiably terminated its delivery of materials under a requirements contract. As a consequence, the manufacturer was unable to supply its retailers; the retailers turned to other sources; and the manufacturer lost business.

You contend that the damage to the manufacturer's business was so severe that recovery will take a long time. Which version is best in support of this point, A, B or C?

Version A:

ABC Corp.'s business will take years to regenerate with its retailers.

Version B:

ABC Corp.'s business with its retailers will take years to regenerate.

Version C:

Regenerating ABC Corp.'s business with its retailers will take years.

Version A is the worst option because it buries the concept of a long recovery in the middle of the sentence and then trails off.

Version B is better than Version A because it places "years" closer to the position of prominence at the end of the sentence, and it ends the sentence with the other important concept—regeneration.

To decide between Version B and Version C, ask which concept is more important—regeneration or the passage of time. You want to show the severity of the damage, so the more important concept is the passage of time, *i.e.*, "years." Version C is better for your purposes because the most important fact—that recovery will take a long time—ends the sentence.

The beginning of a sentence is also prominent but less so than the end. Version C is better than Version B for the additional reason that it begins with the powerful concept of regeneration. The manufacturer's business has been disfigured, like a starfish that has lost an arm, and it must "regenerate."

One More Example

Which is a more emphatic statement of Mr. Big's demand for control, Version A or Version B?

Version A:

Mr. Big insists upon control in all his ventures.

Version B:

In all his ventures, Mr. Big insists upon control.

The point of the sentence is that Mr. Big must have control. The word that embodies the point—control—stands out better if placed at the end of the sentence, as in Version B.

Puzzler

How would you tighten and sharpen the following sentence?

Because the Agency does not have a set of procurement regulations in place, procedures for handling bid protests must be derived from general principles inherent in the common law.

Substitute the shorter and more forceful "has no" for "does not have." Delete "a set of," "in place," "handling" and "general principles inherent" as implicit. Eliminate a prepositional phrase by using "protest" to modify "procedures." Arguably, you don't need "bid" because it will be implicit in context. With "bid" gone, the alliteration of "procurement" and "protest procedures" is tighter.

Say the Agency "lacks" procurement regulations if you wish to suggest that the Agency was remiss in failing to adopt them.

The revised version:

Because the Agency has no procurement regulations, protest procedures must be derived from the common law.

Alternate version:

Because the Agency lacks procurement regulations, protest procedures must be derived from the common law.

Curb Your Editorial Urges

Consider carefully how you describe a court's actions

When you find a favorable precedent, you are ecstatic. Not only are you pleased that the court ruled as it did, but you are certain the court ruled correctly because you believe your client is in the right, or was wronged. Sometimes you express your enthusiasm in an editorial comment, as in the following sentence from a brief:

> *The Supreme Court correctly recognized that any change in the law would have to be made by the legislature.*

The Supreme Court probably was correct, but it is not for you to say. You don't have the stature. Claiming stature you don't have suggests you may claim other things you don't have, such as a good case. It taints your "ethos," your credibility as an advocate.

Suppose you delete "correctly":

> *The Supreme Court recognized that any change in the law would have to be made by the legislature.*

This is still an aggressive approach, but within bounds. To "recognize" something is to observe the truth of it. To say the Court observed the truth of something is to imply that you know the truth and can judge whether others know it as well. In other words, you place yourself in a position from which to judge the Court.

But you don't editorialize; you merely report. You don't say the Court acted "correctly" or "incorrectly" (an adverb). You say the Court "recognized" something (using a verb). In this manner, you suggest but don't actually say that the Court reached its conclusion correctly.

Suppose you back off from the subtle but assertive "recognized" with something more neutral:

> *The Supreme Court ruled that any change in the law would have to come from the legislature.*

"Ruled" is less judgmental than recognized, but it's also less precise. It is akin to "held." But the Supreme Court didn't hold that any change in the law would have to be made by the legislature. The Court didn't have to make that comment to decide the case, so it wasn't a holding. It was "dictum."

A holding or ruling describes the application of law to fact. A typical holding is that a party breached a contract by supplying defective product or that a trial court acted within its discretion in refusing to overturn a jury verdict.

In short, "recognized" is better. Does it push the envelope? A little. Is that bad? No.

Can we find a word less aggressive than recognized but more precise than held or ruled? How about "stated"? Did the Supreme Court state that any change in the law would have to come from the legislature?

It did. But where does "state" get you? It is painfully neutral. A reader may expect you to be more assertive. If the intensity of your advocacy fails to meet expectations, like company earnings that fall short of earnings estimates, a reader may sense weakness.

What about "said"? Can you write that the Supreme Court "said" that any change in the law would have to be made by the legislature?

I wouldn't. It's too informal.

The denotations of "said" and "stated" are much the same, but the connotations are different. The more formal word ("state") shows better manners because it portrays the court in a more impressive light. By showing good manners, you avoid irritating your reader.

Good manners don't make your points better or your opponent's points worse, but they improve your relationship with the reader, especially if the reader is a judge. Choose the formal over the colloquial when describing what a court did.

For all important words, consider all possibilities. Even if you think you have a good vocabulary, keep a thesaurus handy. For the sample sentence above, alternatives for "say" and "state" (from the thesaurus) fall short as follows:

The Supreme Court __________ that any change in the law would have to be made by the legislature.

Affirmed—double meaning
Asserted—too forceful; Court has no need to assert
Averred—word is rarely used
Declared—grandiose
Explained—didn't, really
Opined—true, but probably too formal
Remarked—too casual

The demands of precision are relentless. Above, we examined a substantial menu to choose one word to describe a statement in a Supreme Court opinion. Such issues arise repeatedly. For most projects, you will not have time to resolve them all.

Puzzler

How would you tighten and sharpen the following sentence?

After severing a relationship with a former client, the Supreme Court has forbidden an attorney to use knowledge or information acquired in the previous relationship against the former client.

The main problem is the "dangling participle" (the opening phrase). The Supreme Court didn't sever the relationship with the former client. The lawyer did. Here, the information in the dangling participle isn't even necessary. The word "former" will indicate that the relationship was severed.

I would not keep both "knowledge" and "information" even though the connotations may be slightly different. "Information" covers as much as "knowledge" here.

The five words that conclude the sentence, "relationship against the former client," are awkward because the attorney did not have a relationship "against" the former client. Moving "against" to create the phrase "use against a former client" is a possible solution, but it, too, is awkward:

> *The Supreme Court has forbidden an attorney to use against a former client information acquired in the previous relationship.*

It is awkward because the first question in the reader's mind after seeing the verb "use" is, "Use what?" not "Use how?" Because the "what" is "information," the next question in the reader's mind is, "What kind of information?" Once that question is answered, the reader finally turns to "Use how?" The sequence is as follows:

- Use what? (information)
- What kind of information? (information acquired from a former client)
- Use it how? (in a subsequent matter against that client)

The revised version:

> *The Supreme Court has forbidden an attorney to use information acquired in a relationship with a former client in a subsequent matter against that client.*

Spell Out the Facts Embedded in Your Generalizations

To do the right thing, the court needs to know the facts

Facts are key to the persuasive process because they give the court a basis on which to do the right thing. They are the clay from which the court molds a result. To maximize the value of facts, set them before the court whenever possible.

Suppose you represent the wife in a long divorce litigation. Since the beginning of the litigation six years ago, the family home has doubled in value. It is about to be sold, and you want the wife to share its current value even though the presumptive date for valuing the home in a divorce is the date the complaint was filed. You have to persuade the court that the wife is entitled to half the appreciation in the home despite the presumptive valuation date.

The husband and wife both lived in the family home during the litigation, albeit in separate bedrooms, and the wife continued to clean the house, tend the garden and cook for both her husband and herself. The children had grown and moved out. You contend that the wife should share the home's appreciation during the six years of litigation because, among other things, she continued to contribute to the common venture of the marriage.

Your assigning attorney writes the Statement of Facts for the trial brief. Describing the wife's contribution to the household during the litigation, the attorney states that the wife "continued to clean the house, tend the garden, and prepare the family meals." The attorney chose the word "family" to connote a common enterprise and the phrase "continued to contribute" to create a parallel with the home's continuing increase in value.

You are assigned the Argument section of the brief. You write the following in Point I:

> *During the six-year litigation, Mrs. X continued to contribute to the common enterprise of the marriage as she had before filing her complaint. Therefore, she is entitled to an equal share of the appreciation of the family home during the litigation.*

You feel pretty good about having picked up on the assigning attorney's use of "continued to contribute" and "family," but you don't repeat the ways in which the wife continued to contribute to the common enterprise of the marriage. You figure the facts are already set forth in the Statement of Facts—you don't want to be redundant—and you don't want to appear overzealous, either. Pounding the law, the facts or the table is not your style.

Overcome your reluctance. Where good facts are concerned, be unabashedly overt in your advocacy. If the facts are good, the principle of frequency overrides the principle of brevity. Write the sentence like this:

During the six-year litigation, the wife continued to clean the house, tend the garden and prepare the family meals, contributing to the joint enterprise of the marriage as she had before she filed her complaint.

Articulating the embedded facts is like clicking on the little plus sign in the folders column of your e-mail program, causing a menu of folders to drop down and become accessible to you. When you "argue the facts," you drop down a set of facts from your generalization. Here, the word "contributed" is the generalization, the set, and each of the ways in which the wife contributed is a subset.

Suppose you are lucky enough to have found a precedent, *Smith v. Smith*, where the wife successfully sought a share of the increase in value of the family home during divorce litigation. During the litigation in *Smith*, the wife lived in the family home, cared for the children, did the household shopping and paid the bills.

After citing your precedent, lock in your analogy like this:

Just as the wife in Smith v. Smith was credited with the appreciation of the family home during a long divorce litigation because she continued to contribute to the marital enterprise, so should Mrs. X share in the increased value of the family home during her divorce litigation because she, too, continued to contribute to the marital enterprise, cleaning the home, preparing the family meals and tending the garden.

You may be tempted to extrapolate Mrs. X's role from "tending the garden" to something more impressive, like "supervising the upkeep of the property." Don't exaggerate. Don't try to turn a subset (tending the garden) into a set (seeing to the upkeep of the property). The court will see through it, and you will lose credibility.

Should you concede that Mrs. X contributed to the family enterprise in different ways from the wife in *Smith v. Smith*, who took care of the children, did the shopping and paid the bills, whereas Mrs. X merely cooked, cleaned and tended the garden—duties that arguably are less strenuous than caring for children?

This is a judgment call. Because Mrs. X did less, the difference doesn't help you. The scope of her marital enterprise contracted when her children moved out. Your bottom line is that both women continued to contribute to the marital enterprise, so the result in your case should be like the result in *Smith v. Smith*.

But it's your choice, and maybe you can turn chicken scratch into chicken cacciatore. The other side will almost certainly address *Smith v. Smith* because it is on point. They will look to minimize your client's role, comparing her unfavorably with the wife in *Smith v. Smith*.

Acknowledging the factual difference between the women's roles carries some risk because your client didn't care for children during the divorce litigation; thus, her contribution to the marital enterprise was, arguably, less. But discussing the differences gives you the opportunity to reiterate and thus solidify the analogy between your case and *Smith v. Smith*, as follows:

True, Mrs. Smith and Mrs. X contributed to the family enterprise in different ways, Mrs. Smith by taking care of the children, doing the shopping and paying the bills, and Mrs. X by cooking, cleaning, and tending the garden—her children having grown up and moved out. Both continued to contribute to the household they shared with their husband.

I would confront the distinction head-on. The *Smith* case is sure to be central in the legal debate and thus to be parsed and picked at by the other side, the judge's law clerk and the judge. Show confidence by taking the aggressor's role. Posit the test as "contribution to the marital enterprise" and dare the other side to say that cooking, cleaning and tending the garden aren't a contribution. Bobbing and weaving has its place, but probably not here.

Puzzler

How would you tighten and sharpen the following sentence?

The Legislature adopted the Gaming Act in April which includes a complete ban on gifts to Gaming Commission employees.

Drop the reference to the Legislature as implicit. Because the ban is included in the Act, not in April, drop "which" (eliminating the question whether to place a comma in front of "which"). Reduce the phrase "includes a complete ban on" to "bans all." It's not only shorter but sharper.

The revised version:

The Gaming Act adopted in April bans all gifts to Gaming Commission employees.

Don't Twist Your Prose into a Pretzel

Remedy awkwardly passive phrasing by changing the subject

An awkward construction common in legal writing is the passive verb form followed by an infinitive, which is usually passive as well, as in:

> *The amounts paid to the firm for lobbying and the amounts the firm pays its lobbyists* ***are required to be reported annually.***

The verb is "are required," and the infinitive is "to be reported." The passive voice is created by combining a form of the verb "to be" with the past participle of another verb. For most verbs ("regular" verbs), the past participle is formed with the suffix "-ed."[1]

When verbs are in active "voice," the subject of the sentence is doing something and takes an object ("Plaintiff filed a motion."). In passive voice, the subject is being done to ("The motion was filed by plaintiff.").

Amounts paid for lobbying are, in a sense, "required to be reported," but the grammatical structure is hard for the reader to follow. Generally, the construction "are required" is followed by the infinitive of an active verb, as in "Lobbyists are required to file a notice of representation." The passive verb form "are required" followed by the passive "to be" construction does not immediately compute.

The easy fix is to substitute "must" for "are required to."

> *The amounts paid to the firm for lobbying and the amounts the firm pays its lobbyists must be reported annually.*

A Second Example

Suppose that a buyer and seller enter a contract for sale of a medical testing laboratory. While the deal is pending, the Commissioner of Health proposes to amend regulations to reduce what labs can charge for tests. The proposed regulations would be a materially adverse development for medical testing labs.

The seller does not tell the buyer about the proposed regulations, and the buyer relies on the seller's warranty of no materially adverse changes to the business. When the buyer finds out about the regulations, the buyer sues the seller for a price adjustment. The buyer's brief opposing the seller's motion for summary judgment states as follows:

> *After the Purchase Agreement was executed, and unbeknownst to Buyer, the regulations that govern billing and collection by medical labs* ***were proposed to be amended.***

---

[1] Examples of past participles for irregular verbs include arisen, begun, brought, caught, done, driven, given, known, paid, seen, spoken, stolen, thrown and written.

"Were proposed to be amended" is awkward. Regulations are regularly "proposed," but they aren't "proposed to be amended."

Writers get into these predicaments by following their noses. They write in the order in which thoughts occur. First they place an event in time with, "After the Purchase Agreement was executed," and then they select "regulations" as their subject because the sentence seems to be about regulations. They don't think ahead, and they don't rethink the structure once created.

A formulation such as "proposed to be amended" results when the writer clings to the idea that the regulations have to be the subject of the sentence—the actor in the drama—because the regulations are important and because the writer thought of them first.

Here, the focus isn't the regulations; it's their amendment, which supports the following revision:

> *After the Purchase Agreement was executed, and unbeknownst to Buyer, amendments were proposed to the regulations governing billing and collection by medical labs.*

This is an improvement. "Amendments were proposed" is more accessible than "regulations . . . were proposed to be amended." But you need another sentence to say that the amended regulations would reduce the amounts that labs can charge. Changing the verb from passive (amendments were proposed) to active ("the Commissioner of Health proposed amendments"—see below) would not only increase the vigor of the sentence, but it would tighten the paragraph by allowing the writer to set forth the nature of the proposed amendments where the amendments first appear:

> *After the Purchase Agreement was executed, and unbeknownst to Buyer, the Commissioner of Health proposed amendments to the regulations governing billing and collection by medical labs to reduce the amounts that labs could charge.*

Little change was necessary to make the sentence serviceable rather than awkward, and little additional change was needed to make it sharper and give it more substance. For inveterate Puzzler solvers, here is an additional option: replace "the amounts that" with "what."

Other Examples

The following sentence appeared in a brief seeking injunctive relief:

Defendant's continuing discharge of toxic chemicals must be ordered to stop.

This passive formulation was created because the writer thought, "What is this sentence about? It's about defendant's continuing discharge of toxic chemicals, so I'll begin with the discharge." The writer was then stuck trying to find a verb to explain what must happen to the continuing discharge. The solution is to choose a new subject, such as the court:

The Court should order defendant to cease discharging toxic chemicals.

How would you fix the following?

The issue sought to be barred from relitigation by plaintiff is the validity of the contract.

Try these solutions:

Plaintiff seeks to bar relitigation of the validity of the contract.

Plaintiff opposes relitigation of the contract's validity.

Puzzler

How would you tighten and sharpen the following sentence?

The Municipal Utilities Authority (MUA) decided that wetlands approval can be divided into three steps which are each worth three points toward achieving priority on the list for sewage treatment capacity—submission of an application, hearing process, and approval.

If the MUA divided approvals into three steps, then implicitly it decided to do that. No need for both. Save two more words by replacing "which are" (should have been "that are" anyway) with a comma. Also, drop "achieving" and "on the list" as implicit.

Place quotation marks around MUA or not. I prefer not. The reader will know that MUA is short for Municipal Utilities Authority. The marks are, ever so slightly, an editorial.

Reduce "submission of an application" to "application." Submission is assumed. Similarly, drop "process" from "hearing process" because the hearing assumes a process. These deletions not only reduce words but create better rhythm.

The revised version:

The Municipal Utilities Authority (MUA) divided wetlands approval into three steps, each worth three points toward priority for sewage treatment capacity—application, hearing, and approval.

Use Underlining or Italics for Emphasis, Not for Editorializing

Highlight quotations, not your own prose

Underlining and italics can illuminate quotations, guiding the reader and adding emphasis. But underlining and italicizing don't work so well on a writer's own words. They usually make the writer appear to be trying too hard.

Suppose the defendants are taking a position inconsistent with admissions they made in their answer to the complaint. You are plaintiff's counsel. In a motion brief, you call the defendants' inconsistency to the court's attention, arguing as follows:

> *In their answer, the defendants <u>admitted</u> facts that are undeniably inconsistent with their new defense.*

You underline "admitted" because you are outraged that the defendants changed their position and even more outraged that they did so without acknowledging it. You envision yourself standing at the lectern and gesturing emphatically as you raise your voice to say, "The defendants ADMITTED facts that are inconsistent with their new defense."

On your feet, you can raise your voice, but in print, you are expected to be more reserved. Because you have time to refine a brief, you are expected to make your point without the written equivalent of emphatic gestures. Spikes in amplitude are almost always counterproductive on the printed page.

Underlining portions of a quotation helps the reader, assuming you don't underline ponderous chunks of text, which creates other issues. But underlining your own words suggests that you lack confidence in the articulation of your point. Why else would you augment it with what is essentially a gesture?

Underlining or italicizing your own words can also suggest that the reader isn't bright enough to get your point without a typographical assist. As one member of my informal polling group says, "The effect is that of raising your voice to a not very bright listener, and it insults the reader."

You can make your point just as well without the underlining:

> *In their answer, the defendants admitted facts that are undeniably inconsistent with their new defense.*

"The defendants admitted facts" is clear and forceful. It is just as strong as "the defendants <u>admitted</u> facts," and it is better than the underlined version because it is not tainted by a gratuitous editorial.

In the motion brief, you would set forth the admissions inconsistent with the new defense. The persuasion is in the inconsistency between the admissions and the new defense—in other words, in the facts—not in your conclusory statement that the defendants admitted something. Underlining "admitted" steals attention from the facts by focusing unnecessarily on the conclusion.

Ideally, you will state no conclusion until after you present your facts because the best persuasion occurs when the reader reaches the conclusion independently. If the reader draws a conclusion before you assert it, the reader embraces the conclusion and owns it. You sold it, but the reader owns it. The facts make the sale. The underlining does not.

A Second Example

Suppose you represent ABC Corp. (the "company") in a proxy contest against XYZ Co. (the "dissenter"), which is looking to replace the company's board of directors with its own nominees. The dissenter's initial draft proxy statement, filed with the SEC and available on-line to all shareholders, contains false statements about the character of the company's directors. You successfully petition the court to require the dissenter to amend its draft proxy statement.

The court orders the dissenter to change the text of its draft proxy statement, but the court rejects your request that the dissenter be required to identify and acknowledge the errors in the original text. The dissenter then chooses not to revise the original draft proxy statement but merely to supply an insert with corrected language, leaving the original draft intact.

At the election a few days later, the dissenter's nominees win seats on the board by narrow margins. You immediately seek an order enjoining the installation of the new board until the court can determine the extent to which the hotly contested voting process was tainted by the materially misleading statements that remained in the dissenter's draft proxy statement for all to see. You write the following, underlining the phrase "materially misleading":

> *The cumulative effect of XYZ Co.'s erroneous statements, which this Court concluded were <u>materially misleading</u>, resulted in the election of the XYZ Co.'s nominees by a razor-thin margin.*

You add the underlining for emphasis, thinking you need to drive home the point that the false statements by the dissenter were materially misleading. It is a good fact, and you have noticed that senior lawyers harp on good facts.

Delete the underline. It is diverting and potentially insulting to the court. It is diverting because the court may pause to wonder why the two words are underlined. It is potentially insulting for at least two reasons.

One, it suggests the court is not alert enough to remember—without your help—that it found the dissenter's statements materially misleading. Two, it suggests you may be trying to put one over on the court by means of a diversion, given that the underlined phrase "materially misleading" is off-message.

Your point on this application is that the dissenter's final proxy statement was misleading because the dissenter never revised the text of its draft proxy statement. It merely provided an insert. Emphasizing the falsity of the proxy statement rather than the failure to revise it is a diversion from what you need to prove—that the insert failed to correct the problem. It goes to what you have already proved—that the draft proxy statement was materially misleading.

The court may be particularly sensitive on this application because it looks like an attempt to get a second bite at the apple. Be forthcoming in the difference between what you previously sought (a ruling that the dissident not only make revisions but confess its sins) and what you are seeking now (a ruling that the insert was an inadequate fix).

Can I Ever Underline or Italicize My Own Words?

Upon occasion, you can underline or italicize your own words to good effect. As one member of my informal polling group says, "Sometimes your adversary will make a statement that needs to be rebuffed with a little indignation." He proffers the following example:

Plaintiff's brief: "Joe beats his wife."

> *Defendant's brief: "Plaintiff offers no evidence that Joe beats his wife. In fact, Joe's son confirmed that Joe <u>never</u> beat his wife."*

Using underlining to emphasize negation can work. But do it sparingly, and bear in mind this observation from a very experienced writer of my acquaintance: "When I see underlining other than in a quotation, I tend to think the person who wrote the brief is inexperienced, *i.e.*, a junior attorney."

Puzzler

How would you tighten and sharpen the following sentence?

There is nothing in the contract which suggests that the parties agreed to less than six shipments.

"Which" should be "that," but the whole "There is nothing . . . which" construction should be deleted in favor of one word—"Nothing."

You don't need "that" after "suggests," but it is acceptable. "Less" should be "fewer," which is the preferred usage for numbers, whereas "less" is the preferred usage for amount (*e.g.*, "He brings fewer lawsuits and wins less money.").

The revised version:

Nothing in the contract suggests the parties agreed to fewer than six shipments.

When Working by Analogy, Elaborate the Comparison

Spell out your analogies to make them unassailable

The facts of the cases on which you wish to rely are almost always different from the facts of your case, forcing you to argue by analogy. If the analogy is credible, you can profitably invoke *stare decisis*, the principle that prior rulings in similar cases control what is before the court. The tighter the analogy, the greater the pressure on the court to follow suit.

Suppose you represent a paint manufacturer. A batch of defective pigment ruined several vats of paint, and your client thinks the pigment manufacturer knowingly used substandard materials. You believe your client may have a cause of action under the state's Consumer Fraud Act for an unconscionable commercial practice.

You face two issues: (i) whether the Consumer Fraud Act protects corporations as well as individuals; and (ii) whether a manufacturer buying materials to be incorporated into an end product is a consumer under the Consumer Fraud Act, just as a purchaser of the end product at retail is a consumer.

The first issue was resolved in your favor in *Roe v. Jones*, which you will cite. The available precedent on the second issue is *Smith Air v. ABC Corp.*, in which a sole proprietor who manufactured air conditioning units was permitted to bring an action under the Consumer Fraud Act against a company that supplied defective generators for the air conditioning units. You want to analogize the defective air conditioner generators to defective paint pigment.

Many lawyers drawing this analogy would write something like the following in a summary judgment brief:

> *Just as a cause of action was found against the manufacturer of a defective generator as a component of an air conditioner in* ***Smith Air v. ABC Corp.,*** *so should a cause of action be found against the manufacturer of defective pigment as a component of plaintiff's paint. Both products—the generators and the pigment—are components.*

This is not bad, and kudos to the writer for using "defective" twice and for building parallel structure around the phrase "as a component of." But the analogy concludes prematurely. The adversary will contend that *Smith Air* is not precedential because the generators retained their identity within the air conditioning units, whereas pigment dissolves into paint, loses its identity, and cannot be viewed as a finished product. Arguably, if it can't be viewed as a finished product, then the person who buys it can't be viewed as a consumer.

This may be a distinction without a difference, but it's a predictable response by the pigment manufacturer. Your analogy can defuse this anticipated rejoinder if expanded to include the functions of the component parts so the reader can see that the essence of the analogy is in the function, not the physicality, of the component parts:

> *Smith Air is directly on point. Just as the manufacturer of the generator in Smith Air provided a component of the air conditioning unit, the supplier of pigment provided a component of the paint. Just as the generator by itself was of no use to purchasers of the air conditioning unit, the pigment by itself is of no use to purchasers of the paint. Conversely, the air conditioning unit won't work without the generator, and the paint won't work without the pigment. That the pigment dissolves and the generator doesn't dissolve is of no significance. Both products are integral to the ultimate end product and useless apart from it. Both are supplied at arm's length by independent vendors.*

This paragraph flows easily into your internal summation:

> *An unconscionable commercial practice in the sale of a generator for an air conditioner is no different from an unconscionable commercial practice in the sale of pigment for paint. The point of Smith Air is that the purchase of component products is covered by the Consumer Fraud Act.*

Don't wait for the reply brief to discuss functionality. You may be tempted to lay an ambush by drawing a light analogy based merely on the physicality of incorporation, teasing the other side into arguing that *Smith Air* is distinguishable because the generator does not lose its identity within the air conditioner, whereas the pigment dissolves into the paint. Then you would "really hit them" in your reply brief.

Don't outfox yourself. Make your strongest argument in your initial brief. If the opponent can't overcome your initial argument, the court won't even need to read your reply.

Opposing counsel may also try to cloud the issue by arguing that *Smith Air* is not precedential because it involved a sole proprietor, not a corporation. This is an "apples and oranges" argument. The corporation vs. individual issue is irrelevant to the issue regarding component parts. Anticipating this argument, you could add a paragraph identifying the apples and the oranges:

> *The question whether the Consumer Fraud Act protects corporations as well as individuals is irrelevant to the issue whether the Act covers the purchase of component parts. A component is no less a product if purchased by a corporation than if purchased by an individual. In any case, coverage under the Consumer Fraud Act for corporations as well as individuals was established in Roe v. Jones.*

Suppose the court in *Smith Air* didn't provide a rationale for finding a cause of action against the supplier of the air conditioner generators under the Consumer Fraud Act. The court said only, "The court sees no reason why the Consumer Fraud Act should not apply to the buyer of a component part just as it applies to the buyer of an end product."

Courts sometimes use the "see no reason" approach when they haven't fully analyzed the basis for their ruling. They are going on instinct, which is usually reliable, but a "see no reason" ruling can be frustrating to the winner, who has to unpack the reasoning on appeal, and infuriating to the loser, who is left with an amorphous target. Nothing stops you from completing the reasoning that the court curtailed.

You can explain that the public policy supporting a cause of action under the Consumer Fraud Act for a defect in an end product applies equally to a defect in a component part. In both instances, the integrity of the transaction depends on the honesty of the seller. Though a manufacturer in the role of buyer may be more sophisticated than an individual consumer, the manufacturer is vulnerable to unconscionable conduct because, almost by definition, deceptive conduct negates commercial savvy.

Many writers would simply quote the court's "see no reason" language as if the declarative force of a statement by a court were enough. After all, if the court saw no reason, who are we to look for reasons? You can always find a reason if your equities are sound. You just have to think it through.

Puzzler

Which is correct—Version A or Version B?

Version A:

She is averse to having her drafts criticized.

Version B:

She is adverse to having her drafts criticized.

We are averse to things we find distasteful. The word describes a feeling. It comes from the same Latin root as "avert"—"to turn away or aside (as the eyes)."[1]

We are adverse to our adversaries—persons opposed to our interests. The word describes a position. Version A is correct.

---

1 *Merriam-Webster's Collegiate Dictionary*, 11th Ed.

8

Conventions

Grammar, Usage and Punctuation

Conventions

Grammar, Usage and Punctuation

You want readers to be unaware of your prose. Otherwise, they will be distracted and lose the thread. Your prose should be "transparent." The chapter entitled "Conventions" encompasses three categories relating to transparency and pace—grammar, usage and punctuation. When these elements are handled well, the reader is unaware of them. When they are handled poorly, they bring the reader up short. They interrupt, and they suggest lack of education and training, casting doubt on your argument and on you.

Commas Enhance Clarity and Regulate the Flow of Your Writing

If used improperly, they can confuse and irritate the reader

> When anyone reads anything which he wishes to study, he does not despise the letters and punctuation marks, and call them illusion, chance and worthless shells, but he reads them, he studies and loves them, letter by letter.
>
> —Herman Hesse, *Siddhartha* (New Directions, Paperback, 1957) at 42

Not knowing how to use commas is like not knowing how to catch a baseball. Despite the simplicity and utility of doing it correctly, some people do it wrong anyway.

One catches a baseball by drawing the glove back as the ball approaches rather than snapping at the ball stiff-armed. This softens the impact and reduces the likelihood that the ball will bounce out of the glove. Either you know how to do this, or you don't.

It seems that people either know how to use commas, or they don't. Trying to teach this skill can be as frustrating as trying to teach someone to catch a baseball. Editing drafts doesn't seem to help, nor do principles such as "Use a comma to separate independent clauses connected by 'and.'" The concept of "independent clause" is meaningless to most people who misuse commas (and to many who don't), as is the term "run-on sentence."

Supplying practical reasons for the rules of punctuation may help. After all, commas are practical. They show the reader where to pause, enhancing the rhythm and clarity of the prose.

Three rules for using commas are explained below.

Rule No. 1. Precede tack-on "which" clauses with a comma.

Example:

The trial court granted the motion for summary judgment which the appellate court affirmed.

This one is a classic. I call it the "breathless which clause" because it rushes on as if the writer is overwhelmed by the importance and urgency of the message and hasn't time to catch a breath. Because "judgment" is not followed by a comma, the writer seems to be distinguishing a summary judgment motion that was affirmed from summary judgment motions that were not affirmed. This makes no sense, and the reader will eventually catch on, but not without a moment of confusion, whether conscious and palpable or subconscious and fleeting.

True, the use of "which" instead of "that" could signal that the tack-on clause is intended to modify (describe) rather than identify something in the first half of the sentence, given that the proper way to identify an item in a set is to use "that," not "which" (for example, "the dog that barked," not "the dog which barked"). But writers so frequently use "which" where they should use "that" that most readers would probably figure the "which" to be functioning like "that" and would briefly be confused because the intended message (that summary judgment was affirmed) is at odds with the alternative, albeit illogical, message embedded in the structure (that the trial court granted the motion that was affirmed). Corrected, the sentence reads:

The trial court granted the motion for summary judgment, which the appellate court affirmed.

Getting commas right is not merely an academic exercise. Readers who expect to see proper punctuation may be irritated by an apparent lack of respect for the forms, and even those on whom punctuation is lost will have to sort through the conflicting grammatical messages. As a consequence, your writing may be perceived as substandard, and by dint of association, your argument may be perceived as substandard as well.

Rule No. 2. Use a comma when tacking on an "-ing" clause that modifies rather than identifies something in the first half of the sentence:

The U.S. District Court for the Southern District of New York dismissed the complaint finding that plaintiff had failed to allege a prima facie case.

The writer meant to say the court dismissed the complaint for failure to allege a *prima facie* case. But without the comma, the sentence appears, at least momentarily, to suggest that the court dismissed a particular complaint—the one that made a certain finding ("the complaint finding that plaintiff had failed to allege a *prima facie* case"). Because complaints don't make findings, the reader will figure it out, but at the cost of time and energy. Thus, a comma is needed between "complaint" and "finding":

The U.S. District Court for the Southern District of New York dismissed the complaint, finding that plaintiff had failed to allege a prima facie case.

Again, it is a small bump in the road for the alert reader, but bumps add up.

Rule No. 3. Place a comma between "independent clauses" connected by "and," that is, groups of words that have a subject and a verb and could stand on their own as separate sentences.

As indicated above, lawyers have a tendency to run on as if breathless with the importance and urgency of what they have to say. Maybe they do this for effect, or maybe they fear they will lose the reader's attention if they interrupt the flow. For example:

The attorney work product privilege is not conditioned upon litigation actually ensuing and it will be applied as long as the prospect of litigation is identifiable.

This is a run-on sentence because it runs from one independent clause to another. Readers who are trained in punctuation—and this probably includes most judges—cannot help viewing the omission of the comma as substandard. If they experience the packaging as substandard, then the message is at risk as well. In a close case, this could tip the balance.

A comma in the above sentence would tell the reader to pause and digest an important principle—that work product protection does not require actual litigation—before learning how the principle is qualified, namely, that the prospect of litigation has to be identifiable. Thus, the comma can not only serve as a talisman against reader prejudice, but it can aid clarity as well.

The sentence can be fixed in three ways. You can add a comma after "ensuing," thus eliminating the run-on factor. You can add a semicolon after ensuing and drop the "and," or you can put a period after ensuing and begin a new sentence.

I like the period because it directs the reader to stop completely and absorb the first thought before moving on. The semicolon is a nice touch, but I avoid it because many readers do not know what to make of it, and I don't want to confuse or alienate them. Our job is not to expose readers to the finer tools of writing, merely to persuade them.

Puzzler

How would you tighten and sharpen the following sentence?

A corporation has an obligation to report all campaign contributions that it makes that are over $100.

Reduce the phrase "has an obligation to" to "must" and remove both "that" constructions at the end of the sentence because they are implicit.

The revised version:

A corporation must report all campaign contributions over $100.

Create a Parallel Universe for Rhythm and Reinforcement

A balanced structure can also improve clarity

You may have heard the term "parallelism" in high school English. It describes the repetition of a verbal pattern to create rhythm and to reinforce the message. Parallel construction is a staple of legal writing because lawyers continually present series of principles, reasons and facts.

Here is an example of a sentence using parallel construction:

> *The jury was asked to determine whether plaintiff's sales territory covered all three states, whether plaintiff could be terminated without cause, and, if not, whether plaintiff was properly terminated for cause.*

The parallel element is the repeating "whether" clause.

Here is an example of a sentence lacking parallel construction:

> *The opening statement is intended to inform the jury about the nature of the action, the issues involved, and give the jury an outline of the facts.*

The sequence begins with two nouns ("nature" and "issues"), suggesting that a third noun will be next in the sequence (*e.g.*, the "facts"). Instead, a verb appears ("give"). The two nouns create an expectation of a third, but the expectation is unfulfilled.

Several solutions are possible, including the following:

Version 1:

> *The opening statement informs the jury about the nature of the action, the key issues and the essential facts.*

This version preserves the "Power of Three," that is, the rhythm and reinforcement in a series of three items. It trims the unnecessary words "intended to" and "involved," and, for precision and balance, it describes the issues as "key" and the facts as "essential."

Version 2:

> *The opening statement informs the jury about the nature of the action and the issues, and it outlines the facts.*

This version solves the parallelism problem by eliminating the series of three.

Parallel construction assists the "flow" of writing, that is, the ease with which the reader moves, and the momentum with which the reader is propelled, from one thought to the next. A reader expects items in a series to have the same grammatical structure. The first item in the series creates the expectation, and the remaining items either fulfill it or disappoint it.

If you interrupt the flow with gratuitous changes in syntax, the reader will become hesitant and will reserve energy to deal with surprises. Conversely, if the structure is predictable, the reader will relax confidently into the prose and may gain confidence in you and your ideas.

Clarity Benefits as Well

Reviewing your drafts for parallel construction may have a secondary pay-off. It may alert you to problems with content as well as with flow. Consider the following passage, in which the writer reports what happened at a status conference before an administrative agency:

> *The last issues discussed at the status conference were the submission of additional testimony, protective orders, and whether a public hearing would be scheduled.*

The sequence lacks parallel construction. The first item in the sequence is a conceptual noun ("submission"), the second is a concrete noun ("orders"), and the third is a noun clause beginning with "whether" ("whether a public hearing would be scheduled").

Not only is the sequence eclectic, but it is unclear. The reader cannot tell whether the participants at the status conference discussed the nature of additional testimony to be submitted or whether they discussed whether to submit any additional testimony at all. Similarly, the reader cannot tell what the parties discussed about protective orders. Was it their necessity or their form?

Assuming appropriate facts, the writer could have used the word "whether" as the repeating element of syntax:

> *The last issues discussed were whether additional testimony would be submitted, whether protective orders would be necessary and whether a public hearing would be scheduled.*

With parallel construction, the message became clear: The parties discussed whether to submit additional testimony and whether to use protective orders. True, the writer could have achieved parallel construction by dropping the "whether" and using a series of three nouns ("The last three issues discussed were additional testimony, protective orders and a public hearing"), but the message would have been incomplete and thus unclear.

In the alternative, the writer could have used "whether" just once:

> *The last issues discussed were whether to take additional testimony, use protective orders and hold a public hearing.*

The repeating element "whether" is now consolidated in one use of that word, which works just as well. The construction is still parallel, even though the word "whether" appears only once, because the reader can tell that the word relates to all three items in the series.

Should you repeat the word "to," saying "*to* take additional testimony, *to* use protective orders and *to* hold a public hearing"? It is not necessary, but it is not wrong. The sound and sense work with or without the additional "to's."

Puzzler

How would you tighten and sharpen the following sentence?

A review of plaintiffs' proposed amended complaint reveals that rather than clarify the allegations against ABC Co., plaintiffs have made them murkier.

"A review . . . reveals" is implicit and can be deleted. "Plaintiffs'" is also implicit and can be deleted though you could keep it for alliteration ("plaintiffs' proposed . . . ."). The concept of murkiness can be conveyed by a verb, "obscures," which is more assertive and shorter (and thus has more "punch") than the phrase "have made them murkier." You do not need "allegations against ABC Co." In a complaint, allegations are assumed, and unless ABC Co. is only one of many defendants, it need not be identified.

The revised version:

The proposed amended complaint obscures what it should have clarified.

To Get to the Point, Get to the Verb

Avoid the "start-stop" syndrome

Lawyers write long sentences, which isn't necessarily bad. We write for an intelligent audience that can handle large chunks of information, and we want our prose to seem smooth and sophisticated, not choppy and adolescent.

But the longer the sentence, the tougher the task of organizing it.

Rules of thumb can facilitate this task by eliminating choices. One such rule is to bring the verb as close to the subject as possible so you don't try the reader's patience or let the reader drift. This isn't a matter of grammar; it's a matter of efficiency. Readers generally don't like to wait for the verb.

The common practice of beginning a sentence with a noun followed immediately by an interruptive phrase, set off by one or more commas, violates the guideline that a verb should follow closely upon its noun. The interruption brings an abrupt halt to the story, as in the following example:

> *The Supreme Court, in Smith v. Jones, supra, held that the tort of interference with prospective economic advantage requires a showing of four elements.*

A reader who sees a noun expects a verb. In fact, the reader demands a verb because a verb supplies action. Without action, you tell no story. If you tell no story, you frustrate the reader, who may disengage.

A reader who sees a noun allocates a unit of attention, and thus a unit of energy, to receive a verb. When an interruption occurs, the energy is spent on that; a tempo is lost; and the reader has to "reload" for the substantive message.

Reloading consumes energy, and so does holding the subject in memory ("Supreme Court") until the verb finally arrives. Thus, the interruption not only frustrates the reader by delaying the action, but it forces the reader to spend extra energy to read your piece.

Such annoyances create suspicion about the validity of your thesis. If your prose is awkward, perhaps your thinking is awkward, too.

Fixing the problem is not difficult. Move the prepositional phrase to the beginning of the sentence ("In *Smith v. Jones . . .*"), or cite *Smith v. Jones* at the end of the sentence:

Version A:

> *In Smith v. Jones, the Supreme Court held that the tort of interference with prospective economic advantage requires a showing of four elements.*

Version B:

> *The Supreme Court has held that the tort of interference with prospective economic advantage requires a showing of four elements. Smith v. Jones.*

At the beginning of a paragraph, "In" followed by a case name is generally not an effective transition, but this does not preclude your using that structure within paragraphs. Presumably, your paragraph would have an informative topic sentence.

A Second Example

Which of the following versions is better, A or B?

Version A:

The notice provisions in the insurance policy do not require, either expressly or by implication, that the notice letter demand a defense or indemnity.

Version B:

The notice provisions in the insurance policy do not expressly, or by implication, require that the notice letter demand a defense or indemnity.

Once you say the notice provisions don't do something, the reader wants to know what they don't do. If you delay the verb, the reader may think the notice provisions don't "state" something, or maybe they don't "reveal" or "address" something. Until you supply the verb, the reader can head in any of several directions or may drift, waiting for instructions.

Either way, you aren't in control. You aren't guiding the reader, and when you aren't guiding the reader, you aren't persuading or laying the groundwork for persuasion. Thus, version A is better because the second half of the verb "do require" is closer to the noun it serves.

In the foregoing example, you reduce uncertainty if you tell the reader before the digressive phrase ("either expressly or by implication") that the notice provisions don't require something. That way, the reader will immediately know what function the notice provisions don't perform (*i.e.,* they don't "require" something). The reader still has to wait to find out what isn't required, but with the verb in hand, the wait is tolerable.

Other examples of the "start-stop" syndrome are as follows:

- The parties, with the assistance of the mediator, ultimately agreed.
- The Court, after full briefing, ruled on the motions.

This is "choppy" prose. What should be a two-part sentence is cut in three. Often, the solution is to move the interruption to the beginning of the sentence, *e.g.,* "After full briefing, the Court ruled on the motions."

Puzzler

How would you tighten and sharpen the following sentence?

> *Perhaps no statement of the reasons why a society founded on the principles of free enterprise fears the over-concentration of economic power in the hands of a few and does not tolerate allegedly "benevolent" monopolies is better than Judge Learned Hand's.*

Get right to it and say "the best statement" rather than "no statement" so the reader does not have to wait until the end of the sentence to learn your position. Drop "reasons" because it is implicit in the word "why." The phrase "founded on the principles of" can be replaced by "premised on," and "the over-concentration of economic power in the hands of a few" can be dropped because it is implicit in the word "monopolies." "*Will* not tolerate" seems stronger than "*does* not tolerate." Finally, the quotation marks around "benevolent" make "allegedly" unnecessary.

The revised version:

> *Perhaps the best statement why a society premised on free enterprise fears monopolies and will not tolerate them, even if "benevolent," is Judge Learned Hand's.*

Grammatical Patterns Dictate the Reader's Response

Arrange your sentences to account for embedded reactions

In arranging the elements of a sentence, lawyers sometimes forget to account for the reader's likely reaction to common grammatical patterns. Consider the following "Question Presented" at the beginning of a brief:

> *Is an employee who causes an accident while driving to work acting within the scope of his employment such that his employer might be held liable for torts committed by that employee under the doctrine of respondeat superior?*

Read literally, this sentence says the employee committed torts "under the doctrine of *respondeat superior*," which makes no sense. One does not commit a tort under a doctrine.

The reader will eventually decipher the sentence but may be confused, momentarily, by the illogic of committing a tort "under a doctrine." In that moment, as in every moment of confusion, the reader's attention may be lost.

The author of this "Question Presented" evidently thought the phrase "for torts" should follow the word "liable" because a person is, after all, liable for torts. But the precise question is not whether someone may be liable for torts but whether someone may be liable under the doctrine of *respondeat superior*. Therefore, the phrase "under the doctrine of *respondeat superior*" should come immediately after the word "liable."

This is accomplished by dropping the phrase "for torts committed by that employee," which is unnecessary anyway because it is implicit in the reference to the employee causing an accident.

The revised sentence reads as follows:

> *Is an employee who causes an accident while driving to work acting within the scope of his employment such that his employer might be held liable under the doctrine of respondeat superior?*

The writer knew that the concluding phrase "under the doctrine of *respondeat superior*" explained the word "liable," and the writer assumed, incorrectly, that the reader would automatically make that connection despite the intervening phrase "for torts committed by that employee."

But a reader doesn't have the writer's intimate knowledge of the material and won't necessarily make connections that override grammatical signals. Here, the phrase "torts committed by that employee" indicates that a description may be forthcoming of how, when, where or why the employee committed torts, as "torts committed by that employee in a negligent manner"; "in his vehicle"; "on public streets"; or "in a fit of rage."

The writer doesn't mean it this way, but the reader experiences it this way because the reader responds instinctively to the grammatical signal in the phrase "torts committed by that employee."

Such mistakes can be avoided by reviewing each sentence from the reader's perspective. To attain such a perspective, try sounding the passage out in your mind. Misplaced phrases should have a hard time getting past that screen.

A Second Example

Another example of improper sequencing is the following effort to qualify (describe, limit) a group of restaurants:

> *Defendants submitted affidavits showing the existence of restaurants within walking distance of the office that would have been open at the time of the accident.*

The writer meant to limit the category "restaurants" in two ways: (1) to a subset of restaurants within walking distance of the office and (2) to a subset of restaurants open at the time of the accident.

But the sentence refers not to a restaurant being open but to an office being open (" . . .the office that would have been open at the time of the accident"). The sentence should be revised as follows:

> *Defendants submitted affidavits showing that restaurants within walking distance of the office would have been open at the time of the accident.*

The key to this revision is the deletion of the passive, nondescriptive phrase, "the existence of." The word "that" can then be moved from after the word "office" to before the word "restaurant," resolving the problem.

Verbal communication follows rules, just as baseball is played according to rules, or music is written according to rules. The implicit rules of verbal communication are described in grammar books that lawyers don't read, which doesn't really matter because we internalized the rules of grammar when we were very young.

One such rule is that a "that clause" following a noun modifies (describes) the noun. In the above example, the noun followed by a that clause is "office." The reader's instinctive reaction to the that clause ("that would have been open") is that the clause modifies office because it immediately follows office.

This is an embedded reaction. You can anticipate it because you would have the same reaction if you were the reader. Because the reaction to grammatical structures is embedded not only in the reader but in you, you can preview the passage as the reader would receive it and can determine if the passage could be misunderstood.

Puzzler

How would you tighten and sharpen the following sentence?

If a trial had occurred, after cross-examination of all experts, it is unclear as to what position any of the parties would have taken on these issues.

This sentence makes the reader wait for the main idea by beginning with a secondary thought (if a trial had occurred), then narrowing to cross-examination of the experts and finally ending with the gist of the sentence—the uncertainly regarding the parties' positions.

Try beginning with the key idea, "uncertainty." Words and phrases that can be dropped as implicit include "all," "as to," "any of" and "on these issues." Depending on the context, "at trial" may be implicit as well.

The revised version:

It is unclear what positions the parties would have taken had they cross-examined the experts at trial.

If you dislike the "It is" construction, you could write:

We do not know what positions the parties would have taken had they cross-examined the experts at trial.

You May Need to Reorganize Your Thoughts After Recording Them

Be wary of digressions, which divert the reader

Tape recorders and word processors allow writers to capture ideas almost in real time. The price of this fluidity may be disorganization—an undulating mix of thesis statements, supporting points, background facts and even irrelevancies. Writers who "go with the flow" usually record digressions as well as progressions, creating disjointed paragraphs and pretzel-like sentences in which the ends curl back into the middle and the beginnings are trapped at the end.

The lure of being able to keep up with one's thoughts is palpable—a writer can cobble together work product in less than an hour. But it involves a trade-off: In return for speed, you may sacrifice order. If you write as you think, some of your writing will inevitably digress.

In personal conversation, we can stray from the point and still hold the listener's attention with tones and gestures that acknowledge the detour and assure the listener that we intend to return to the path. In writing, we don't have that luxury.

Writers cannot bring tones and gestures to the printed page. We have no way to urge the reader to bear with us while we explore a tangent or add a qualification or two, other than to announce, awkwardly, that we intend to digress.

The underlined portion of the following sentence is an example of a typical digression:

> *An officer of the defendant mortgagor allegedly entered into an oral agreement with the plaintiff mortgagee, <u>in consideration of the mortgagee's agreement to forbear from foreclosing</u>, that he would pay the principal and interest due on the note within a few months.*

The underlined phrase splits the description of the oral agreement in two. The first part of the sentence says the mortgagor allegedly made an oral agreement with the plaintiff mortgagee. A reader would expect at that point to be told what the mortgagor agreed to do. But the reader does not learn until the end of the sentence that the mortgagor promised to pay the principal and interest on a note.

The digression in the middle ("in consideration of the mortgagee's agreement to forbear from foreclosing") delays the reader's finding out what the mortgagor promised. On the way to describing that promise, the writer seems to have remembered the consideration for the promise and decided to report that first.

When I first read the passage, the digression appeared to be the end rather than the middle of the sentence. I was surprised to see a comma, not a period, after "foreclosing," and I reread the sentence to see if I had missed something. Some readers would just move on.

As with most digressions, the problem can be solved by rearranging. You can move the statement about consideration to the end of the sentence, where it no longer interrupts:

> *An officer of the defendant mortgagor allegedly entered into an oral agreement with the plaintiff/mortgagee to pay the principal and interest due on the note within a few months, in consideration of the mortgagee's agreement to forbear from foreclosing.*

In this restructured sentence, the reader learns first what the mortgagor allegedly agreed to do—pay principal and interest on a note—and then what the mortgagee allegedly agreed to do—forbear from foreclosing. Had the writer tested the passage against the reader's expectations, as all writing should be tested, the digression might not have occurred.

Chances are the writer didn't realize that the sentence digressed. The writer was probably so familiar with the subject matter that the order in which the facts appeared seemed irrelevant. The writer's mind supplied all the connections. Most readers probably won't make those connections because they are less familiar with the material and don't know the writer's intent.

One could eliminate the digression another way—by beginning the sentence with what used to be the interruption—"In consideration." Assuming the sentence structure isn't dictated by the shape of the sentence before it, I don't favor this approach. I prefer to tell the reader about the mortgagor's promise first because it is the principal subject of the sentence.

A Second Example

In the following sentence, the writer is trying to say that the rules of a stock exchange may deem a director to be "outside" (that is, independent) even if the director provides non-directorial services to the board, for example as a consultant, and receives compensation in addition to director's fees:

> *The rules of the stock exchange permit persons who provide additional services to the board for separate compensation, except for persons who regularly serve as professional advisors, legal counsel or management consultants, to qualify as outside members.*

The writer's point is that persons who provide additional services to the board of directors may still qualify as independent directors unless the services are of a particular kind and are regular. But the idea is broken in two by an "except" clause. The first part of the sentence tells the reader that the rules of the stock exchange permit something, but the next part of the sentence fails to tell the reader what the rules permit.

Instead, the interruption states that the rules have an exception. So the reader knows that rules exist and have an exception, but until the reader completes the sentence and "puts two and two together," the reader doesn't know what the rules allow. By requiring the reader to solve this puzzle, the writer has committed one of the cardinal sins of persuasive writing—making the reader do extra work.

The sentence can be improved by shifting the parts around:

The rules of the stock exchange permit persons who provide additional services to the Board for separate compensation to qualify as outside directors unless the persons regularly serve as professional advisors, legal counsel or management consultants.

The concept of persons being permitted to qualify as outside directors is now a unit at the beginning of the sentence. The interruption has been removed by shifting the qualification to the end of the sentence, and no information has been lost.

Puzzler

How would you tighten and sharpen the following sentence?

The court ruled that plaintiff could not establish that defendant had any duty whatsoever to preserve the evidence where plaintiff failed to ask defendant to do so.

"Plaintiff could not establish" can be dropped. If the court ruled that the defendant had no duty, then the plaintiff implicitly failed to establish a duty. The intensifier "whatsoever" (first cousin to "in any way") is unnecessary. "Where plaintiff failed to ask defendant to do so" can be shortened to "without being asked." "Unasked" is even shorter, but it could, at least momentarily, be taken to modify "evidence" rather than "preserve."

The revised version:

The court ruled that defendant had no duty to preserve the evidence without being asked.

Use Brackets to Alter a Quotation

You can substitute words to improve clarity

I have been asked how to use brackets in a quotation to show changes from the source text. Suppose, for example, that a sentence from a judicial opinion reads as follows:

> *Furthermore, disclaimers of the obligations that normally attend a sale are not favored and are strictly construed against the seller.*

You wish to omit "Furthermore" but otherwise quote the sentence verbatim. To indicate that the sentence in the original text did not begin with "Disclaimers," bracket the "D" in Disclaimers:

> *[D]isclaimers of the obligations that normally attend a sale are not favored and are strictly construed against the seller.*

The brackets show that the "D" in disclaimers was lower case in the text from which you took the quotation.

This works in reverse as well. Suppose the text you wish to quote did not include the word furthermore and began with Disclaimers. If you wish to precede the original quotation with Furthermore, bracket the lower case "d" on disclaimers to show that it was a capital D in the original text:

> *Furthermore, "[d]isclaimers of the obligations . . ."*

Brackets Can Be Used for Clarity

Brackets can also be used to add or substitute words in a quotation to improve the flow and ensure clarity. Suppose that your quotation includes a proper name likely to confuse the reader because the person was not previously identified. You can include an identifier in brackets, with or without the name:

Version A:

> *Plaintiff testified as follows: "Then Smith [another riveter] almost lost his balance."*

Version B:

> *Plaintiff testified as follows: "Then [another riveter] almost lost his balance."*

The bracket in Version A tells the reader that Smith—never before mentioned—is a riveter, which explains why his losing his balance is an important fact. Version B identifies Smith by his job instead of his name.

Either version can work. The context will indicate whether the bracketed reference is explanatory, as in Version A, or whether it replaces a name, as in Version B. You would use the version that seems likely to help the reader most. Depending on the context, you might wish to include Smith's name for flavor.

You can also use brackets to indicate a change of tense from the original text:

He "guess[ed] that the mechanic failed to check the gauges."

Or you can use brackets to add a word that was implicit to the person being quoted but is needed in the quotation for clarity, as in the following:

Counsel conceded that "the court's order did not mention the method of [wastewater] disposal."

Similarly, the material you wish to quote may omit an important term because it was used earlier in the material from which you are quoting. In the following example, you intend to quote the second of two sentences from a court's opinion, but you wish to use the term "administrative agency" from the first sentence instead of the phrase "such a body" in the second. The two sentences read as follows in the original text:

We are concerned with a determination made by an administrative agency. When such a body acts within its authority, its decision is entitled to a presumption of correctness.

You can incorporate the reference to an administrative agency into your quotation of the second sentence by using brackets:

The court opined: "When [an administrative agency] acts within its authority, its decision is entitled to a presumption of correctness."

Don't Bracket Obsessively

You can overdo bracketing in an effort to be true to your source. Suppose that you wish to say the frustration of purpose doctrine will be applied if the principal purpose of a contract was "totally or nearly totally" frustrated.

A treatise says that the frustration of purpose doctrine applies where the purpose of the contract "met with total or near total" frustration. In the flow of your argument, you want to use the words totally or nearly totally, not total or near total. In other words, you want to add "ly" to the two words from the treatise and still cite the treatise.

Forget about quoting. Don't add a bracketed "ly," as in "total[ly]" or "nearly total[ly]." Just say the treatise stands for the proposition that the frustration of purpose doctrine can be applied if the principal purpose of the contract was totally or nearly totally frustrated.

You don't need the force of an exact quotation, and a reader who checks the citation won't be upset that you added "ly." But the reader might be annoyed and distracted by unnecessary bracketing.

Puzzler

How would you tighten and sharpen the following sentence?

To advance a successful cause of action under quantum meruit, one must show that: (1) the plaintiff performed certain services for the defendant; (2) the reasonable value of the services; (3) that the services were rendered at the defendant's request; and (4) plaintiff was unpaid.

This is principally an exercise in parallel construction. Look to create parallel structure by converting the elements of the cause of action to the same part of speech. Nouns work well here: performance, value and nonpayment. (You'll see what we do with "request.") Among other things, the nouns solve the problem of the unbalanced "thats."

You can save words by substituting "establish" for "advance a successful cause of action." Also, in (1), the plaintiff and the defendant are understood, and "certain" adds nothing; you can drop them. In (2), you can save words by using "their" to reinvoke "services" from item (1).

In (3), "were rendered" is unnecessary and is the wrong part of speech for the parallel structure we are developing. Finally, in (4), one word—nonpayment—substitutes for three.

I would reverse items (2) and (3) because the request for services is closely related to performance. You can run (1) and the old (3) together ("the performance of services at defendant's request"), but the elements of performance and request should be numbered separately because they require different proofs. Arguably, the parallel structure based on nouns is sustained by elements (1), (3) and (4).

The revised version:

To establish quantum meruit, one must show (1) the performance of services (2) at defendant's request; (3) their reasonable value; and (4) nonpayment.

Alternate version:

To establish quantum meruit, one must show (1) the performance of services; (2) defendant's request for the services; (3) their reasonable value; and (4) nonpayment.

Discretionary Punctuation Should Achieve Clarity and Flow

You may have a choice of where to put the last comma in a series

An associate asked me whether she should use a comma after the next-to-last item in a series—the one before the "and" or the "or." She said she leaves the comma out, but others put it in, and this bothers her because she believes everyone should do it the same way. She says that legal writers have enough choices without commas adding to the uncertainty.

I told her that omitting the comma after the next-to-last item in a series is optional unless the comma is needed for clarity. I said she can use whichever convention she prefers as long as she is consistent.

Freedom to choose didn't satisfy the associate, who still felt that everyone should follow the same rule.

In grade school, I was taught that a comma is required after the next-to-last item in a series, as in the following:

The court dismissed the first, second, and third counts of the complaint.

As a lawyer, I bowed to and finally embraced what seems to be the dominant practice in legal writing—not to use a comma after the next-to-last item in a series.

Usually, that comma is not needed for comprehension. Because of the initial items in the series and the comma or commas between them, the reader already knows that a series is being presented. The words "and" or "or" signify that the series is about to end.

The extra comma will only slow the reader down.

In the above example, the pacing with the extra comma is as follows: "The court dismissed the first (pause) second (pause) and third counts of the complaint." Without the last comma, the pacing is faster: "The court dismissed the first (pause) second-and-third counts of the complaint."

Generally, the pace of legal writing should be brisk though not breakneck. Some lawyers eschew nearly all commas to create the illusion, I suspect, of being breathless with the importance of what they have to say or to cause readers to move so rapidly through the argument that they overlook its flaws.

Readers know that writers do this—omit commas to create the illusion of power—but I don't think the distrust thereby developed for comma-less prose will carry over to the omission of the last comma in a series. That comma is only a small element in a larger scheme.

As long as clarity is unaffected, consider omitting that comma. It increases the pace and will rarely confuse. Just be consistent. Don't give voice to your ambivalence by arbitrarily using the comma sometimes and not other times so that both sides of your ambivalence are represented.

Sometimes You Need the Last Comma

You may wish to use the extra comma for clarity in a series such as the following:

The complaint alleged tortious interference with prospective economic advantage, intentional infliction of emotional distress and defamation.

Without the comma after "distress," a reader could read "intentional infliction of defamation," which makes just enough sense to cause momentary confusion.

Similarly, a comma after "case" in the following sentence precludes the reader's seeing "dismissal of default judgment":

Sanctions can include monetary fine, dismissal of case or default judgment.

Another good spot for a comma before the conjunction would be after "accuracy" in the following:

E-records are created to promote information functionality, not trustworthiness, accuracy or evidential significance.

This sentence followed a statement that paper documents usually say why they were created, whereas electronic documents do not. The concept of trustworthiness is so strong as a counterpoint to functionality that the reader may deem the thought concluded right there and may think, initially, that "accuracy or evidential significance" begins a new thought.

But it doesn't, which means the reader will be taken aback. In contrast, if a comma follows "accuracy," the reader's eye will catch it, and the reader will suspend closure.

Conventions of punctuation should serve your rhetorical (persuasive) purposes. They should guide the reader, or they should appeal to the reader's aesthetic sense. If a comma assists those purposes, then use it. If not, then don't.

I know that good authorities, including Strunk and White, recommend using a comma after the next-to-last item in a series. I doubt that most readers notice the absence of these commas unless it makes the reading difficult.

Omitting the extra comma as a general rule but including it for clarity takes extra effort because you have to make a decision for each series. Sometimes, reasonable minds can differ, and you may not make the best choice.

Nevertheless, if you are comfortable with this challenge, I suggest you accept it. You won't have many hard choices, and the process will have a secondary benefit. Each time you ask yourself how the reader will perceive a sentence, you will reinforce the reader-centric mindset necessary for successful writing.

Of course, if dropping a comma would violate a hallowed rule of punctuation and could offend or confuse readers, then you must follow the rule. For example, if you are connecting independent clauses with "and," you must use a comma. Otherwise you will have a run-on sentence, as in the following:

They moved for summary judgment on all counts and in the alternative they moved for bifurcation of the trial.

A reader trained in the use of punctuation—as most judges are—may notice the improper omission of the comma after "counts" and may subconsciously conclude that if your punctuation is substandard, then your argument is substandard as well. Justified or not, this can undermine your credibility as an advocate.

This is a truth that persons who refuse to take punctuation seriously seem not to understand. Bad punctuation sends a message, albeit subliminal. At a minimum, it suggests you don't care enough to attend to detail. Though incorrect punctuation has nothing to do with the merits of your case, it sends the wrong message about your commitment and capacity to think things through.

Puzzler

How would you tighten and sharpen the following sentences?

The plaintiff made two separate charges in her court case against defendant alleging racial and sexual discrimination. However, the sexual discrimination charge was the only one filed with the EEOC.

Your initial reaction may be to place a semi-colon after "discrimination" because one should not begin a sentence with "however." Instead, just eliminate the however and make one sentence by beginning with "Though," which ties the second part of the message to the first by signaling a change of direction from the outset.

The rearrangement also keeps the subjects parallel ("plaintiff" and "she"). You would lose rhythm and momentum by switching subjects in successive clauses. The phrase "against defendant" is implicit and can be dropped.

The revised version:

Though the plaintiff alleged both racial and sexual discrimination in her court case, she filed only the sexual discrimination charge with the EEOC.

You Need to Sweat the Small Stuff

Minor usage mistakes can be major blemishes

Just as you shouldn't wear a shirt showing food spots, you shouldn't submit a brief with usage mistakes. They create a bad impression.

Usage conventions such as dropping the "of" from "all of" are not, in the larger scheme, as important as organization, analysis or theme. But adherence to such conventions may be more important than you realize because violating them can irritate a reader who believes that adherence to the rules is a virtue, and that non-adherence is a vice. Such readers often view writers who fail to follow usage conventions as sloppy, ignorant or both.

Treat the following usage mistakes like spots on clothing and clean them out.

CATEGORY I: Excess words that offend the ear.

"Off of." Delete "of" as unnecessary. Do not say "off of the work site." Say "off the work site." To the trained writer—which includes nearly all judges—"off of" sounds bad.

"All of." "All" is sufficient.

BAD: Plaintiff satisfied all of the elements of the test.
BETTER: Plaintiff satisfied all the elements of the test.

You can retain the "of" where it serves another word, as in "some or all of the cost."

"As to whether." Delete "as to."

BAD: Smith was unsure as to whether Jones made the promise.
BETTER: Smith was unsure whether Jones made the promise.

CATEGORY II: Words that drag but probably don't offend the ear.

Even writers who never use "off of" or "all of" can be seduced by the following:

"Whether or not." "Or not" is understood.

BAD: He debated whether or not to exercise the option.
BETTER: He debated whether to exercise the option.

"The fact that." "That" is usually enough. "Fact" is understood.

BAD: He was aware of the fact that . . .
BETTER: He was aware that . . .

"In order to." "To" is generally sufficient.

BAD: In order to make a prima facie case . . .
BETTER: To make a prima facie case . . .

CATEGORY III: Words with Rogue Connotations.

Several words are substandard where their use creates ambiguity.

"Due to." Say "because of." "Due to" not only sounds bad, but it can mislead the reader—albeit momentarily—because it has connotations not only of causation but of owing, as a debt.

BAD: He was unable to process the application due to a clerical backlog.
BETTER: He was unable to process the application because of a clerical backlog.

"While" for "although."

BAD: While the case law is clear that . . .
BETTER: Although the case law is clear that . . .

The temporal connotations of "while" create an ambiguity that the reader has to solve before proceeding. The task may be minimal, but it is a diversion, and, like "due to," it could trigger a prejudice, causing the reader to perceive your writing and your argument as substandard.

"Over" for "more than." "Over" is spatial. Use "more than" for quantity.

BAD: The house has over 4,000 square feet.
BETTER: The house has more than 4,000 square feet.

"As" for "because." "As" is principally a temporal word. In a causative role, it grates on the traditionally trained ear even more than "due to." Actually, "grates on the ear" is being kind. When you breach a usage rule, you risk being viewed not only as inattentive to form but as inattentive to the substance of your argument. If your language is deemed substandard, your argument may be deemed substandard as well.

BAD: He could not attend the meeting as he was out of town.
BETTER: He could not attend the meeting because he was out of town.

I say that a phrase grates on the "traditionally trained ear" because such phrases do not seem to grate on the ears of those who use them. Much to the distress of writing teachers and assigning attorneys, "as" in a causative role sounds fine to those who use it. In fact, one former "as user" considered me a fuddy duddy for insisting that she use "because" rather than "as" in the causative role.

Really, I'm just trying to be helpful. As long as because—rather than as—is standard in a causative role, you have to use because. (Query how long "as" will remain substandard in a causative role with business answering machines urging, "Please listen closely as our prompts have changed.")

"Since vs. because"—a classic conflict. Our English teachers admonished us not to use "since" in lieu of "because," given the temporal connotations of since. Consequently, many readers react poorly to since in a causative role. For some readers, it is a pet peeve.

Yet scholars say that since has deep causative roots and should be perfectly fine for such use, *e.g.,* "Since the company's debts far exceed its liquid assets, bankruptcy may be imminent."

I suggest you favor "because" over "since" in a causative role because you never know where prejudice may lurk. Because people in this business care about words, you have to be careful with them. Ideas are more important than word choice, but subtle influences can have significant effect in a close contest. Don't give the other side an edge.

Puzzler

How would you tighten and sharpen the following sentence?

The cases hold that, to the extent that electronic data is inaccessible, there may be good reason to shift some or all of the cost of retrieval to the requesting party.

Remove the interruptive phrase beginning "to the extent that" to get more quickly to the point that cost may be shifted. Replace the qualifying phrases "to the extent that" and "some or all of" with "in whole or in part." The expression "there may be good reason" is implicit and can be dropped.

Pausing after the word "shifted" in the revised version doesn't weaken the powerful phrase "may be shifted." It provides dramatic buildup for the concluding phrase, "to the requesting party."

The revised version:

The cases hold that the cost of retrieving inaccessible electronic data may be shifted, in whole or in part, to the requesting party.

Alternate version:

The cases hold that some or all of the cost of retrieving inaccessible electronic data may be shifted to the requesting party.

Free Yourself from the "It" Syndrome

A missing antecedent may give the reader pause

We flow easily into expressions where the pronoun "it" has no antecedent, as in, "It would be inequitable to deny him the commissions he earned," or "It would be extraordinary if the court ruled for plaintiff." In legal writing, this common construction can sidetrack the reader.

Consider the following:

If the documents may be important to the lawsuit, it would be unreasonable to discard them.

The writer means that discarding documents would be unreasonable if the documents may be important to the lawsuit, but the sentence initially directs the reader away from that idea because readers are programmed to associate pronouns with nouns. A reader seeing the pronoun "it" immediately after the noun "lawsuit" will associate "it" with "lawsuit" and will assume, albeit momentarily, that the subject of the second clause of the sentence is the lawsuit.

Obviously, when the reader sees "would be unreasonable to discard them," the reader will realize that the subject of the second half of the sentence is not the lawsuit. One would not speak of a lawsuit being "unreasonable" where the discussion is about documents, nor would one normally associate the word "discard" with a lawsuit. Consequently, the reader will quickly deduce that "it" cannot refer to the lawsuit.

But this self-correction requires work, and while the work is being done (that is, while the reader is thinking, literally or figuratively, "Whoops. The word 'it' doesn't refer to the lawsuit"), the reader is not following the writer's point.

Editing the sentence is not difficult:

Discarding the documents would be unreasonable if they may be important to the lawsuit.

Now the pronoun ("they") has an antecedent ("documents"). Not only does this revision remove the misdirection caused by "it" without an antecedent, but it strengthens the sentence by featuring the action—the discarding of documents.

Let's try another example:

The form in which electronic data is stored may make it difficult to access the information.

The writer means that accessing electronic data may be difficult because of the form in which it is stored, but a reader may instinctively associate the pronoun "it" with the closest noun, "data," and may be nonplussed by the concept of data being difficult. Although the reader will quickly figure it out, the reader will waste energy and, for a moment, will lose the train of thought.

Possible re-writes include:

The form in which electronic data is stored may make accessing the data difficult.

The form in which electronic data is stored may impede access to it.

"It" without an antecedent may also create an ambiguity that the reader cannot solve, as in the following example:

A court may require a search for a critical piece of information at the responding party's expense even if it is uncertain whether the information exists.

What is uncertain? Is the court uncertain, or is the existence of the information uncertain? The more I read the sentence, the less sure I am of the answer.

At first, I thought the writer used "it is uncertain" to mean "nobody knows." But the writer could also have meant the court was unsure. The difference is subtle but potentially meaningful.

A possible clarification is as follows:

A court may require a search for a critical piece of information at the responding party's expense even if the existence of the information is uncertain.

In this version, the uncertainty clearly relates to the existence of the information, not to the court's state of mind.

Sometimes the independent "it" is not only ambiguous but grammatically wrong:

When examined carefully, it becomes clear that every case cited by defendant is distinguishable.

The writer meant that cases were examined carefully but said that "it" was examined carefully, whatever "it" might be.

Sometimes an "it" that lacks an antecedent isn't confusing, merely unnecessary:

It is the senior management of a corporate party that bears the ultimate responsibility for developing and implementing procedures to ensure the preservation of relevant evidence.

Remove "It is" and "that." Resist the temptation to use the kind of emphatic with which you might season a speech, thrusting your forefinger toward the sky as you hold forth in front of a packed auditorium. Physical actions can keep listeners interested and drive home your point, but such gestures are lost on readers, who cannot see you.

Puzzler

Which Version would you use, A, B or C?

Version A:

This Responding Brief will in Point I address the defendant's analysis of the jurisdictional question.

Version B:

Point I of this Responding Brief will address the defendant's analysis of the jurisdictional question.

Version C:

This Responding Brief will address the defendant's analysis of the jurisdictional question in Point I.

Keep the verb intact, as in Versions B and C ("will address"). Version C has two infirmities. It suggests, inadvertently, that the defendant performed an analysis in Point I ("the defendant's analysis . . . in Point I") or that a jurisdictional question can be found in Point I ("the jurisdictional question in Point I"). It also cedes the featured position at the end of the sentence to "Point I," which isn't as important as "jurisdictional question." Version B is cleaner, better balanced, and still direct ("Point I . . . will address").

Typos Undermine Your Credibility and Your Case

To catch mistakes, let your product sit or find a second set of eyes

Old-timers are dismayed at the sloppiness of today's written work. They say people were more careful when mistakes had to be corrected by hand, not only on originals but on carbon copies. They say (as they have said forever) that the younger generation shows no respect.

Old-timers are not wrong to be dismayed. A sloppy presentation makes a bad impression. Misspellings, omitted words, random punctuation and other typographical errors (collectively, "typos") reflect lack of effort, which suggests your case isn't worth the effort. They also reflect lack of care, which suggests you lack respect. Typos are the spot on the blouse or the dust bunny on the floor. They stand out.

Most courts will tolerate a few typos. In fact, a former appellate law clerk told me that the occasional typo actually humanized the larger firms. (Now that's a soft heart.) But the same clerk also told me that if a brief was riddled with mistakes, "You sort of assumed that the substance would be equally haphazard." This echoes what a sitting judge told me: "Carelessness of form implies carelessness of thought."

Sloppiness will mar not only submissions to a court but also submissions in draft to a supervising attorney. You may be "among friends" within the firm, but you are still making an impression on persons who control your fate. Be careful.

If courts and supervising attorneys are irritated by typos, clients are enraged. They expect a well-packaged product for the generous fee they pay. Typos suggest the firm doesn't care enough about the client to be attentive.

I asked my informal polling group about the causes of typos and their cures. One person said that typos occur because "I think faster than my fingers can type." Another blames the vagaries of dictation. When the writer reviews the draft, he sees what he remembers dictating. "My mind compensates for mistakes in the text." In subsequent drafts, he doesn't reread passages—especially quotations—that he doesn't plan to change.

Ironically, the spell-check programs that prevent mistakes in spelling cause different problems. Spell-check highlights nonwords (like "answr") but not wrong words (as in "he has more money then she"). Relying on spell-check, typists don't read for meaning. Writers do read for meaning, and as a consequence, they unconsciously fill in gaps and read right past mistakes.

One associate says that mistakes don't get corrected "if I am pressed for time." In his universe, neatness receives low priority as the deadline looms. I would reallocate those priorities. One rarely improves core arguments in the hour before a brief goes out, but one can irritate a lot of people with missed typos.

One way to catch typos is to bring in a fresh pair of eyes, either your own—by putting the document aside and coming back to it—or someone else's. Law review editors read aloud to each other, cross-checking as they go. Probably, you won't have this luxury. At best, you will have a proofreader.

Some writers perform a final review just for misspellings and other typos, not for substance. This reduces the chance that the sense of a passage will carry the reader right past a mistake.

Unfortunately, some lawyers proof indifferently. Some are impatient, and some consider their time too valuable for this task. They rationalize, "It's the secretary's job to avoid typos, not mine. If the firm wants perfection, it should give me help."

My advice is this: Include proofing on the list of tasks for which you will do what it takes to get the job done. Either delegate proofing to a person on whom you can rely implicitly, or rely on yourself. In the words of one writer, "You need to do old-fashioned, finger-tracing-of-each-word proofreading."

Comic Relief

The following errors resulted from dictation and were caught, several of them after passing through spell-check:

- You have asked for a budget for attorneys fees for pursuing a separate depilatory judgment action in the trial court.
- Section 92 of the Casino Control Act names only those service industries that traditionally were more likely to harbor organized crime, such as Garbor Chandler's [garbage handlers], vending machine providers . . . [and so forth].
- This is a public document request under New Jersey's Right-2-No-Laws.
- I knew I was doing something wrong, but I did not realize that the man would shrude up my era [the magnitude of my error].
- Desperate treatment wherever it appears presents a naughty problem.
- In this case, the gain just does not seem worth the scandal.
- The absence of evidence to the contrary casts dispersion on the jury's verdict.
- The trial court did not even pay lift service to the analytical framework for evaluating a retaliatory discharge claim.
- The Supreme Court reversed, adopting the Appellate Division's descending opinion.
- Please read the letter and mole over your response.
- If an employee rats on a co-worker and breeds dissection, the employer can fire him or her for that.

- The locust of power is always subject to change.
- That statement is a known sequitur.

The following errors escaped scrutiny and went out, to the embarrassment of one party and the amusement of the other:

- The United States Supreme Court is the final orbiter on questions of federal constitutional law.
- This permit super seeds permit #45443.
- In a form of order submitted to the court: It appearing that such relief is in the best interests of the estate, and for good insufficient cause appearing therefore . . .
- Letter to the judge: We would appreciate your stamping one of the copies of the Affidavit "received" and returning to our office with our messenger.
- To a job candidate: We are deferring (check spelling) a decision on the paralegal position for six to eight weeks.
- Section heading in an answer to a complaint: Twelevth Separate Dedfense
- Concluding a letter: Thank you for your corporation.

Mistakes may be funny when others make them, but not when the assigning attorney appears at your door with the tainted document in hand. Make diligent proofreading part of your prefiling routine.

Puzzler

Which is better, Version A or Version B?

Version A:

XYZ Corp.'s argument blurs the distinction between breaching express terms of a contract and breaching the implied covenant of good faith.

Version B:

XYZ Corp.'s argument blurs the distinction between breaching an express covenant and breaching the implied covenant of good faith.

Version A focuses on four variables, two of which are adjectives and two of which are nouns: (1) express; (2) term; (3) implied; and (4) covenant. More variables mean more work for the reader. To help the reader, reduce the variables.

You can eliminate a variable by bringing both the express and the implied elements under the rubric "covenant," as in Version B. You are concerned with the substantive distinction between express and implied terms, not the semantic distinction, if one exists, between terms and covenants.

Some Commas Should Neither Be Seen Nor Heard

Don't place a comma between subject and verb

An earlier column discussed three situations in which commas are wrongly omitted: the "breathless which clause" (*e.g.,* "The trial court granted the motion for summary judgment which the appellate court affirmed."), the descriptive "-ing" clause (*e.g.,* "The court dismissed the complaint finding that plaintiff had failed to allege a *prima facie* case."), and the run-on sentence. This discussion addresses a circumstance in which commas are wrongly added between subject and verb, as in the following:

> *Under the Sarbanes-Oxley Act of 2002, employees in publicly traded companies who allege retaliatory discharge or other discrimination, may file a complaint, first with the Department of Labor and then, if necessary, in Federal court.*

By the eighteenth word in this long sentence ("discrimination"), the writer evidently felt the need for a comma, particularly after a "who clause," which in other circumstances might be bracketed by commas (*e.g.,* "Judicial clerks, who work for peanuts, can't begin repaying their college loans until they enter the private sector.").

In the sentence about the Sarbanes-Oxley Act, the comma after "discrimination" serves no useful purpose. It unnecessarily interrupts transmittal of the information regarding what employees in publicly traded companies can do under the act (they can file a complaint).

The rule is that one should not place a comma between subject and verb. It's a good rule—practical, not vestigial like the rule against splitting infinitives, and not merely conventional like the rule that periods go inside rather than outside quotation marks. The rule is premised on the reader's instinctive reaction to the relationship between subject and verb.

When a reader sees a subject, the reader not only expects but demands a verb. The longer the verb is delayed, the more impatient the reader becomes. This is why you shouldn't put long interruptive clauses between subject and verb, as in "ABC Co., looking to strengthen its position among the leaders in the industry by way of merger as well as internal growth, made a tender offer for the stock of XYZ Corp."

Generally, a comma means you have finished at least a portion of a thought. Placing a comma between subject and verb sends the reader a mixed message. On the one hand, the comma says you have finished a thought. On the other hand, the nonappearance of the verb indicates that the thought isn't finished. The reader has to sort out the mixed message before moving on.

Compound Verbs

A typical mistake is to add a comma between a subject and the second of two verbs in a compound verb, as follows:

Dr. Deductible specializes in hemophilia, but treats many different blood disorders.

The compound verb consists of "specializes" and "treats." (The term "compound verb" is somewhat counterintuitive because it calls two verbs one.) The comma after hemophilia is inappropriate because you don't want the reader to pause between the subject (Dr. Deductible) and the second part of the compound verb (treats). You want the reader to find out as quickly as possible that Dr. Deductible's practice is broader than just the one disorder.

Few writers would place a comma between Dr. Deductible and the first part of the compound verb, "specializes" (*i.e.*, "Dr. Deductible, specializes . . ."), but many would think a pause appropriate before beginning the second thought, namely, that not only does the doctor specialize in hemophilia, but he treats other blood disorders as well. Corrected, the sentence has no comma:

Dr. Deductible specializes in hemophilia but treats many different blood disorders.

A writer who adds the comma after hemophilia may be reasoning from the premise that changes of idea should be marked by commas. Because the sentence contains a change of idea from "specializes in" to "treats many," the writer adds a comma. The flaw is in the premise, not the logic. Not all changes of idea need to be marked by a comma.

The reaction to a comma is so deeply embedded in a reader's consciousness that a comma sends a signal whether the writer means to or not. The comma says "pause." A pause can, theoretically, aid comprehension, but not when inserted between subject and verb.

Here is another example of a comma improperly placed between a subject and the second part of a compound verb:

The police took the suspect into custody, but released him after they determined he was not in town on the day of the crime.

The subject is the "police," and the verbs are "took" and "released." The comma after custody improperly separates the subject from the second verb, "released." A speaker might pause after "custody," but a reader would not—unless forced to by the comma.

The competing principles in this sentence are (1) place a comma between the old thought (took into custody) and the new thought (released) and (2) don't place a comma between subject and verb. Here, the second principle controls. If the new thought doesn't include a new or repeated subject, then the thought shouldn't be preceded by a comma.

One more example of a comma improperly placed between the subject and the second part of a compound verb is as follows:

The Code does not make clear whether a machine that can function as a pari-mutuel ticket issuing machine, and be adapted as a slot machine is illegal.

Significant ideas appear on both sides of the "and," but the relevant subject—"that" in the embedded "that clause"—is not restated. The verbs in the compound verb are "can function" and "be adapted." Because the second verb in the relevant clause is acting for the single subject, the verb should not be preceded by a comma.

Puzzler

How would you tighten and sharpen the following sentence?

What is the threshold that has to be passed to create critical mass?

The most obvious initial change is to take out "is the" and "that," reducing the sentence to "What threshold has to be passed to create critical mass?" Because the idea of something having to be passed is implicit in the concept of threshold, you can drop the phrase "has to be passed to create" if you put back "is the."

The revised version:

What is the threshold for critical mass?

Alternate version:

What is the critical mass threshold?

"Threshold" may not be the best metaphor to pair with critical mass. At a threshold, one is on the brink but has not entered. When you have reached "critical mass"—a term generally associated with nuclear explosions—you have entered a new plane of existence (or nonexistence). The reader probably wants to know the first point past the threshold, where critical mass has been reached.

Try this:

At what point [or When] do you reach critical mass?

Mind Your P's and Q's and the Apostrophes That Go with Them

The little mark is a detail worth attention

> The confusion of the possessive "its" (no apostrophe) with the contractive "it's" (with apostrophe) is an unequivocal signal of illiteracy and sets off a simple Pavlovian "kill" response in the stickler.
>
> —Truss, "Eats, Shoots & Leaves" (2003) at 43.

Misplaced apostrophes may not confuse, but they irritate, and they make your writing seem careless. It is not wise to irritate readers who have power over you, like partners, clients and judges, and it is similarly imprudent to appear sloppy. Imprecision in form suggests imprecision in substance. It sows a seed of doubt that may sprout with the first gap in your logic. Even minor irritants may bother a reader who is already on edge.

For example, I was recently grumbling over an associate's misinterpretation of a case when I noticed that his version of the phrase "attorneys' fees," referring to our firm's aggregate charges, placed the apostrophe after attorney and before the "s," like this:

attorney's fees

Fleetingly, I had the thought "can't even get apostrophes right." I tried unsuccessfully to stifle it, then to ignore it, and finally to put it into perspective, but reactions are reactions. I can't always suppress them, nor can other readers.

The singular possessive "attorney's fees" works only if one attorney performs all the services. In a large firm, especially in litigation, that is unlikely. Fees generated by a firm are attorneys' fees because they aggregate the work of several lawyers and other billing professionals, like paralegals. In the absence of evidence that only one lawyer is involved, follow the convention of "attorneys' fees."

In fairness, many experienced attorneys don't know where to put the apostrophe in attorneys' fees, either. Some even hedge their bets, doing it both ways in the same document. First, they place the apostrophe before the s, then after the s, then before the s, and so on, which ensures that they get it right about half the time.

For conventions like the apostrophe in attorneys' fees, you must learn the custom. For ministerial facts that you don't know, such as whether a company's name ends with "Corp." or "Corporation," choose one form and stick with it. Don't show your uncertainty.

Chances are, if you write it consistently one way, the reader won't question whether you are right. If you waver, writing "ABC Corp." one time and "ABC Corporation" another, the reader will sense that you don't know the company's name and may consider you either weak-minded for failing to commit to a name or careless for failing to complete your due diligence.

Misplacing the apostrophe in "attorneys' fees" is usually a matter of ignorance, as is misplacement of the apostrophe in worker's compensation. The convention for that possessive is singular, not plural.

In contrast, misplacing the apostrophe for the possessives of "plaintiff" or "defendant"—one of the most common typographical errors—is usually caused by inattention. Writers often make the possessive singular when it should be plural and vice versa.

Apostrophes get misplaced in dictation when the lawyer doesn't verbalize them, and the typist, preferring to keep pace rather than pause to make judgments about punctuation, guesses wrong. Surprisingly, apostrophes are also misplaced by lawyers who type directly onto the computer.

Proof your drafts carefully for this mistake. Misplaced apostrophes annoy readers, especially perfectionists and curmudgeons, and they leave bad impressions even on benign, forgiving readers.

The Great Debate

I will not join, but I will visit the fringes of, the debate whether to add just an apostrophe or both an apostrophe and an s to form the possessive of singular nouns ending with an s or z sound, like witness, class, or Jones. Most writing manuals recommend that you add s for the possessive, as in witness's, class's or Jones's, but newspapers omit the s. If I wrote "witness's character" without quotation marks in this column, the editors would change it to "witness' character."

I have no problem with either convention, s or no s, but for legal writing, I prefer to add the s if I would pronounce it. Prose is less likely to call attention to itself if the appearance tracks the pronunciation. For example, I would say "wit-nis-sizz character," so I write "witness's character." I would say "Jone-zizz contract," so I write "Jones's contract." I would not say "Jones contract," so I don't write "Jones' contract."

Even manuals that recommend adding the s after the apostrophe make exceptions for names that would sound strange with the extra s. The examples commonly given are Moses (for whom the extra s would create "Mo-ziz-izz") and Jesus (for whom the extra s would create "Je-zuz-izz"). Consequently, the possessive of Moses is Moses', and the possessive of Jesus is Jesus'. The rule would apply to "Kansas" as well.

Multisyllable names with an unaccented "eez" ending also drop the extra s for the possessive. For the name Maimonides (accent on "mon"), for example, a reader who sounds out words would struggle with the pronunciation "My-MAH-ni-dee-zizz" based on the incorrect possessive, "Maimonides's." The same would hold for Greek names like Archimedes and Euripides.

I don't know what the rule is for the plural possessive of "Hobbits." Following my pronunciation approach, I would omit the extra s to avoid the sound "Hobbitzizz" (Hobbits's), which is what Gollum called Frodo and Sam in Tolkien's Trilogy of the Ring—"nasty Hobbitses."

Additional Hints

Use an apostrophe or not—it's your choice—to form the plurals of dates, words referred to as words, words comprised of capital letters, and capital letters, as in:

the 1990's or the 1990s

six however's or six howevers

ATM's or ATMs

RFP's or RFPs

P's and Q's or Ps and Qs

Just be consistent. To form the plural of small letters, use an apostrophe:

a's, b's, c's

For the plural of proper names, do not use an apostrophe:

The Smiths made a down payment on the house.

For joint possession, use the possessive form for the last word only:

Smith and Jones's partnership

For individual possession, use the possessive form for each noun:

Smith's and Jones's securities

Puzzler

How would you tighten and sharpen the following sentence?

The statute applies to public officials and acts as a complete bar to gifts of any sort.

If you must record your thoughts in the order you have them, so be it. But be critical thereafter. Look for ways to bring your point forward. The first thought the writer had was that the statute applies to public officials, so he wrote that. His second thought was that the statute bars gifts to public officials. So he wrote that, and for emphasis he said the bar was "complete" as to gifts "of any sort." He was tempted to write "absolutely a complete bar to gifts of any sort," but he resisted the impulse.

The sentence did not begin with the point—that the statute bars gifts to public officials. True, the statute "applies" to public officials, but the point of the sentence is that the statute bars gifts. Move that idea to the beginning of the sentence.

Shorten "complete bar to gifts of any sort" to "bars all gifts."

The revised version:

The statute bars all gifts to public officials.

"Which" Is Often Incorrectly Used in Place of "That"

Get the words straight to please the purists

I found an old memo on sewage treatment capacity in which I used "which" instead of "that" in sentences like the following:

The consultants wrote the plan for allocating the sewage treatment capacity which will become available when the treatment plant expands.

The application for final approval required an engineering plan which is more refined than the plan submitted for tentative approval.

In the above examples, "which" should have been "that" because my intent was to differentiate an item from others of its kind. In the first sentence, the item is sewage treatment capacity—the specific capacity, and no other, that would become available when the sewage treatment plant expands. In the second sentence, the item is an engineering plan different from an engineering plan submitted earlier.

As used above, "which" or "that" is called a "relative pronoun." You need not remember the term, but you should know when to use "that" rather than "which" as a relative pronoun because deviation from the preferred usage is likely to irritate finicky readers (who largely think of themselves as "well-educated" readers). Several judges have told me that finding a "which" where a "that" belongs is among their pet peeves.

Nobody has told me that finding "that" where "which" belongs is of any concern. From this I conclude that as a matter of prudence if nothing else, we should know how to use that and which.

As a novice brief writer, I used "that" as a relative pronoun because it sounded better. Then I noticed that a partner whose judgment I respected used "which" rather than "that." Figuring to make a small stride forward in my legal writing, I began using which, just as I later fell briefly into the bad habit of using "commence" because (what else?) a good writer used it, and it sounded impressive.

After a couple of years, I stumbled on the preferred usage of that and which, probably in Strunk and White's *Elements of Style*, which says, "Careful writers, watchful for small conveniences, go *which*-hunting, remove the defining *whiches*, and by so doing improve their work."[1] Almost immediately on learning the preferred usage, I became intolerant of the other, like a newly rich person suddenly looking down on a middle class neighbor.

With a history as an offender, maybe I should be more tolerant; but I can't help myself. I wince when someone uses which where that is preferred. If I wince,

---

[1] Strunk and White, *Elements of Style* (4th Ed.), p. 59.

others wince, too. That is why you should use the preferred form—so your readers, especially your less tolerant ones, don't wince. As I repeatedly advise, a reader's discomfort interferes with your ability to persuade.[2]

The oft-stated rule for using "that" and "which" as relative pronouns is that the clause should be introduced by "which," preceded by a comma, if you can omit the clause "without materially changing the meaning of the sentence." If you cannot omit the clause without materially changing the meaning of the sentence, then use "that" without a comma.

I do not find that explanation helpful. A lawyer should use words only if they add meaning. Otherwise, the words are just filler. If the words add meaning, then omitting them changes the meaning of the sentence, presumably materially, whether the words are preceded by "that" or by a comma and "which."

The best I can do in terms of articulating a rule is to recommend using "that" when you wish to distinguish one item from others in the same category, as in "the appeal that was dismissed," which tells the reader that other appeals were not dismissed. If you say "the appeal, which was dismissed," then the reader understands that you are speaking of only one appeal. If you say "the appeal which was dismissed," the reader doesn't know whether you can't punctuate correctly or whether you mix up that and which.

Sometimes "which" is correct but mispunctuated. Consider the following:

Immediately after the closing, Smith recorded the deed which included covenants of seisin.

The which in the above sentence is correct—it shouldn't be "that"—but it should be preceded by a comma. Grammatically, the which introduces a "nonrestrictive" or "nondefining" clause, meaning, essentially, that the clause merely describes what precedes it. It doesn't set its antecedent apart from something similar, but different.

If the sentence had said, "Smith recorded the deed that included covenants of seisin," then the deed he recorded—the one that included covenants of seisin—would be distinguished from some other deed. Above, only one deed is at issue.

Here is a similar example:

Most courts will admit this type of statement as an excited utterance which is an exception to the hearsay rule.

"Which" is fine. Just place a comma after utterance.

Sometimes, neither which nor that is necessary, as in the following:

---

2 Some Internet commentators don't fuss over that and which, but then they don't have to write briefs for finicky (well-educated) judges. See www.wsu.edu:8000/~brains/errors/which.html (last visited January 22,2007) ("I must confess that I do not myself observe the distinction between "that" and "which."); and http://andromeda.rutgers.edu/~jlynch/writing/t.html (last visited January 22, 2007) ("According to the more quibbling self-styled grammar experts, *that* is restrictive, while *which* is not.").

The factual scenarios which are to be framed as causes of action in the Amended Complaint arose as a result of newly discovered information.

The bacteria which are used in the sewage treatment process consume oxygen in the stream.

Forget about changing "which are" to "that are." Just drop "which are," leaving "The factual scenarios to be framed" and "The bacteria used."

Another way to delete "which" is to use the "-ing" construction, as here:

Transfer of venue is limited to causes of action which arise under Title 11 in the United States Bankruptcy Code.

The procedural issue which has caused conflict among the Circuits is whether the school district bears the burden of proof at the administrative hearing.

Change the phrase "which arise" to "arising" and the phrase "which has caused conflict" to "causing conflict."

Puzzler

How would you improve the following sentence?

The license application was rejected due to an insufficiency of information.

"Due to" is considered substandard. "Because of" is preferred. "Insufficient" is shorter and sharper than "an insufficiency of."

The revised version:

The license application was rejected because of insufficient information.

Be Cautious Using Nouns as Adjectives

A string of modifying nouns makes a heavy meal

Adjectives describe nouns. In grammatical jargon, we say they "modify" nouns. One noun can support more than one adjective, as in "a vicious, interminable quarrel." The adjectives "vicious" and "interminable" characterize the intensity and duration of the quarrel. A series of adjectives can be an effective way to home in.

But a series of adjectives won't work as well when the adjectives are nouns used as adjectives ("noun adjectives"), such as "venue" in "venue motion" and "settlement" in "settlement talks." Strings of noun adjectives are not reader-friendly. They repeatedly offer the reader false closure, as in the following sentence regarding electronic discovery costs:

> *The court ordered further proceedings to determine electronic document production expense allocation.*

The topic is cost allocation for producing electronic documents. Four modifiers precede the noun "allocation": electronic, document, production and expense. Of those four, only one is an adjective by nature. The other three are nouns used as adjectives: "document," "production" and "expense."

Readers seeing the verb "to determine" instinctively begin looking for a direct object—something that answers the question "determine what?" A reader's initial reaction on seeing a noun in that slot is to view it as an object, not a modifier, because nouns that follow verbs tend to serve as objects.

The first noun after the verb is "document," momentarily suggesting that the court ordered further proceedings to "determine [an] electronic document." For several reasons, the reader will quickly deduce that "document" has been used as an adjective: The "an" is missing; one doesn't "determine" documents; and the sentence continues with another noun. But the deductive process will, naturally, require effort.

The reader will then look to the next noun, "production," as a possible object of the verb "determine." Momentarily, the reader will think the court ordered further proceedings "to determine [an] electronic document production."

That makes some sense, but the "an" is still missing, and another noun follows. So the reader will conclude that "production" is not the direct object of "determine" and will move on to "expense," still looking for the direct object, thinking briefly that the court determined "electronic document production expense."

But one more noun follows: "allocation." Now the reader can sense that some sort of allocation of cost is involved, but the work required to glean that insight has been substantial. By this time, the reader has had enough of the sentence. The string of three noun adjectives is oppressive.

Noun adjectives not only confuse the reader grammatically, but they tend to be conceptual rather than descriptive, and thus they fail to home in. Consider the nouns used as adjectives in the above sentence: document, production and expense.

"Document" covers a lot of ground. It is inclusive rather than descriptive. "Production" is a process and thus amorphous, conceptual rather than visual. Similarly, "expense" creates no images. The multiple denotations and connotations potentially associated with these open-ended words allow the reader to drift from the desired path.

To fix the sentence, we can bring "allocation" forward so that it appears immediately after "determined," applying the rule of thumb that a direct object should come as soon as possible after the verb:

> *The court ordered further proceedings to determine the allocation of electronic document production expense.*

Now the reader quickly learns that what has to be determined is an allocation. The order of information is more attuned to the reader's hard-wired expectation that the direct object will immediately follow the verb.

But the reader still has to wait for the answer to the question "allocation of what?" Two noun adjectives (document and production) still precede the noun that says what was allocated (expense).

We can move the concept of expense forward and change "expense" to "cost," which is more precise, one syllable shorter and rhythmically better. Also, instead of "allocation," we'll use "how to allocate," which is sharper:

> *The court ordered further proceedings to determine how to allocate the cost of electronic document production.*

Now the reader immediately learns that what has to be determined is how to allocate cost. What cost? The cost of electronic document production.

But wait. We can also bring forward the word that tells the reader what the cost is associated with, that is, the production of documents:

> *The court ordered further proceedings to determine how to allocate the cost of producing electronic documents.*

Now the reader learns in rapid sequence that what has to be determined is (i) how to allocate (ii) the cost (iii) of producing documents. Only one word is a modifier—electronic—and it's an adjective by nature. The phrase "electronic documents" also finishes well. It's crisp and strong in a position of prominence at the end of the sentence.

One further thought. "To determine how to allocate" is implicit in the verb "allocate." Shortening the sentence works even better:

> *The court ordered further proceedings to allocate the cost of producing electronic documents.*

Puzzler

How would you tighten and sharpen the following sentence?

The matter of eligibility for a casino license is specifically addressed in Section 82b of the Act, which identifies those persons who are "eligible" to hold a casino license.

If we wish to use the opening clause of this sentence, we can delete "The matter of" and begin with "Eligibility" because no reader cares that eligibility for a casino license is a "matter." We can also delete "specifically" because the word "identifies" tells the reader that the Act specifically states who is eligible to hold a casino license.

But we don't need the opening clause. Except for the section of the Act, the information it conveys is provided later.

In the clause that remains, drop "who are" as unnecessary and retain "those" to make clear that Section 82b covers all persons eligible, not just some persons eligible.

The revised version:

Section 82b of the Act identifies those persons eligible to hold a casino license.

Alternate version:

Section 82b of the Act specifies who is eligible to hold a casino license.

Follow *Blue Book* Style; It's Not That Hard

Add another skill to your résumé as a writer

After years of working hard to see the forest for the trees, I have been less than excited about dealing with the tiniest of the trees—the *Blue Book* rules. In fact, for a long while, I had an aversion to the rules because they seemed to demand so much attention for so little rhetorical gain and because *Blue Book* style varies in several arbitrary though relatively insignificant ways from the style followed by the New Jersey courts. I resented having to sweat the details.

Recently, I made my peace with *Blue Book* style, my rite of passage eased by former law review editors who showed me how second-nature the Rules can become, once learned.

The rule that triggered this column is the "consecutive capital" rule for citational spacing. I was gratified to learn after years of citing the Federal Reporters that I had correctly been omitting space between "F." and "2d" in "Federal Second":

F.2d

The *Blue Book* dictates that space be omitted between adjacent single capital letters, as in "D.N.J." Individual numbers (actually, number-letter combinations), such as "2d" in F.2d or in N.Y.2d, are treated as single capitals, which means that no space is inserted, for example, between the Y. and the 2d in "N.Y.2d."

This is contrasted with the abbreviation for "Southern Second" (So. 2d), which includes a space between the "2d" and the period after the little "o." A space is inserted because the little o is not a capital letter.

An exception is made to the consecutive capital rule when the second part of the abbreviation is longer than one letter (*e.g.*, "Supp." or "Conn."), as in:

F. Supp.

D. Conn.

Brief writers often fail to leave a space between F. and Supp.

Redundant Periods?

An arcane but interesting *Blue Book* rule directs that a full sentence quoted in a parenthetical receive a period inside the parenthetical, to end the enclosed sentence, even though the period outside the parenthetical ends the overall sentence, which includes the parenthetical. For example:

The court similarly so held in Smith v. Jones, 555 N.J. 1021 ("We see no reason to vary from the general rule governing the doctrine of anticipatory breach.").

In the above example, the sentence quoted within parentheses ends with a period, and the overall sentence ends with a period as well. I used to omit the period within the parenthetical, figuring that the period after the concluding parenthesis would do double duty, terminating both the sentence within the parenthetical and the overall sentence.

That doesn't make complete sense, when you think about it, because the concluding quotation mark inside the parentheses isn't sentence-ending punctuation. The message sent by that quotation mark is that the material just presented was taken verbatim from another source. The rule that a full sentence within a parenthetical should be terminated by a period evidently considers the message sent by that period helpful enough to justify the apparent redundancy of the second period.

Ellipses

Another arcane and frequently breached convention is the spacing for an ellipsis—the series of three periods that indicates an omission from the text. The ellipsis should include spaces between the end of the text and the first period, between the periods, and before the first word after the last period in the series. In other words, you don't hit the period key on your keyboard three consecutive times. To create an ellipsis, you hit space, period, space, period, space, period, space. "Space" is the watchword for ellipses, as in the following quotation:

> *Foreseeability . . . is important but not dispositive.*

When omitting language at the end of a quoted sentence, the ellipsis goes between the last word quoted and the final punctuation of the sentence quoted:

> *The latter standard requires a more obvious and manifest breach of duty by a public entity and imposes a more onerous burden of proof . . . . [omitting the concluding phrase "on the plaintiff"].*

Some lawyers ask whether the effort needed to comply with the *Blue Book* rules is worth it. They figure that judges look more to the substance than the form, and that as long as a writer doesn't misspell words and overlook obvious typographical errors, like inadvertent duplications or omissions, the writer should be fine.

As a general rule, I agree. Judges largely keep their eye on the mark, which is to do justice. They look to the merits, and as long as you don't insult them by being messy, which manifests disrespect, you should be all right.

That said, some judges are *Blue Book* trained, and of those, some are *Blue Book* snobs. They get irritated when people breach *Blue Book* form. I don't think many judges fall into this category, but some do.

Blue Book style is not hard to learn, even if you have to overcome an innate aversion to regimentation. Take it from one who strayed. Once you learn the drill, it stays with you.

And learning the rules may have collateral benefits. You can garner a psychic boost from knowing that you know these special rules, and you may become known within the firm as someone who can conform a brief to *Blue Book* style. This is a nice addition to your résumé. It makes you more useful, and it may suggest that you served on a law review even if you didn't.

One of our associates who was the managing editor of his law review says that he can't get the *Blue Book* rules out of his head. For hours on end, all he did was make *Blue Book* corrections to law review articles. He even attended a seminar on how to get the *Blue Book* changes right. I admit to thinking, "better him than me," but I am grateful for his knowledge of the rules, which helped ease my way back into the fold.

Puzzler

Assuming that a proposal responding to a town's request for proposals (RFP) for a bridge repair project must conform in all material respects to the specifications in the RFP, how would you tighten and sharpen the following sentence?

The bidder's response did not fail to conform to the RFP in any material way that required the town to reject the proposal.

Given that a material deviation from the specifications in an RFP requires a public entity to reject a proposal, the "that" clause in the above sentence is misleading. It incorrectly suggests that some material deviations may not require rejection, which makes the writer look ignorant of the law and slick.

Also, as a matter of precision, the bidder's response didn't conform "to the RFP," which contains more than just specifications. It conformed to the specifications in the RFP.

Generally, be affirmative rather than negative. Say, "The bidder's response conformed" to the specifications rather than "The bidder's response did not fail to conform" to the specifications. It's more assertive and easier to understand. Reluctantly, I add "in all material respects" to the end of the revised version even though it suggests nonconformity, weakening the assertion. Apparently, the response in this case included one or more non-material deviations from the specifications.

The revised version:

The bidder's response conformed to the specifications in the RFP in all material respects.

9

Institutional Concerns

Writing as Seen from the Firm's Point of View

Institutional Concerns

Writing as Seen from the Firm's Point of View

A strong writing sample does not guarantee that an applicant will succeed as a lawyer, nor does a weak writing sample presage failure (except, perhaps, failure as a writer). A strong writing sample won't overcome a bad interview, nor will a weak writing sample negate a good one. A typical evaluation of a writing sample ends something like this: "The piece has some strengths and several flaws, but if you feel strongly about the candidate, I wouldn't reject him for his writing."

Teaching practicing lawyers to write is an uphill battle. Improvement is hard to measure, and participation in an organized program is hard to command in a billable hour environment. Consequently, formal writing instruction is usually more for show than for effect. Writing improvement is ultimately the responsibility of individual lawyers and their mentors. If the latter wish to teach, and the former wish to learn, they may have a beginning.

Evaluating an Applicant's Writing Ability

A writing sample can provide a window into a job candidate's skills

The job interview is a notoriously unreliable predictor of an associate's ability to function effectively in a law firm. The firm can bridge a portion of that gap with the insight provided by a writing sample. Writing is, after all, something lawyers do often.

Below is a list of questions to help reviewers evaluate writing samples. For writers, it is a guide with which to measure their own work.

1. Does the writer engage you quickly?
2. Is the writing forceful and direct, exuding confidence, or does it stumble along? Does the writer appear to be in command?
3. Is the writing lean or verbose? Do the words grip, or do they get in the way?
4. Do you understand the message?
5. For briefs, and to a lesser extent for memos, is the writer an effective advocate? For example, does the writer:
    - Hit hard and early with good facts?
    - Present good law without stretching?
    - Distinguish bad law on material grounds?
    - Confront difficult issues head-on?
    - Use repetition and internal summary to reinforce points?
    - Choose words with precision, sensitive to their connotations?
    - Provide back-up for each assertion by way of supportive facts, legal citations or deductive reasoning?
6. Does the writer know how to sum up?
7. Is the writing organized, section by section and paragraph by paragraph?
8. Does each paragraph have a tight logical progression, or does the sentence order seem to be "b, e, d, c, a"?
9. Does the writer show the courage and ability to state a point rather than just suggest it? Are the topic sentences forceful?
10. Is word position used to achieve emphasis? For example, are important words given prominence at the ends of sentences?
11. Are the case discussions crisp and to the point, or are they long-winded, full of marginally relevant facts and findings?

12. Does the writer seem attuned to concerns of fairness, justice and public policy, or does the writer merely invoke *stare decisis*?
13. Does the writer maintain flow and aid comprehension by the deft use of transitions, grouping, internal summaries and parallel construction?
14. Or does the writer frustrate you, insult your intelligence, and ultimately lose your attention with verbosity, ambiguity, illogic, undefined terms of art, interruptive phrasing, gratuitous footnotes, typos, misspellings, bad punctuation, dangling modifiers, nonagreement of subject and verb, exaggerations such as "clearly," "obviously" and "simply," editorials such as "astonishingly" and "incredibly," and the unrelenting drone of "there is" and "there are"?
15. Does the writer apply the tactics of brief writing, including (but not limited to):
    - Introducing quotations rather than forcing the reader to read them cold?
    - Using underlining within quotations to highlight what is favorable?
    - Including rationales in point headings so the table of contents will function as an argument?
    - Providing explanatory parentheticals after case citations?
16. Does the writing suffer from usage problems, especially the annoying ones, such as:
    - Improper use of which and that?
    - Using as for because?
    - Using while for although?
    - Using due to for because of?
17. Do the citations follow *Blue Book* form or at least remain consistent within themselves?
18. Notwithstanding flaws in the writing, does the writer get the job done? In other words, is the writing effective?
19. Did the writer think the problem through?
20. Would you like to have this person writing for you?
21. Does the writing appear to meet your firm's standards at this person's level?
22. Does the writer appear to have what it takes to write for your firm without undue training or attention?
23. How confident are you that the writing sample is representative of this applicant's skills?

Like any evaluative process, especially truncated ones, writing sample evaluation is imperfect. If the sample is strong, the analysis may have been performed on a closed universe of facts and law, as in a moot court exercise, or the writer may have had help. If the sample is weak, the writer may have potential that hasn't matured.

When a writing sample is flawed, I look amid the clutter for a willingness to confront the tough issues. A lawyer with the courage and self-honesty to battle an opponent's strength is halfway there. I also look for a knack for discussing the facts because persuasion ultimately lies in the facts. These signs give me hope that the writer has a feel for what lawyers do.

Above all, I look for clarity and logic. If the writer seems to have the talent and instinct for that, everything else may fall into place. As they say in basketball, "You can't teach height." The analogy isn't perfect, but some things are more easily fixed than others.

Puzzler

Which is better, Version A or Version B?

Version A:

Work hard to assure success.

Version B:

Work hard to ensure success.

To ensure is to make secure or certain. To assure is to impart confidence and relieve doubt, but it can also mean to guarantee, make certain. To ensure success, you must work hard. To assure your boss that you will succeed, you must work hard. The words overlap in meaning and are often confused. Version B is better because ensure does not have competing connotations.

Law Firm Writing Programs Are a Challenge

The results are uncertain, and the time is non-billable

Let's put legal writing in perspective. It is neither the most important nor the least important lawyering skill. One does not have to write well to advance to the highest levels of the profession. Persons who originate business, negotiate big deals or direct major litigations are the most valuable lawyers in the firm and thus the most highly compensated.

On the other hand, bad writing is bad for business. A weak brief becomes target practice for a court and opposing counsel, and it leaves a bad impression. After several poor products, a court may lose faith in the writer, thereafter presuming, until persuaded otherwise, that the writer's arguments are flawed.

Bad writing also sours relations with clients. In-house counsel easily see past the "indeed's," the "clearly's," and the "It-has-long-been-held's." Even unsophisticated clients can sense when a brief or memo is confused or pretentious. The client who discerns a lack of skill loses confidence in the writer and the firm.

Clear writing reflects clear thinking, and usually, muddled writing reflects muddled thinking. What many lawyers don't consider is that unclear writing not only reflects, but is a hiding place for, unclear thinking. It gives the writer false comfort. Verbosity, disorganization, exaggeration, and lack of transition, among other things, conceal the absence of a point not only from the reader but from the writer.

Bad writing also sours the working atmosphere. It irritates assigning attorneys, who criticize the work and lose faith in the writer. The writer in turn loses confidence and grouses about the hypercritical atmosphere. All this is bad for morale.

Good writing, on the other hand, is a useful tool. Or to use a metaphor more in keeping with the litigator's image, it is a useful weapon. The more powerful the weapon, the more formidable the advocate who commands it. A litigation team with a good writer has more tactical options because maneuvers that depend on clear, forceful writing have a greater chance of success. Good writing builds confidence and empowers the team.

Given the importance of persuasive writing, one would expect law firms to have flourishing writing programs. But most don't. Trying to sustain a law firm writing program is like trying to grow grass in a dead spot on your lawn. Each year, you throw in more seed; the grass springs up and looks good for a while; and then it wilts. The next year, the dead spot is still there.

Writing programs fail to take hold for many reasons, not the least of which is the billable hour. Few lawyers are willing to spend time teaching or learning writing if they are paid in proportion to the time they bill. Even those with the teaching gene are discouraged.

Law firms won't elevate writing instruction to billable status any time soon. Though writing ability is useful if not essential for an associate's early survival, it is secondary in the climb up the pecking order. To attain partnership, associates must originate business or do an excellent job in the first chair.

For that, associates need much more than writing ability. They need to relate effectively to people; to be assertive and tenacious (to have "fire in their belly"); and to be quick on their feet. They need good judgment, a sense of strategy, and vision. They also need good follow-through.

Skill at writing does not ensure any of these abilities. To the contrary, the better writers are often viewed as the "intellectuals," who may be less suited for origination or the first chair. Ironically, this tends to give good writing a bad name.

Not only does writing ability fail to ensure personal success, but it is hard to impart. Even with special attention, some lawyers seem not to improve. Gains come slowly, if at all, and they are unpredictable. Evidence of improvement may not emerge for months or years.

Motivation is also a challenge. Though criticism can euphemistically be called "constructive," it still diminishes the self-image. After a few uncomfortable feedback sessions, some associates have an aversion reaction and give up.

Others don't want to admit that they need help; they think they can't be helped; or they are under pressure and won't spare the time. The instructional process doesn't provide enough satisfaction to offset the expected discomfort and the loss of billable time.

Good writing doesn't even guarantee a good brief. Writing is only the last step in the long process of developing an argument. First, the writer must take the assignment—getting it straight is a tall order for some.

Then the writer has to find case law and analyze it, extracting value from good cases, distinguishing harmful ones and finding common threads. If the analysis is wishful or incomplete, the writer's argument may fail whether the prose is fluid or not.

Lawyers also have to gather facts, organize them, and tell a good story. They need to know what will sell. Above all, they need the courage to confront the other side's best argument and deal with the weakness in their own case.

All these tasks—research, case interpretation and thematic analysis—require complex abilities and diligent effort even before the lawyer begins to write. Why fuss over the icing (the writing) if a lawyer can't bake the cake (everything else)?

In sum, formidable barriers discourage writing programs: Writing is only one of many important skills; though helpful, it is not essential to attain partnership; instructional success is far from assured; and writing programs consume billable hours. The cream of the associates will rise to the top with or without a writing program, and the less able and less motivated will move on. Even assuming associates could be trained to write, why train them for someone else?

If a writing program lasts, several things are probably true: The lawyers who run it are dedicated and skilled; the program is directed at the right audience; the firm demands participation and expects results; and the firm rewards or at least recognizes the efforts of those who teach and who are taught.

This is asking lot of a firm and its lawyers. Partners and senior associates looking to launch a writing program have to sell it to management and then sustain the sell with results. I don't have a problem with that. It's business.

Puzzler

How would you revise the first of the following two sentences?

It is important to note that the lack of a fiduciary duty is instrumental to plaintiff's claims. Without such a duty, plaintiff's claims for constructive fraud and breach of the covenant of good faith and fair dealing fall away.

Delete the opening phrase, "It is important to note." Your saying that something is important does not make it so. To the contrary, it may make the reader suspicious. If you have to try to jack up the significance of your facts with editorials, maybe your facts aren't so good.

"Lack of fiduciary duty" and "instrumental" are not a match. Instrumental is a supportive word whereas the lack of a fiduciary duty undermines plaintiff's claims. I like "absence" better than "lack" because the latter suggests that the claims rather than the defendant might bear the duty.

The revised version:

The absence of a fiduciary duty is fatal to plaintiff's claims.

Alternate version:

Fiduciary duty is a necessary element of plaintiff's claims.